INTRODUCTION TO
BLACK
SOCIOLOGY

Robert Staples

Graduate Program in Sociology
University of California at San Francisco

D0060791

McGraw-Hill Book Company

New York   St. Louis   San Francisco   Auckland
Düsseldorf   Johannesburg   Kuala Lumpur   London
Mexico   Montreal   New Delhi   Panama   Paris
São Paulo   Singapore   Sydney   Tokyo   Toronto

E
185.86
.973

Introduction to Black Sociology

1234567890M U M U 798765

This book was set in Press Roman by Allen Wayne Technical Corp.
The editor was Lyle Linder;
the designer was Allen Wayne Technical Corp.;
the production supervisor was Judi Allen.
The cover was designed by Joseph Gillians.
The Murray Printing Company was printer and binder.

Library of Congress Cataloging in Publication Data

Staples, Robert.
    Introduction to Black sociology.

    Bibliography: p.
    Includes index.
    1. Negroes—Social conditions—1964-
2. Sociology.   I. Title.
E185.86.S73   301.45'19'6073   75-11571
ISBN 0-07-060840-7

The colonized man who writes for his people ought to use the past with the intention of opening the future as an invitation to action and a basis for hope. But, to insure that hope and to give it form, he must take part in action and throw himself body and soul into the . . . struggle.

Frantz Fanon

Contents

Preface

This book is the first of its kind to apply many of the notions about the Black perspective in a specific social science discipline. It is a beginning attempt to provide a new perspective on Black life and culture in the United States. Since it is an initial effort, I have confined myself largely to using secondary data and fitting them into the Black perspective. Because this discipline is in the embryonic stage, many subjects are only surveyed and not investigated in depth. Some topics are rarely touched upon, for example, demography, ecology, research methodology, etc. But a primary objective of this work is to stimulate other scholars to further explore the ideas contained within this perspective and to systematically develop theories and methodologies consistent with the goals of Black sociology.

Even though this book may be regarded as revolutionary in some respects, it is first and foremost intended as an introductory text for the undergraduate student. Specifically, it is organized along the same lines as general sociology texts, but with topics and content that are particularly relevant to the Black experience. The writing style is geared toward students at beginning levels. It will be of use in introductory social science survey courses, race and ethnic relations classes, and what are generally called sociology of the Black community courses.

This volume makes no claim to being the definitive work on Black sociology. Basically, it is an attempt to provide a fresh, and more relevant, perspective of Black life in America. For that reason, it is ipso facto polemical. The criticism of it will come from both Black and White sociologists and must be anticipated. Much of the criticism will be valid, since there are bound to be flaws in developing a new perspective on a subject where there is little unanimity on either the cause or the nature of the problem. But, this is a foundation upon which those who are committed to Black liberation can build, and it had to be initiated by some scholar. Whatever it accomplishes, at least an alternative will have been presented to the prevailing sociological interpretation of Afro-American life.

In this effort I have drawn upon elements from the three models mentioned in the first chapter. Although it was suggested, I have refrained from developing a syncretic model, because theory construction is a long and laborious task. I have, thus, limited myself to applying elements of the three conceptual models, combining them in some cases, and in others describing phenomena without a priori concepts in the best way I could. This book has to be read with these limitations in mind.

Some will argue that Black sociology is a racialistic version of sociological concepts and will be quick to point out that I have used the works of White sociologists in the book. If it is not clear in the first chapter, let me now state that I have reserved judgment on whether only Blacks can practice Black sociology. I do maintain that they can bring a special interest and skill to the study of Black sociology if they are so inclined. Moreover, in some cases where I have used the research of White sociologists, it has been a matter of reinterpreting their data to fit the Black perspective. This highlights one of the issues in the confrontation between Black and White sociology: that of interpretation of data. If you have the value orientation of Black sociology the data often conforms to that perspective, and vice versa for White sociology.

In this groundbreaking book, I have used many of the scholarly resources available to me. St. Clair Drake, Gerald McWorter, and Joyce Ladner provided me with the original inspiration for the work as well as their own ideas on the structure of a Black sociology. Others who helped by reading portions of the manuscript were: Wendell Brooks, Ralph Gomes, Nathan Hare, Alex Swan, Carol Stack, and James Turner. My appreciation to those sociologists who read the entire original draft and made extensive suggestions, which improved the book immeasurably: Robert Allen, Robert Blauner, Douglas Davidson, and Rutledge Dennis.

During the writing of this book I had the invaluable assistance of my typist, Vicki Pegullian, and my research assistant, Gay Yambert. Jim Mirrieles of McGraw Hill prodded me into writing the book; Dave Edwards, the former sociology editor, put his personal commitment into the project; and Lyle Linder speeded up the process of completing it by his prompt attention to details and by his encouragement.

Finally, Dennis Forsythe must be singled out for his special contribution. He made suggestions before, during, and after the writing of the chapters. And his imprint can be seen in each page of the book. Since the rewards of a single-author book are so weighted toward the author, I will follow the custom of accepting all responsibility for its faults, while acknowledging that its merits are the result of a collective effort.

Robert Staples

The Nature of Black Sociology

THE SOCIOLOGY OF AFRO-AMERICAN LIFE

A study of the sociology of Afro-American life emerges from a distinct set of intellectual needs. One of the most important reasons is the void in the sociological literature of any systematic analysis of Black society, culture, and personality. While a considerable body of knowledge on Blacks can be found in sociological research, it is not a sociology of Black life, but a sociology of race. Blacks have been studied as an integral part of America's race relations problem. Rarely has the Afro-American population been investigated as a separate cultural grouping whose structure and dynamics are in themselves a focus of sociological concern. This is an attempt to remedy that oversight by describing the origins, nature, structure, and dynamics of Black life in America from a Black perspective.

Since the analysis of Black life emanates from the perspective of Black sociology, the question will inevitably rise as to whether this is really sociology. There are sociologists who will claim that the discipline of sociology is, or should be, devoid of racial labels, that its goal is to study all men and their social relations. Why not call it a sociological study of Black life without the implications that it is a Black sociological perspective? The answer is fairly simple. Sociology, as it relates to Black people, has been characterized by an ethnocentric bias, which has easily earned it the title of White sociology. In its earlier period (i.e., 1880–1960) it furnished much of the ideological ammunition for the status quo level of race relations—White privilege and Black deprivation. Contemporary sociology (post-1960) continues to define Blacks as a source of tension in the social structure whose demands for inclusion in mainstream society represent one of America's greatest social problems.

Black sociology proceeds from the premise that Black and White peoples have never shared, to any great degree, the same physical environment or social experiences. People of different cultures relate to one another and to their physical environment differently. The result is a different behavior pattern as well as different values, norms, and mores that should be analyzed independently of preconceived notions of superior and inferior cultures. Black life must be viewed in its total spectrum, and this includes looking at the variations in Black culture. At the same time, the subjugated status of Afro-Americans must be seen from the eyes of the oppressed as well as of the oppressor. The knowledge of Black sociology must function as a means of change, not of control. It should be a science of liberation, not of oppression.

While the above statements may surely be characterized by some as nonsociological, the sociology of Afro-American life is deeply rooted in the sociological tradition and will use the rules of sociological method. Undergirding this effort to redefine the interpretation of the Black experience is the sociology of knowledge model. The basic principle of this model is that knowledge is a function of environment and the individual's place in that environment. In essence, individuals hold to the beliefs and ideas that their society socializes them to have.[1] During one period, Blacks were conceived of as biologically inferior and the sociology literature, although ostensibly objective, reflected those beliefs. In the present era, it is fashionable to consider them as a group subjected to social discrimination and prejudice who must be absorbed in the society since they have no culture or values (positively constructed, that is) of their own.[2]

The sociological method of Black sociology is also firmly grounded in the tenets of traditional sociology. Relevant data will be collected, organized, and classified. Certain aspects of Black life will be conceptualized and subjected to empirical verification. Where it seems relevant or necessary, the quantitative method will be employed so that the conditions of Black life can be accurately determined. However, the nature of our methodology must be compatible with the philosophy of our discipline: that knowledge must serve the cause of Black freedom and not the sanction of the present social order. Or, in other words, the research design should not be constructed to find evidence of Black pathology which will later be used to demonstrate that the problem is located in individuals—rather than in the racist social structure.

In the pursuit of this goal, Black sociology is continuing in the tradition of Marx, Weber, Durkheim, and DuBois. Each, in his own fashion, saw the study of society as being time-contained and subject to the changes taking place in the world. Their sociology developed in response to the needs of the epoch. For Marx, it was the economic conditions of the working classes; Weber's concern was the rise of bureaucracy in Germany, Durkheim focused on the alienated in France, and DuBois dealt with the race problem in the United States. At this time, Black sociology arises out of the need to study Black American life and culture as an internal social system while understanding the external constraints on Black lives and institutions. In order to move from tradition to rationality, sociology must go from White myths to a Black knowledge and interpretation of Black life in America.

It was W. E. B. DuBois who provided the foundation for Black sociology, both in terms of subject and methodology. Over 75 years ago he noted that the past studies of Afro-Americans had been characterized by a lack of detail, failure to be systematic, and a tendency to be uncritical. Hence, he advocated basic research on Blacks that would separate opinion from fact. The task for sociology, he said, was to put science into sociology through the study of the condition and problems of Blacks. Moreover, he opposed the idea of a value-free sociology as it is generally defined. Instead, the sociologist should be oriented toward a humanistic perspective of his society. What he wanted was a shift from the negative values held by social scientists, which tended to support the oppression of Blacks, to more positive values that allowed Blacks to maintain their cultural patterns unrestricted by the laws and social customs of the White majority.[3]

BACKGROUND OF WHITE SOCIOLOGY

The problem of Whites studying Blacks is not unique to sociology or to the question of race. Intellectual elites have traditionally come from the group in control and have tended to dominate the interpretation of a minority group's behavior. Thus, we find most studies of women have been by men, the middle class interpret lower-class behavior, and Europeans develop the body of knowledge about Africans and Asians. Our earliest knowledge of slavery, for example, is based on the slaveholder's interpretation and reports. As Blauner and Wellman (1973) have noted, "When the objects of investigation are poor or people of color, then the research relationship itself falls into the structure of class relations or race relations."[4]

As a result of the industrial revolution and the French revolution, sociology was initiated in Europe for the purpose of understanding the nature of society and the structure of social relations. At that time, there was a general consensus among European intellectuals that Europe represented the highest form of civilization. Even the radical, Karl Marx, believed that nations of colored people were still in a state of barbarism.[5] The founder of sociology, Auguste Comte, ignored peoples of color when he chose to study societies that had made progress.[6] His successors, Spencer, Ward, and others, belonged to the evolutionary school of thought. Basically, they ignored non-Whites in their study of human society because they conceived of them as being at a lower stage of evolutionary development. Herbert Spencer, in particular, saw those individuals who were poor as being unfit to compete in the society and thereby being confined to their "natural" level. The alleged peculiar aspects of Black behavior were explained in terms of biological characteristics.

Around 1880 the perspective of social Darwinism began to dominate sociology and was the primary element in evolutionary theory. Basically, it saw the racial situation as part of the struggle for survival within the species of homo sapiens. The White race had achieved supremacy because it was the fittest of the two racial groups. For years sociologists located Blacks lower than Whites in the chain of evolution because they were thought to be less capable of surviving in Western civilization. Until recently racial problems were defined in terms of biological factors, a tendency directly attributable to the influence of social Darwinist theory.[7]

Although sociologists would be expected to consider culture in the patterning of human behavior, Black-White differences were usually interpreted as resulting from unique biological factors in the Black personality. While the works of DuBois on race were ignored during the early part of the twentieth century, the *American Journal of Sociology* printed articles stating that "the average Negro is still a savage child of nature that the North and South can be brought to unite in work to uplift the race."[8] Even the "liberal" sociologists, Park and Burgess (1924), once described Black temperament as "consisting of a few elementary but distinctive characteristics determined by physical organization and transmitted biologically."[9]

It is not that these men were motivated by any particular malice toward Blacks. Many of them were considered devoted to "uplifting" Blacks. However, a social analysis by a White sociologist tends to reflect and reinforce the racial values of the group to which he belongs. Mannheim (1936) once observed that "the ruling groups in their thinking become so intensively interest bound to a situation that they are simply no longer able to see certain facts which would undermine their sense of domination."[10] Thus, it is not surprising, as Mintz (1970) has stated, that "it must be one of history's deftest ironies that oppressors have always sought to rationalize their oppression by blaming the oppressed."[11]

Lest we appear to be indicting all White sociologists, it should be noted that not all of them have participated in the academic assault on the Black population. And, a few Black sociologists were part of this process. Part of the problem lies in factors beyond their control. The depiction of Blacks as problems of deviancy was controlled by government and foundation funding sources. Money was available to study Blacks as problems or culturally deprived, but not as a culture with its own normative values, behavioral patterns, and institutions.[12] Liberal reform was accomplished through much of this research, but another result was the continuation of stereotypes that saw Black life as a cultural nonentity or inferior vis-à-vis middle-class White culture.

Even the radical sociologists tended to undermine the value of Black culture. One finds in the works of radical sociologists some significant commonalities with Black sociology. The radical sociologists have correctly identified the ideological use of sociology in fostering class and racial oppression. Yet, their history is permeated with the same ethnocentric bias of establishment sociologists. Their very emphasis on the class struggle tends to confine Blacks to the category of a superoppressed class who must subordinate their movement for group self-determination to the class struggle. Additionally, their own group membership and experiences prevent them from capturing the subjective aspects of Black life.[13]

One of the basic ways to define the behavior of man is through concepts. It is in the concepts of White sociology that we see the ideological use of this discipline. The social theories developed to explain the race problem have never adequately dealt with the daily functioning of the Black social system or specified the nature of the political and economic oppression to which Blacks are subjected. The problem has always been framed in ways that discuss the tragic effects of slavery on the slaves, but omit the atrocities of the slavemaster. We hear of the problems that Afro-Americans encounter but little of the pathology of White racism.

WHITE SOCIOLOGICAL THEORIES

Immigration-Assimilation Cycle

This is one of the most prominent theories used to explain race relations. Developed by George Simmel in Europe and applied by Robert Park it pinpoints a cycle of race relations based on initial stages of racial contact, competition, accommodation, and eventually terminating in the final stage of assimilation.

In the first stage, *contact,* different racial groups meet in a new setting and must relate to one another. The second phase, *conflict,* emerges when there is a scarcity of resources for which the races must compete. *Accommodation,* the third stage, results when one group accepts a lower status in the social order. And, eventually, *assimilation* occurs when the different races fuse culturally and physically and lose traits of their original distinctions.[14] This theory was first applied to

White European immigrants who came to this country voluntarily, shed their major marks of distinction from the native White American majority, and were absorbed into American society. It assumed that being integrated into mainstream society was the ultimate goal of any minority and that immigrants would not be interested in preserving any distinctive cultural values and institutions.[15]

Moreover, this particular theory could be used to sanction the existing social order. Whatever state of race relations exists is acceptable because it is a part of a natural process that is inevitable whenever two different cultures come into contact. Change is expected, but it will come according to its historically determined pace. Therefore, Blacks could hold out for the raceless society predicted instead of trying to change the fate determined for them.[16] This theory was also applied to Black-White relations, although Blacks had come here some three hundred years earlier than other assimilated immigrants.

Structural Functionalism

This conceptual model was not specifically designed to explain the race problem, but it has significant implications for the understanding of Black life. It is one of the most important theoretical frameworks in contemporary sociology. In this model order, consensus, stability, and integration are stressed. Elements in the society are considered functional because they meet certain needs. An unequal distribution of wealth, for instance, is required in order to ensure that vital tasks are performed. Only by allocating higher rewards of status and money can people be motivated to fulfill these necessary functions.[17] The obvious racial implication in this theory is that Blacks have less rewarding positions because they perform less valuable services for the society.

This conceptual model originated in the biological sciences and it emphasizes the integration of parts within a whole, the social system to which the parts belong. Within this framework, behavior and institutions are considered to be functions of one another. Each one has a reciprocal relationship with the other. The main principle governing social relationships is that they are always striving for the equilibrium (balance) of society. When it is used to study Blacks, their behavior is usually described in relation to the values of American society rather than to any distinct cultural values or needs of their own. Or, their behavior is viewed as dysfunctional when it does not conform to the American social system and its needs.[18]

One of the eminent theoreticians belonging to this school is Talcott Parsons (1966). His view of the race problem is that a revolution is unnecessary since the mechanisms for correcting America's greatest social evil are available. Blacks will ultimately receive full citizenship because the value system of America is committed to granting these rights to all Americans. Although the pace may be slower for Blacks than other ethnic groups, they will eventually be incorporated into the assimilation process once they have acquired the capacities that qualify them for civic inclusion.[19]

Structural-functional analysis is another example of sociology's sanction of the present social order. Change will come naturally, and there is no need for collective action to influence it. This school accepts the prevailing social system as meeting the needs of all its members. There is little room for conflict within society since values and goals are collectively shared. Its perspective gives little insight into the existence of racial inequalities except as a normative part of the social structure. No consideration is given to the possibility that the political system does not represent the interest of racial minorities and that change has historically not taken place without a struggle. Under this framework, the only solution for Blacks is to wait for America to live up to its democratic creed.

The Culture of Poverty

A conceptual model considered to be a "liberal" approach to the race problem, this theory stresses the pathology of Black life by explaining that poverty is originally induced by inequalities in the opportunity structure but subsequently becomes self-sustaining. Just like any other culture, the culture of poverty is transmitted from generation to generation, thus further preventing the members of this culture from escaping their deprived circumstances. The term, *culture of poverty,* leads to an emphasis on negative qualities of the poor such as apathy, intolerance, lack of motivation, disorganization, and fatalism. Changing the values of the poor is often seen as the crucial practical problem in attacking poverty rather than eliminating basic inequalities in the social structure.[20]

The weakness of this model is that, while it stresses the economic basis of poverty, it does not impute any worth to the values and behavioral patterns of Blacks. In fact, its essential function is to illustrate how Afro-Americans are only White men with Black masks. They are regarded as holding strongly the values of White Americans, which, of course, denies the existence of a Black value and cultural system despite the fact that significant differences are found between lower-class Blacks and Whites. In its own way, it lends support to the thesis that the oppressed are responsible for their own condition.[21]

THE PERSPECTIVE OF BLACK SOCIOLOGY

Afro-American sociology is characterized by a number of assumptions uncommon to the traditional field of sociology. While some sociologists maintain that sociology should be strictly a science and avoid making a choice among values, Black sociology makes no such claim to value neutrality. Our position is best summed up by Charles Hamilton (1973):

> The Black social scientist in this country is a member of a race that is subjected and oppressed. He is subjected and oppressed. It is impossible to be "objective" about that any more than it is possible for a white social scientist, who has benefited directly or indirectly from racial oppression, to be objective about his position of preference, whether he admits it or not. Each brings insights from his own vantage point of reality to his work. Each brings preconceived value judgements.[22]

The values that the Black sociologist must bring to his work must be Black values. Those values must be humanist orientations to Black and White society. Just as White sociology has been put to political use by making legitimate the institutions of White America, Black sociology must sanction the positive values and institutions in Black life. We must describe the richness and diversity of Black life and the ingenuity which is demonstrated in creating institutions and lifestyles that enabled Blacks to cope and survive in a hostile society. In the use of Black sociology, there must be a commitment to promoting social change in the interests of Black people. Within the context of these goals, we can maintain scientific traditions by using sociological concepts and methods in our study of Afro-American life.

This is not an attempt to undermine sociology as a science. There is no unanimous agreement among sociologists that the study of human beings can be scientific. C. Wright Mills (1959) once stated that "the behavioral sciences are simply impossible."[23] Science in sociology consists of the method. It is the responsibility of the social scientists to collect, organize, and classify the data. But, in their interpretation, the specific conclusions reached will be related to social goals and personal values. And, sociologists are not inclined to reach conclusions from their research that tend to diminish the credibility of their own self-conceptions and institutional loyalties. Hence, while the method may be impersonal and universal, group membership and the values resulting therefrom are decisive in determining the use to which research will be put.[24]

Numerous examples of the influence of values on sociological research can be found in the history of sociological studies of Blacks. When White society held Blacks to be inferior, White sociologists conducted studies that confirmed this belief. To racial prejudice was added impartial scientific validation.[25] As the civil rights and Black nationalist movements changed the structure of race relations, so did the sociological literature undergo a modification. With a few rare exceptions, Blacks were no longer studied to prove their biological inferiority, but the new studies still did not call into question the preferential power of Whites. The Black condition was ascribed to the history of slavery, which led to inferior education and other behavioral traits whose elimination could bring Blacks to parity with Whites in a system of equal opportunity for achievement.

BLACK SOCIOLOGY VERSUS WHITE SOCIOLOGY

Sociology consists of a set of concepts used to explain social behavior. These concepts derive from a certain philosophy which seeks to interpret social reality from the perspective of privileged political and economic elites to whom such "knowledge" provides an ideological justification for their power and authority in a given society. A comparison of certain concepts, as interpreted by Black and White sociology, will illustrate some of the crucial differences in the two perspectives.

White sociology	Black sociology
Race is defined as a distinctive combination of physical traits.	Race is a political status which determines the individual's life chances.
Members of a social class view one another as equals.	White society regards all Blacks as unequal regardless of education or income.
Changes in technology bring about a society based on achieved rather than ascribed status.	Automated production and mechanized agriculture will create a permanent army of unemployed Blacks.
Blacks must be integrated into the present values of White America.	There must be a new America before Blacks will choose integration. What is wanted is Black self-determination.
Education is the best way of achieving racial equality.	The more education a Black person receives, the greater the gap between him and his White counterpart.
The female-headed household is a deviant form of the family.	Black women heading households represent a positive form of role integration in the Black community.
Blacks are discriminated against and lead joyless lives.	Blacks are oppressed but manage to have more fun on Saturday night than many Whites have in their lifetime.

GOALS OF BLACK SOCIOLOGY

Sociology often defines itself as a pure science in that it seeks to objectively study group life without much concern for its practical use. Afro-American sociology is an applied science because it has as its primary objective the application of sociological knowledge to the development of the Black community. It is not interested in the accumulation of data unless that information can prepare Black people to function in the struggle for survival. At the same time, Black sociology along with radical sociology can serve as the intellectual vanguard for a humanist society.

Among some of the other methods and goals of Afro-American sociology are:

To introduce the concept of cultural relativism into the study of Black life. Black culture should be viewed as a social system whose function and meaning are relative to the existing environment. Black and White cultures can be seen as different without being categorized into inferior or superior divisions.

To study the dynamics of White racism in American society and how it is related to the functioning of Afro-Americans in the Black and White world. While such an analysis will prepare Blacks to deal with the effects of White racism, it can also help to sensitize Whites to the subtle but harmful impact of racism on their own lives. At least they can become more aware of the relationship between Black status and White racism.

To reevaluate White sociological theories and studies. It is not sufficient to build an Afro-American sociology without showing the inadequacy of existing White models. The failure to do so will only maintain the credibility of those models for Whites and some Blacks who are willing to consider other options.

To use Black norms and perspectives when analyzing the data. One can best understand Black life by taking into consideration the meanings, interaction, and language as felt and experienced by those in Black society. As W. I. Thomas once stated, "If men define situations as real, they become real in their consequences."

To provide a historical analysis of the Black condition from a Black perspective. Historical studies anchor all research on man in society. In studying Black life historically, we can examine the changing elements of racism and its dynamics. We can analyze the Black response to these situations and the collective values and institutions that emerged as assets in the struggle. Additionally, we should look at the past struggles for freedom in other lands, their strategies and goals, failures and successes.

To study Blacks from a pan-Africanist comparative perspective. We need to know the continuities of African traits in Afro-American culture. A kind of historical anthropology is needed whereby we can assess exactly what happened to the Africans who were brought to the North American shores. What African traits in Black lifestyles have survived is a question to be posed and answered.

To use statistical investigation to get at the truth of the Black population. While statistics have been manipulated to show that Blacks are inferior, deviant, and deprived, a Black quantitative approach will use Black norms in determining what facts to collect and how they will be interpreted. Using statistics to determine the nature of the Black population can be helpful in formulating Black goals, developing priorities, and evaluating programs.

CONCEPTUAL MODELS IN BLACK SOCIOLOGY

Certain existing models have elements that are useful in the development of a Black sociology. In fact, it is by combining the elements of these theories that we have the perspective of Afro-American sociology.

The Colonial Model

The colonial model views the Black community as an underdeveloped, exploited colony controlled by individuals outside the community. This is a theory that has traditionally been applied to the relationship between a foreign country that takes over the control of political and economic institutions in another country. Former examples of this relationship could be found in the African countries dominated by Europeans. In the most recent period, colonialism has meant the dominance of White Westerners over non-White peoples in other parts of the world. The characteristics of colonialism are: (1) the colonized subjects are not in the social system voluntarily but have it imposed on them; (2) the subject's native culture is modified or destroyed; (3) control is in the hands of people outside the native population; and (4) racism prevails, i.e., a group seen as different or inferior in terms of alleged biological traits is exploited, controlled, and oppressed socially and psychologically by a group that defines itself as superior.[26]

An important feature of this model when applied to the United States is its technique of combining racial and class oppression into one theoretical framework. It also illustrates the institutionalized patterns of racist oppression. Instead of focusing on individual attitudes of racial prejudice, it treats racism as a political and economic process that maintains domination of Whites over Blacks by systematic subjugation. By employing this model, it is possible to refocus certain issues such as education, politics, crime, etc., as part and parcel of a colonial relationship. It illustrates that Black deprivation is not a result of the Black individual's limitation or the White person's lack of racial tolerance. The Black condition can be more realistically viewed as a pattern of systematic subjugation maintained by those people who stand to profit the most from it.[27]

Examples of domestic colonialism are abundant, although not necessarily in the pure classical form found in other societies. In education, for instance, Blacks find their cultural values unexpressed in the classroom or in their books. This is because a colonial society accords no legitimacy to the values of the natives. What is termed *acculturation* could as easily be labeled *colonization.* Those Blacks who receive a higher education internalize the values of the colonizer even more strongly. In any colony, there is always room for bright natives to hold responsible positions—though not at the very top.

Since the educational system imposes the values of White society on Black students, it is those values they represent as they serve the colonial powers.

The colonial model is significant because it views racism in its political and economic dimensions. It also serves to develop the formulation of solutions to Black deprivation. If colonization is the essence of the race problem, decolonization is the remedy. This is reflected in the Black demand for community control. However, this theory must be developed and refined before it is applied indiscriminately to the interpretation of the Black experience. One problem with this model is its emphasis on the negative results of racial oppression. While it is important to see Black life in the context of systematic racial oppression, we also need to understand that within this limitation Black people also have some options in the social world. Some of their adaptations have been innovative and positive parts of their lives. What may have emerged out of hardship can become functional aspects of Black life.

The Marxist Model

Marxism was very influential as a conceptual model in the earlier period of sociology, and the school of radical sociology is strongly influenced by Marxist ideas. Basically, Marx conceived of societies as always being divided into two classes, the exploited and the exploiters. In modern capitalist countries, the owners of the means of production (the bourgeoisie) exploit the working classes (the proletariat) by retaining a large amount of their production in the form of profits. The working classes accept this situation because they do not have the class consciousness to become aware of their exploitation and their capacity to take over the means of production in the service of the people rather than for the profits of an elitist class of landlords and industrialists.[28]

The Marxist analysis does not address itself directly to the question of racial oppression. Marx himself wrote little on the subject. Contemporary Marxists are inclined to see racism as a tool used by the capitalist class to divide Black and White workers. Black workers are seen simply as the most oppressed segment of the working class. They are exploited more because racism in employment practices makes it easier to pay Blacks less by relegating them to hard and menial jobs that have little status in the society. According to Marxist analysis, only the unity of Black and White workers can bring about liberation for both groups. Once the economic basis for racism is destroyed, racism itself will slowly wither away.

This type of analysis of race relations has a certain importance for an Afro-American sociology. It stresses the political and economic control that influences the location of individuals in the social structure. One can perceive of racism as more than a natural part of human society, i.e., just one element in human evolution. In this theory it is conceptualized as a *key* element in the structure of class exploitation. The historical analysis in the Marxist model allows us to see the relationship between economic conditions and racial oppression in terms of changing elements. It also has predictive power in that as economic changes occur, so will the nature of race relations.

Even more useful is the conflict orientation of the Marxist model. Whereas establishment sociology has viewed human society as an evolving structure based on a natural progression from one stage to another, the Marxist theory is that societies are composed of classes in conflict. While establishment sociology sees society as being bound together by a consensus anchored by a common value system, Marxists conceive of it as being permeated by conflict, although muted, that will ultimately be resolved by revolution. Sociologists who perceive this society as having integrated elements that constitute some kind of equilibrium are, in essence, giving sanction to the present social order. The notion of conflict, however, allows us to analyze the existing social system as being incompatible with Black needs. It also puts into a correct perspective the relationship of political and economic institutions to the Black condition.

There are some imperfections in this model for the understanding of Black life. Its value lies chiefly in analyzing political and economic factors as they affect the status of Blacks. However, it does not address itself to the question of Black culture. In fact, nationalism does not have an important role in Marx's theory. The solution implied by his analysis points to racial integration rather than cultural pluralism or Black self-determination. Marx also does not deal adequately with the question of racial conflict as an overriding factor in the class struggle. It is difficult to foresee a unity of Black and White workers when racist attitudes are most strongly ingrained in the working class stratum of American society. Although economic conditions may have created the need for a racist ideology, that ideology may persist long after it has outlived its purpose. Thus, eliminating capitalism will not necessarily destroy racism.[29]

The Pan-Africanist Model

This is not a conceptual model as such. It is primarily a political perspective and program. If we applied it to the study of Black life in American, our focus would be on the continuities in African cultural strands among the Afro-American population. Pan-Africanism sees all people of African descent as having a common history, experience, and culture. Hence, Afro-Americans are considered dislocated Africans (i.e., a diaspora). The elements of African culture remain the same, although the form may have changed through the adaptations imposed upon Black Americans. A basic assumption is that a culture group never completely loses its cultural heritage, it simply fuses into another form.

An important value of this model is the focus on the comparative study of African and Afro-American cultures. It provides an important link to the past and serves as the foundation for any analysis of Black cultural values and patterns. Some significant work has already been done in the area of music, speech, and family patterns. However, much historical research is needed in order to determine the origin of African cultural traits, the means of transmitting them among Africans in another country, and in what form they exist among contemporary Afro-Americans.

Some problems exist with this model. One difficulty is that Africa itself has a diversity of cultural values, languages, and behavioral patterns. Another limitation is that, as an analytical tool, this model emphasizes the study of cultural forms rather than political and economic analysis. It lends itself easily to cultural nationalist ideology which would have us focus on our cultural subjugation rather than the political and economic oppression to which Blacks are subjected. Revolutionary Pan-Africanists, however, struggle against more than cultural imperialism.

METHODS AND PROCEDURES OF BLACK SOCIOLOGY

We have already sketched in broad outline the research goals of Black sociology. This section is designed to specifically detail some of the special research problems and methodological techniques of Black sociology and the procedures to be used in carrying out relevant research on the Black community. Although there is no research technique specific to Blacks, some existing techniques may be more productive than others.

Methodological Techniques

Definition of Concepts   Since concepts are terms that convey value orientations as well as perspectives of social behavior, it is important to frame concepts in Black sociology that are relevant to the Black reality. Hence, we might substitute the concept of *role integration* for the term *matriarchy* so often used in White sociological research on Black families. The former term reflects the fluidity of roles in the Black family while the latter suggests family disorganization and pathology. The concept of *cultural deprivation* can be reinterpreted to mean *culturally disposed* or *culturally different.* Such euphemistic terms as *economically disadvantaged* groups can be replaced by *economically exploited* groups.

Framing Questions   Since the questions asked in social research often reflect what the researchers believe are the relevant aspects of a given problem, it is essential that the questions reflect a Black perspective of the research purpose. For instance, instead of going out into the Black community and asking the question, Why are there so many illegitimate children who only increase the welfare rolls? we should be asking how these children born out-of-wedlock are cared for, in what way, and by whom. Such questions lead us to examine kinship structures, economic cooperation, and cultural lifestyles rather that sexual morality, birth control practices, and the stigmatization of children.

Problems of Verification   Much of the previous research on Blacks has been unreliable for a number of reasons, some of which we have already noted. A significant factor has been what is called the Black "put-on." This is a response that Blacks have developed and refined particularly for Whites. Historically it has been a part of their survival strategy. In research interviews or questionnaires, it involves telling a White person (or his Black emissary) what he believes is appropriate.

In its extreme form it is a very exaggerated response designed to deceive (e.g., telling a sex researcher that he had 150 sexual partners in a given year).

Some of the problems of verification can be resolved by using the method of participant-observation, i.e., the researcher takes part in whatever he is studying. Obviously, the White researcher would be at somewhat of a disadvantage in using this method. The Black sociologist, however, can bring special skills to this method of research by his knowledge and insight into the community of which he is a member. Although criticisms have been made of this research technique because it may be too subjective or because it lacks generalizing power for other groups and situations, it is eminently superior to questionnaires. Most questionnaires used on Blacks have been developed and designed by and for Whites. They often contain language or concepts Blacks do not understand, and when they are sent out by mail, the researcher often gets an astonishingly low rate of return.

Another way to improve verification is to put more emphasis on Blacks' telling their stories themselves. Data can be collected in the form of letters, autobiographies, poems, folk tales, songs, proverbs, films, and music. It has been noted that some of the best sociological accounts of Black life have come from nonsociological sources such as the works of James Baldwin, Claude Brown, Malcolm X, etc.

Historical Analysis The use of a sociohistorical approach marks a break with White sociological theory. Much current sociological theory is present-oriented and does not make the crucial historical connections so essential to a full understanding of the dynamics of human behavior, cultural change, and intergroup as well as intragroup changes. It is essential to our understanding of Black life to examine the historical forces that shaped the present structure of the Afro-American community. An important historical technique, especially for Blacks, is the gathering of oral data. Among Blacks historical knowledge has been passed from one generation to another by word-of-mouth, through storytellers and musicians. The rich oral history of Blacks has yet to be tapped.

Analysis Although statistical analysis may be helpful in limited studies of the Black population (e.g., differences in jail sentences for Blacks and Whites), it has been more often used to victimize the

Afro-American community. Through manipulation of statistical data, sociologists have tried to identify all sorts of pathological elements in the Black group—from unwed mothers to dope addicts. However, statistical information is almost meaningless when applied to a population about which little is known of its internal functioning. To tell us that there are large numbers of female-headed households among Blacks does not give us insight into how that group functions. Black sociology must emphasize qualitative analysis and develop its theories and hypotheses as it is conducting its research rather than going into a setting with preconceived notions about what is supposed to happen.

PROCEDURES IN BLACK SOCIOLOGICAL RESEARCH

The researcher should feel responsibility toward the subject group rather than the research project itself. Several suggestions have been offered and tried by a few sociologists, but the time has come to alter the unilateral value of research on the Black community. What most often happens is that the researcher of Blacks gets in exchange for his work a Ph.D., a promotion, published writings, etc., while the subjects get nothing, and are sometimes victimized in the process by their identification as a pathological group. The researcher must become involved and accountable to his subject community. If he does not voluntarily make this commitment, it will probably be imposed on him anyway. White researchers, in particular, are encountering increasing resistance in Black communities. Many of them are now resorting to hiring Black interviewers. In Roxbury, Massachusetts, a Black community group is demanding veto power over any foundation grants to researchers conducting investigations of their community.

In carrying out their research on a Black community in a California city, Blauner and Wellman (1973) were made aware of the exploitative nature of White research on Blacks. Interviews were becoming hard to obtain. As a result they abandoned their position as dispassionate, objective social scientists and committed themselves in various ways to those from whom they wanted interviews. They volunteered their work and technical assistance to community groups; prepared research which these groups saw as important; made phone calls, wrote letters, and drove people to their appointments. At the end of this experience they concluded that a new organizational format was needed, a center or institute that would integrate social action with the empirical goals of the researchers. Academic research projects would have to be related to the interests of oppressed communities and be understood, discussed, and approved within the community.[30]

A similar view is held by Jackson, Slaughter, and Blake (1974). They advocate barring scholars, Black or White, who do not subordinate their research interests to service to the Black community. Any scholar who desires to study the Black community must work with the residents to assist them in meeting their needs as they perceive them. The most effective way of doing this, they say, is through coordination with community-controlled local agencies and by providing effective services to the communities. The research of scholars in Afro-American communities should be coordinated research so that the agencies can get needed materials and data at the same time the scholars are getting the results they seek.[31]

Other additional research procedures would be to provide feedback and data to groups that do not form a geographically distinct community. Research on prisoners, for instance, can be coordinated with the efforts of prisoners' unions. Scholars can also write articles for popular magazines in order to publicize the findings of their research. Some scholars have even started fund-raising drives to help the oppressed communities they have studied. Such practices should be a normal modus operandi in Black sociology research. It is part and parcel of our premise that sociology must have a unity of theory and action.

SUMMARY

Afro-American sociology has emerged out of the need to develop countertheories about the nature of Black life in this country. In White sociology's efforts to legitimate the present order, the Black condition can only be seen as part of a human evolution in which status and class are fixed and unchangeable elements in the social structure. To a large extent, Black deprivation is viewed as a function of flaws in Afro-American culture. This is about all that we can expect from establishment White sociology since other theories tend to call into question the legitimacy of the present political and economic system and threaten the belief that White Western culture is the highest form of civilization known to mankind.

In its development, Black sociology continues in the tradition of other Black sociologists who saw sociological knowledge of Black life as a tool to improve the Black condition.[32] Just as they worked in their own way to promote sociology as an agent of change, so must we use this discipline as an instrument of Black liberation. White Americans can also benefit from an Afro-American sociology that will provide a realistic picture of different cultural forms and describe the political and economic elements involved in racial oppression. There is much that Whites can learn from Black humanism and creativity. More important, however, is the task of developing a sociology that can provide a balanced perspective of Blacks and not theories that are peculiar to the needs of an oppressive social system.

Hence, the purpose of Afro-American sociology is to study Black life and culture which when seen from a new Black perspective can serve to correct myths about Afro-Americans found in the sociological literature and to further study Black life as it is affected by political and economic factors. While we may find a pattern of systematic racial oppression, there also exists a rich culture that has emerged from the African traditions and American experiences. We need to know the elements of that culture in order to separate those cultural traits that are negatively imposed on Blacks by domestic colonialism from those that have served as an asset in the struggle for survival.

This is a task that will be carried out mainly by Black sociologists. Although there is nothing in race per se that makes the Black sociologists more competent, it is their special obligation to fulfill this important role. Just as the White sociologist has made his scholarship a servant to the vested interests in his racial group, so must Black sociologists use their knowledge in the service of the Black community. As White sociology has been a tool of oppression, Afro-American sociology must become an instrument of liberation.

NOTES

1 Karl Mannheim, *Ideology and Utopia*, Harcourt, Brace and World, New York, 1936.
2 Nathan Glazer and Daniel P. Moynihan, *Beyond the Melting Pot*, M.I.T., Cambridge, Mass., 1965, p. 53.
3 W. E. B. DuBois, *Dusk of Dawn*, Schocken, New York, 1968, p. 51.
4 Robert Blauner and David Wellman, "Toward the Decolonization of Social Research," in Joyce Ladner (ed.), *The Death of White Sociology*, Random House, New York, 1973, p. 315.

5 Dennis Forsythe, "Radical Sociology and Blacks" in Ladner, op. cit., p. 228.

6 Robert Staples, "What Is Black Sociology: Toward a Science of Liberation," in Ladner, op. cit., p. 165.

7 Stanford M. Lyman, *The Black American in Sociological Thought: A Failure of Perspective*, Putnam, New York, 1972, pp. 27–70.

8 Elliot Rudwick, "Notes on a Forgotten Sociologist: W. E. B. DuBois and the Sociological Profession," *The American Sociologist*, vol. 4, pp. 303–306, November 1969.

9 Robert Park and Ernest Burgess, *Introduction to the Science of Sociology*, University of Chicago, Chicago, 1924, pp. 138–139.

10 Mannheim, op. cit., p. 36.

11 Sidney W. Mintz, "Slavery and the Afro-American World," in John F. Szwed (ed.), *Black America*, Basic, New York, 1970, p. 40.

12 Chuck Stone, "The White Foundation's Role in Black Oppression," *The Black Scholar*, vol. 3, pp. 29–31, November 1971.

13 Forsythe, op. cit., p. 225–226.

14 Robert Park, *Race and Culture*, The Free Press, New York, 1950, pp. 15–151.

15 Nathan Hare, "The Sociological Study of Racial Conflict," *Phylon*, vol. 33, pp. 27–32, Spring 1972.

16 Lyman, loc. cit.

17 Kingsley Davis and Wilbert Moore, "Some Principles of Stratification," *American Sociological Review*, vol. 10, pp. 242–249, May 1945.

18 Bernard Barber, "Structural-Functional Analysis: Some Problems and Misunderstandings," *American Sociological Review*, vol. 21, pp. 129–135, April 1956.

19 Talcott Parsons, "Full Citizenship for the Negro American: A Sociological Problem," in Talcott Parsons and Kenneth Clark, (eds), *The Negro American*, Houghton-Mifflin, Boston, 1966, pp. 709–754.

20 Charles Valentine, *Culture and Poverty: Critique and Counter Proposals*, University of Chicago, Chicago, 1968.

21 Douglas Davidson, "Black Culture and Liberal Sociology," *Berkeley Journal of Sociology*, vol. 15, pp. 164–183, 1969.

22 Charles V. Hamilton, *"Black Social Scientists: Some Contributions and Problems,"* in Ladner, op cit., p. 472.

23 C. Wright Mills, *The Sociological Imagination*, Grove, New York, 1959, p. 18.

24 James A. Tillman, Jr. and Mary Norman Tillman," Black Intellectuals, White Liberals and Race Relations: An Analytic Overview," *Phylon*, vol. 33, pp. 54–66, Spring 1972.

25 Rhett S. Jones, "Proving Blacks Inferior: The Sociology of Know-
    ledge," *Black World*, vol. 20, pp. 4–19, February 1971.
26 Robert Blauner, *Racial Oppression in America*, Harper & Row,
    New York, 1972, pp. 84–85.
27 Ibid.
28 Irving M. Zeitlin, *Ideology and the Development of Sociological
    Theory*, Prentice-Hall, Englewood Cliffs, N.J., 1968, p. 83–108.
29 Robert Staples, "Race and Ideology: An Essay in Black Sociology,"
    Journal of Black Studies, vol. 3, p. 395, June 1972.
30 Blauner and Wellman, op. cit., pp. 321–330.
31 Juanita Jackson, Sara Slaughter, and J. Herman Blake, "The Sea
    Islands as a Cultural Resource," *The Black Scholar*, vol. 5, p. 38,
    March 1974.
32 John Bracey et al. (eds.), *The Black Sociologists: The First Half
    Century*, Wadsworth, Belmont, Calif., 1971, pp. 11–12.

SUGGESTED READING LIST

Blackwell, James E. and Morris Janowitz: *Black Sociologists: Historical
    and Contemporary Perspectives*, University of Chicago, Chicago,
    1974.
Blauner, Robert: *Racial Oppression in America*, Harper & Row, New
    York, 1972.
Blauner Robert and David Wellman: "Toward the Decolonization of
    Social Research," in Joyce Ladner (ed.), *The Death of White
    Sociology*, Random House, New York, 1973, pp. 310–330.
Bracey, John, et al. (eds.): *The Black Sociologists: The First Half Cen-
    tury*, Wadsworth, Belmont, Calif., 1971.
Clarke, Cedric X.: "The Role of the White Researcher in Black Society:
    A Futuristic Look," *Journal of Social Issues*, vol. 29, pp. 109–118,
    Winter 1973.
DuBois, W. E. B.: *Dusk of Dawn*, Schocken, New York, 1968 edition.
Fanon, Franz: *The Wretched of the Earth*, Grove, New York, 1963.
Gary, Lawrence E. (ed.): *Social Research and the Black Community:
    Selected Issues and Priorities*, Institute for Urban Affairs and Re-
    search, Washington, 1974.
Hare, Nathan: "The Sociological Study of Racial Conflict," *Phylon*,
    vol. 33, pp. 27–32, Spring 1972.
Lyman, Stanford M.: *The Black American in Sociological Thought: A
    Failure of Perspective*, Putnam, New York, 1972.
Mannheim, Karl: *Ideology and Utopia*, Harcourt, Brace and World,
    New York, 1936.

Rex, John: *Race, Colonialism, and the City,* Routledge and Kegan Paul, London, 1973.

Rex, John: *Race Relations in Sociological Theory,* Schocken, New York, 1970.

Ryan, William: *Blaming the Victim,* Pantheon, New York, 1971.

Thompson, Daniel: *Sociology of the Black Experience,* Greenwood, Westport, Conn., 1974.

Sociology of Race and Racism

In a general sense, sociology is concerned with the social relations that prevail in human society. It focuses on the institutional arrangements and roles that satisfy human needs; on the ordering of symbols to facilitate communication; and on the underlying processes that characterize the dynamic aspects of human interaction.[1] The problem we face is specifying those aspects of sociology that describe the few elements of social reality with which Black people deal. With rare exceptions, White sociology has not given to Black people any systematic theory concerning the nature of their oppressed status, its historical antecedents, or the process by which their deprivation has been stabilized in the social structure.[2]

A relevant sociology dealing with race should reveal that the economic and political organization of a society is the primary force in determining the basic patterns of human behavior. While this proposition is accepted by some sociologists, their analysis of human society is frequently limited to the political and economic structures rather than the behavior they generate. This would appear logical in the sense that one usually studies the cause of a disease rather than its symptoms.

Black sociology, however, must study both the cause and effect of White racism. If, for instance, capitalism is the ultimate source of racism, how are some of the dynamics of racism related to the capitalist system? Why, for example, have some White capitalists been vehement supporters of racist institutions and practices while others of their class have just as strongly opposed them? Perhaps the answer lies in the fact that whereas capitalism may initially provide fertile soil for a racist ideology, racism may continue independent of the economic reason for its existence.

In addition to studying the interrelationship of political and economic variables with racist behavior, the institutions and behavioral patterns that Blacks have developed should be analyzed in terms of their interrelationship with the system of White racism. Although these areas comprise an important part of the sociology of race, a central focus of this chapter will be the history of racism and the role of ideology.

From the beginning of sociology, with Auguste Comte (1877),[3] the historical method has been an essential tool for studying human institutions and behavior. History is the foundation of all well-conducted studies of man and society.[4] By studying America's cultural antecedents from a historical perspective, it is possible to analyze not only the historical function that racism fulfilled but also to study the changing relations of the elements and forces of which racism is composed. In this way, one may assess the regularities of a racist system and make some predictions as to its future course. This analysis of the trend of racism by the historical method may be used by Black people to direct the nature of their struggle for liberation.

The role of ideology is important since it forms the basis for justification of racist institutions and practices. According to Marx (1904), the ideas of a society are by necessity the ideas of its ruling class.[5] This means that people hold beliefs they feel are functional for retaining their privileges in a society. The belief, for instance, that Whites are superior is not limited to a certain stratum of the White ruling class, but to Whites in general because they believe that they benefit from the subordination of Blacks. Ideology, then, is a form of social control exercised by the entire White society to retain its privileges in a system partially sustained by this ideology.

Black nationalism is presently a countervailing ideology to White racism. Once it acquires a large following among the Black masses, the system of White supremacy will be more dependent upon political and economic control for its maintenance. In conformity with the purpose of Black sociology the general characteristics of the system of White racism will be examined as it developed from the beginning of Black-White relations in this country. The model presented here provides a chronological scheme for the study of the problem and represents a logical method for studying the changing character of the oppressed conditions of Black people.

From a historical perspective, one must examine the relationship between the oppressed condition of Black people and the political and economic organization of American society. While White racism plays an important role in sustaining and perpetuating the oppressed status of Blacks, it is impossible to understand the interrelationship of White racism and Black oppression without examining the politico-economic system of this country and the historical context in which it existed.

Originally, Blacks entered the New World as indentured servants— a status that many Whites shared. Indentured servants were people who had their passage paid to this new continent and were contractually obligated to work for their sponsors for a certain period of time. Once their debtors were reimbursed, the indentured servants were free to pursue their own interests. According to historians of this period race played a significant, but not central, role in the social relations between White and Black indentured servants. They worked together as equals and even intermarriage between the two racial groups were tolerated during this period.[6]

It was the development of tobacco and cotton that created the need for a large-scale labor force to cultivate these products, preferably an inexpensive work force. The idea of a captive labor force was not new. It existed in earlier societies such as the Greek and Egyptian civilizations. The matter was simply economics. Slavery, despite the problems it posed in terms of regulating human labor in a coercive relationship, was the most profitable source of labor available.[7]

There was little concern, in the beginning of the slave system, for the racial composition of the bondsmen. The slaveholders initially tried

Whites and America's native population—the Indians. However, there were certain difficulties surrounding the use of these two groups. Whites, being part of the same racial group, easily escaped and avoided detection by assimilating into the nonslave society. Also, they disappeared into the frontiers of the unknown West where their recovery was improbable. The Indians were soon found unsuitable for this type of labor, although thousands were killed in the attempt to enslave them.[8]

It was on the continent of Africa that the new bondsmen were to be found. From the beginning of the slave trade until its actual end, estimates are that as many as one hundred million Africans were sold into slavery. It is also reliably reported that many of the slaves did not survive the trip—the majority of them perished en route.[9]

Before this massive depopulation, the African nations had a flourishing civilization. Most of the slaves were taken from the west coast of Africa where they had their own languages, mores, and folkways for regulating the behavior of their members, communication systems, and extensive network of trade relations throughout the African continent. These civilizations drew upon a very rich and long cultural heritage that existed in Africa.[10]

While slavery was not new to mankind nor endemic to the United States, the enslavement of Africans and their brutal transplantation to this country marked a new chapter in the history of man's inhumanity to man. Previous slave systems were not characterized by distinctions of race.[11] Brown (1949) describes the slave system in Greece:

> The slave population was enormous, but the slave and the master in Greece were commonly of the same race and there was no occasion to associate any given physical type with the slave status.[12]

Similarly, in Rome, slaves were not differentiated from freemen in their external appearance. As authorities on the subject have noted, any citizen might conceivably become a slave; almost any slave might become a citizen.[13] The blocked mobility of slaves was also peculiar to the United States. In Latin America, for instance, the slave lost his freedom but retained the right to regain it. In the United States, Blacks were consigned to a slave status from birth to the grave.[14]

The American slave system abrogated all rights the Africans had as human beings. Slaveholders could not be punished for the way they treated their slaves; families were broken up by the sale of members; there was no legal marriage for slaves; the children of a slave mother were automatically slaves; and the status of slave was a position from which little mobility was permitted.[15]

The treatment accorded Blacks, the subversion of their culture, the disruption of their family life were due to a sancrosanct American value—profit. The racial homogeneity of the slave class was initially an insignificant factor. As Eric Williams (1944) writes:

> Here, then, is the origin of Negro slavery. The reason was economic, not racial; it had to do not with the color of the laborer, but the cheapness of the labor. As compared with Indian and White labor, Negro slavery was eminently superior. . . . The features of the man, his hair, color and dentifrice, his "subhuman" characteristics so widely pleaded, were only the later rationalizations to justify a simple economic fact: that the colonies needed labor and resorted to Negro labor because it was cheapest and best.[16]

The labor of the bondsmen was essential to the development of America's economic structure. Slavery as an economic system provided the initial capital, raw materials, and flow of materials needed for economic stability and growth during its existence in this country. This was particularly true of America's cotton production. Tabb (1970) states that cotton was a strategic material that paid for American imports. The United States was highly dependent upon the income received from the cotton trade with foreign nations, and slavery was the basis of cotton production.[17] This often ignored fact of American economic history reveals the importance of slavery and Black labor to the development of American capitalism and in part to the high standard of living enjoyed by many contemporary Americans.

In ancient societies, and in the colonial period, slavery was justified by the "just" war theory: a nation victorious in a war was justified in enslaving the heathens. Various rationalizations arose in the

United States to justify slavery. As its importance and profit value
increased in the South, the ideology that supported slavery changed.
One theory was that Blacks were heathens and that slavery meant
their conversion to Christianity: the slaveowners were saving souls.[18]

However, the racist theory, based on the putative inferiority of
Blacks, became the predominant ideology supporting slavery. There
is no unanimity of opinion on the origin of racism. According to
Ashley Montagu (1964), "A study of the cultures and literature of
mankind, both ancient and recent, shows that the conception of natural or biological races of mankind differing from one another mentally
as well as physically, is an idea not born until the latter part of the
eighteenth century."[19]

This racist theory was embellished with pseudoscientific tracts and
biblical quotations and posited as a self-evident truth beyond cavil.
It created a certain racial mythology that has lingered on into the
postslavery twentieth century and prevails in the racial ethos of
modern-day America.[20] But with the emergence of the Northern
industrialist class, economic interests hostile to the slaveholders brought
forth new theories and ideas and challenged the supremacy of the
slaveholders on all fronts including ideology. The ensuing class struggle
between the Northern capitalists and Southern slaveholders culminated
in a Civil War and resulted in the destruction of an already declining
slave system.[21]

A popular myth that prevails in this country is that White America
fought an internal war to free its slaves because of its moral outrage
at the continued existence of this peculiar institution. Contrary to
this benign history of slavery, the slave trade was not abolished by
any country until the economic value of slavery declined. Slavery
ended in the United States as a consequence of many factors including
the low productivity of forced labor, lack of markets, low industrialization, etc.[22]

Moreover, Blacks played an important role in bringing about the
downfall of the slave system. There was the day-to-day resistance
of the slaves that resulted in sabotage. The slave avoided work by
pretending stupidity, ignorance, or laziness. Stealing and arson were
common on plantations; tools were broken; mules and horses were
abused or killed.[23] In some cases mothers killed their babies so they
would not grow up to be slaves. In addition to this covert resistance,

the slaves put together a number of elaborate conspiracies and insurrections. According to Aptheker (1963), over 250 slave revolts were planned.[24]

The Civil War was fought, in part, not over the principle of slavery, but over the issue of the extension of the slave system. The question was whether the new Western frontiers would be opened up by freemen or by slaves. The Southern slave states had a need to expand because slave labor rapidly exhausted the soil. After exhausting the land in the East, the planters could only move on, with their slaves, farther and farther west. Northern capitalists, however, wanted to colonize the West for their own profit interests. They also saw the abolition of slavery as enabling them to make inroads into the Southern states, using them as a source of raw materials, a market for their manufactured products, a field of investment for their capital, and a reservoir of cheap labor.[25]

Once they entered into a civil war, the Northern industrialists could not have won without the participation of Blacks. When the war began, the Black slaves deserted the Southern plantations in droves and joined the Northern armies. While they were first rejected as undesirable, they subsequently were employed both as soldiers and laborers. What amounted, then, to a general strike by the bondsmen, was crucial to the result of the war. It greatly weakened the Southern economy while reinforcing the military and economic power of the North. It was this direct action of the Blacks that finally elicited from the previously reluctant Lincoln the Emancipation Proclamation of 1863.[26]

RECONSTRUCTION

After slavery, the Northern industrialists attempted to gain power from the former slaveholding class. The best way to attain their goals, they believed, was by taking the vote from the rebellious Southern aristocrats and giving it to the former bondsmen. For a brief period this meant the establishment, under protection of a military dictatorship and by means of universal suffrage, of a political democracy with no distinction as to color. However, this new condition of freedom for Blacks was not to last long.[27]

In an agrarian society, the greatest need of the freed slaves was land. In some cases, Blacks were allowed to take over the abandoned plantations of their former owners. Northern capitalists, too, wanted land and their desire for property increments took primacy over the freed slaves' need for land in order to get started as capitalists themselves. The efforts of certain congressmen to have Congress adopt a proposal to give 40 acres and a mule to every slave family failed. Blacks, who for years had cultivated the land, remained on the plantation, but as manual laborers, not landed gentry.[28]

Thus, slavery was replaced by sharecropping and debt peonage for the landless Blacks. Their status changed from slaves to sharecroppers; the slave barracks near the big house became dispersed wooden shacks; money lending charged against the value of the sharecroppers' share of the crops became an economic surrogate for slavery. Through constant indebtedness, the freedmen were as tied to the land and the landlord as they were under slavery. The planter saw to it that there was always a debt and therefore an obligation to remain. And if necessary, he did not hesitate to use force to discourage his tenant from escaping.[29]

Also, the period of political and economic equality for Blacks was coming to an end. Through a compromise between the North and South, the protectors of Black voting rights—the federal armies—left the occupied areas of the South. Blacks were left to the mercy of their former owners. One Southern state after the other adopted laws designed—by one means or another—to deprive Blacks of their voting rights.[30] White supremacy was restored in the South and a new organization was created as the instrument for its maintenance—the Ku Klux Klan. Their goals, as stated in their program were: to restore the former privileges of the planters, protect their property against the land hunger of the Blacks, and reduce Blacks to the status of servile labor; and in order to achieve these goals, to rob the freedmen of their political rights.[31]

Political disenfranchisement, then, was only part of the total scheme to put Blacks in "their place." Another one was "Jim Crow," as physical segregation by race became known in the South. This practice of racial segregation did not begin until the turn of the twentieth century. Until that time the political leaders attempted to maintain their power in Southern states by manipulating the Black vote against the poor Whites.[32]

One countervailing factor to the divide-and-conquer policy of the Southern Bourbons was the existence of the populist movement in the 1890s, which was a struggle of the landless poor Whites against the planters and the new commercial and industrial interests. The leaders of the populist movement succeeded to a large extent in bringing about cooperation between Blacks and Whites. Eventually, it failed because Southern politicians were able to convince the poor Whites that their condition was due to the competition of Blacks.[33] Thus, they established a system of legal segregation of the races designed to maintain the social and economic subordination of the Afro-American. In order to rationalize the Jim Crow system, an extensive propaganda campaign was carried out to prove that Blacks were subhuman, morally degenerate, and incapable of intellectual development.[34] This is the ideological heritage of twentieth-century White America.

After the turn of the twentieth century, new events marked the Black man's struggle to survive in White America. In the period between 1910 and 1920, a combination of natural disasters in the South, increasing mechanization of agriculture, World War I and the demand for labor, and industrial expansion in the North, generated the dispersal of over a million Blacks across the nation and correspondingly reduced the Black percentage in the South. Black migration was a function of increasing urbanization of both the South and the North along with the expansion of war industries that required that cheap Black labor be recruited.[35]

After World War II, some of the vestiges of Jim Crow were eliminated by the 1948 integration of the armed forces, the 1954 Supreme Court desegregation of schools ruling, the Montgomery bus boycott, and the civil rights movement of the late fifties and early sixties. But the objective condition of the masses of Black people was still abject poverty, persistent high rates of unemployment, substandard housing, etc. The cause of this condition is commonly attributed to the lingering effect of America's racist heritage.

RACISM IN AMERICA

Most students of the subject are in agreement on the economic origin of racism. According to Oliver Cox, before Columbus discovered America in 1492, the world had never known racism. It was the product of the system of forced Black labor which eventually was justified by the color of the laborers.[36] Present-day racism, however, can be studied as a phenomenon in itself. DuBois (1940), while in agreement on the economic origins of race prejudice, believed that a racial folklore was gradually superimposed on the conscious determination of the Whites to exploit Blacks, a folklore which was based on centuries of irrational instincts and mental habits and which eventually sank into the depths of the subconscious.[37]

That White America is a racist society is no longer a moot issue. The National Advisory Commission on Civil Disorders concluded that the root cause of the riots in American cities was White racism.[38] While the Commission's revelation was nothing new to Black people, it meant that with the peace of this nation being shattered by the upsurges of the urban victims of racism, this segment of White America's leaders decided to admit to the racist character of their society.

In the book, *Black Power,* Carmichael and Hamilton (1967) delineate two forms of White racism: individual racism and institutional racism. The former refers to individual Whites acting against individual Blacks while the latter relates to acts by the total White community against the Black community. They explain it this way:

> When White terrorists bomb a Black church and kill five Black children, that is an act of individual racism, widely deplored by most segments of the society. But when in that same city— Birmingham, Alabama—five hundred Black babies die each year because of the lack of proper food, shelter and medical facilities, and thousands more are destroyed and maimed physically, emotionally and intellectually because of conditions in the Black community, that is a function of institutional racism.[39]

INSTITUTIONAL RACISM

This form of racism is significant because it is embedded in American institutions in a subtle form that allows the White-dominated society to not only exploit but dehumanize Afro-Americans in a systematic manner. Among their functions are the maintenance of racist practices that create and sustain White privilege at the expense of Black equal opportunities, a situation from which White Americans benefit in a variety of ways.

Educational Institutions

Educational institutions represent one of the most important instruments of colonial rule and lie at the heart of the colonial process. Ever since the Black arrival on these shores, it has been an important issue in the Black/White confrontation. For the majority of Americans education has always been regarded as the major means of upward mobility in the class structure. Hence to limit the access of Blacks to educational systems is to maintain the racial privileges of the White majority. It is rarely stated in that way but rather is widely regarded as a result of Black inability to take advantage of educational opportunities due to their inherent intellectual deficiencies.

During the days of slavery Black access to education was rare and since then it has been inadequate in the racially segregated schools of the South. It is believed that Blacks did not receive any formal education until the eighteenth century in colonial America. Informal education was little more available as many slaveholders were opposed to their slaves' learning to read. The quest for a decent education has been a long, bitter struggle for Blacks. Free Blacks did receive some instruction from free schools set up by religious societies in the eighteenth and nineteenth centuries, but as the Southern race system of Jim Crow grew harsher the education of Blacks was increasingly restricted.[40] Up to the present time the standards of education for Blacks remains low because of the belief that they are incapable of profiting from an education.

The statistical evidence seems to bear this out when it is revealed that Blacks score lower on every index of school performance than Whites. There are differences of opinion on why these racial gaps in educational achievement exist. One school of thought is that the deprived family and socioeconomic background of Black children means they enter the school setting with certain deficits that make it difficult for them to compete equally with White children.[41] Others believe that the primary effect of poverty and race is the attitudes it creates in White or middle-class teachers. When the teacher is led to expect a poorer performance from a child because he is poor and Black, that attitude is what determines a child's performance. A Black child enters school with a real zest for learning but he soon discovers that the teacher expects little of him and subsequently he begins to expect little of himself.[42]

An authority on education, Kenneth Clark (1965), notes that the belief that Black children are culturally deprived only serves as a rationalization of the educational neglect of those children.[43] Such theories perpetuate the inferior education Blacks receive at every level and maintain their colonial status. These theories only entrench racial differences in class positions and make of the schools an instrument in fostering class inequalities based on race in the larger society.[44]

That is precisely the role educational institutions play in colonial societies. In addition to maintaining the inferior status of its subjects, it acts as a formidable instrument of political power in its role as a transmitter of goals, values, and attitudes of the colonial order. The educational system selects those values and attitudes favored by the ruling class and teaches them as universal truths.[45] School remains one of the major institutions for socializing colonial subjects into the values of the colonizer. According to Cleaver (1969), "They teach the exploited and the oppressed people to virtually love the system that is exploiting and oppressing them. The oligarchy has an interest in seeing to it that the curriculum is to its liking and that it does not expose the true nature of the decadent and racist society we live in."[46]

Although it is generally believed that school desegregation was designed to better educational opportunities for Blacks, it has produced some latent benefits for internal colonial rule. One study, for instance, found that Blacks in segregated schools are more politically aware and more inclined to participate in politics than are Blacks in integrated schools. The research's conclusion was that political action has been more effective in improving Black socioeconomic status than racially integrated schools. The study also noted that racial integration made Black people less politically conscious. Racially segregated schools, it seems, are positively beneficial for Black students in terms of political orientations and behavior.[47]

For most Americans better jobs and a higher income are considered the most desirable rewards of an education. For Blacks education has never given them economic parity with Whites. A Black graduate, for instance, still earns three-quarters the income of a White person with a similar education.[48] Moreover, the effect of school desegregation in 17 states was the loss of the jobs of 31,500 Black teachers at a cost to the Black community of $240 million. Since the 1954 school desegregation decision Southern school systems have dismissed, demoted, dispatched, and discriminated against a large number of Black teachers.[49]

Entertainment

Although entertainment is generally considered an industry rather than an institution, its importance to Blacks in providing some basic institutional functions merits its inclusion in this category.

Being an entertainer is one of the few accessible means of gaining economic success for Blacks. It is also one of the few sources of White approval for their parity with, or even superiority over, Whites. With the exception of sports, Blacks have more significant participation in this area of the White world than any other. The economic gains associated with success in this sphere makes them all the more acceptable to Whites as members of the native elite. However, even in this industry they have been subjected to some aspect of White colonial rule and exploitation.

In one of the most important areas, movies, Blacks have been blatantly subjected to exploitation and dehumanization. More than any other media the film industry has shaped and reflected racist attitudes toward Blacks. Sterling Brown (1933) has listed seven stereotypes of Blacks found in literature and films: the contented slave, the wretched freedman, the comic Negro, the brute Negro, the tragic mulatto, the local-color Negro, and the exotic primitive. In these types one finds the characteristics of laziness, filth, sensuality, and crime.[50] Until 1954 these were the images of Blacks projected in American films and they served to create and maintain the myth of White purity and superiority.

During the latter part of the fifties and early sixties, Blacks were portrayed as social problems and super heroes. Seldom did one ever see an average Black family that worked hard, engaged in normal love and marital behavior, or enjoyed life.[51] It was in the late sixties that a new form of exploitation emerged in the shape of Black films directed toward increasing Black audiences who were hungry to see their image on the cinema screen. Most of these movies (e.g., *Superfly, Shaft,* etc.) contained heavy doses of sex, crime, violence, and drugs in a way that suggested approval of them.[52] In most cases they were nothing more than a continuation of past stereotypes of Blacks as criminal and sexy savages, related this time to the nitty-gritty Black cultural lifestyle.

Most of the producers of these films were Whites who claimed that Black audiences desired these types of films. Few Black leaders outside the movie industry agreed. One reviewer asserted that they were not only an insult to Black intelligence but subtly harmful to the interests and well-being of Blacks and Whites alike.[53] He nevertheless defended them because of his belief that it is unfair to expect the downtrodden to be more upright than the oppressor. The Blacks who participate in the production of Blaxploitation films are in reality that sector of the native bourgeousie which has internalized the values of the colonial ruling order. Hence, they have seized the chance to make a profit out of movies that encourage drug use, crime, and the sexual exploitation of Black women. Recent trends indicate that Black audiences are tiring of the constant diet of sexual violence as the only content of most Black films. Hence, a new trend is emerging exemplified by films like *Claudine, Uptown Saturday Night,* etc.

In the other significant media, television, Blacks have generally been excluded until recent years. Since commercial television exists primarily to sell products, not to entertain, Blacks were not employed simply because they were not salable. Sponsors objected to their presence because they felt there was little to gain in additional sales and they would drive away part of the White audience.[54] Although Blacks actually watch television more than Whites they were rarely considered an important market for a sponsor's product. It was assumed they did not have enough money to buy what was advertised on television and even if they did, no special attention need be given to their desires since there was no competition among sponsors for their business, and they had nowhere else to go. Moreover, Blacks had such little value as a source of special markets that they were not even represented in the national rating services in proportion to their numbers in the population.[55]

When Blacks finally entered television with widespread White audience approval, it was as a middle-class White woman in a Black skin. The television show "Julia" offered little that most Blacks could identify with. Probably the greatest breakthrough was the "Flip Wilson Show," which reflected some aspect of Black culture. Yet, White audiences accepted him with glee because he confirmed a racist stereotype of Black people in the characters he played. One veteran observer noted that he mocked Black culture rather than sentimen-talize it.[56] The latest trend in commercial television is to portray Blacks as protectors of White society. Hence, we are deluged with a number of Black cops-and-robbers shows. Needless to say, Blacks have absolutely no control over this industry.

Economics

The area of economics is such an all-encompassing and basic element in the institution of White oppression, it cannot be dealt with ade-quately here. Probably the most relevant person in this context is the White ghetto merchant. In terms of overall sales, Whites dominate the businesses in Black ghettos. Rarely do they ever live in the area of their business operations, which means that the profits from their exploitative economic practices are spirited out of the Black community at night. The economics of the ghetto are very similar to that of classical colonial societies. Inhabitants of the ghetto are primarily workers who earn low wages and are dependent on the small stores in their community for goods and services. Lacking transportation and awareness of prices elsewhere for comparable merchandise, they are particularly vulnerable to the salespitch of the ghetto merchant who sells them inferior merchandise at higher prices.[57]

Among the many practices typical of the ghetto merchant is the sale of goods on credit installments with very high interest rates. Knowing that he is dealing with an uneducated, powerless native the ghetto merchant often uses deceptive advertising and misrepre-sentative sales contracts, refuses to return deposits, and employs co-ercive efforts to collect nonexistent debts. These techniques are much more prevalent in the ghetto because the natives are powerless to stop them. When the native refuses to pay, or is unable to, the legal system allows the ghetto merchant to attach the native's meager wages to recover his costs while providing the native with no redress from these unethical business practices.[58]

Military

Blacks have allegedly experienced less discrimination in the military than in any other sphere of American life. Historically Blacks have been subjected to racist stereotypes and treatment to the same degree in the armed forces as in other American institutions. Due to the belief that they did not have the ability to make good combat soldiers, attempts have been made to exclude them from participation in all of America's wars except the last two. During the time of the Civil War and for eighty years afterward, Blacks had to fight for the right to fight. The refusal to allow them participation in combat duty really reflected their colonized status since war duty was a symbol of American citizenship.[59]

Patriotic service in the military was highly valued until the last two wars and especially the one in Indochina. Until those two wars Blacks served in segregated military units where they worked at menial tasks as was common in civilian society. In most cases they were supervised by White officers and the few Black officers rarely rose above the rank of Captain. When the armed services were desegregated in 1948, the subsequent wars became less popular and Whites less willing to fight in them.

One result of the unattractiveness of American wars was the increasing use of Blacks and other racial minorities to fight them.[60] The draft became the main instrument of building up combat troop strength. Most of the draftboards were composed of Whites and ever since 1965 the proportion of Blacks drafted has exceeded their percentage in the general population. Middle-class White youth were able to escape military service through college and occupational deferments. Another important technique of evasion was enlistment in the reserves or National Guard. Whites were four times as likely as Blacks to use those means to evade the draft. The ultimate result of White disdain for war was a much larger number of Black draftees and a significantly higher casualty rate.[61]

Life in the Army is still unpleasant for Blacks. In recent years a number of Black servicemen, in all branches of the military, have rebelled against their treatment. Among some of the problems they experienced were racial slurs, the wearing of Confederate flags by White soldiers, intimidation for wearing Afro haircuts, assignment to more dangerous duty than Whites, and failure to get assignments, medals, and promotions on an equal basis with Whites.[62] As they have belatedly learned, the military is merely an extension of colonial society. The so-called volunteer Army has radically increased the number of Black enlistees. In July of 1973 over 35 percent of the new recruits were Black. During that same year 51.8 percent of all Blacks eligible for reenlistment did so compared with 32.5 percent of the eligible Whites. An obvious reason for Blacks entering the armed forces in such large number is their fear of entering the ranks of the underclass in the civilian world. Although Blacks make up almost 20 percent of the enlisted men, they represent only 3.9 percent of the officer corps.[63]

Legal System

Law is another institution popularly regarded as acting favorably on behalf of Black equality. The Supreme Court in particular was considered the catalyst of the civil rights movement in the sixties. Upon closer investigation, their landmark 1954 ruling on school integration came as a result of the heightened expectations of Black people at the end of World War II, along with the colonial order's fear that its educational apartheid system would mar its image among the newly emerging nations of the world. The Supreme Court should be given proper credit for being more responsive to the moral imperatives of destroying the caste system than other American institutions. Yet, the Court's ruling on school integration was so vague and protracted one can only assume it placed a higher priority on buttressing the potential loss of White privilege than the continued damage to the colonial subjects who could not get a proper education. It had been noted that in fields other than race relations, the Court has been very decisive and acted without regard to public opinion.

In the lower courts Blacks continue to experience the treatment normal for colonial subjects. Most judges are political appointees and carry out the wishes of the political state. The legislative branch of government has passed a number of laws that border on the absurd since the victims bear the responsibility of providing proof of discrimination in an admittedly racist society. For example, in a community of 100,000 people where not a single Black person has been able to rent or buy a home, the Black victim has to pay for legal expenses and lose time from work in order to seek redress in the courts. This can only lead one to the impression that the legal system is geared toward maintaining the interests of White values and institutions rather than the rights of the oppressed.[65]

Politics

The political arena represents another area where American institutional oppression is of significance to Afro-Americans. Race is an important factor in the body politic. Politicians use the promise of government intervention to speed up racial progress to gain Black votes. In a more subtle way, at least today, they promise White voters a halt in Black advances to gain their votes. On the national level the same politicians have used both means to gain elective office.

Primarily in the North, Blacks have been manipulated by White politicians in order to gain enough votes to swing an election. This was a successful tactic as long as Whites remained neutral to it. But, when a liberal stance on civil rights began to alienate White voters, who were fearful of losing their racial privileges, White politicians either ignored racial issues or adopted commonly known racist code words such as law and order or they went on record as being opposed to busing so as to let voters know where they stood. Black votes were important only as long as there was no appreciable loss of White votes.

Blacks have been wedded to the Democratic party since the Roosevelt Administration. However, one result of their putting Democrats into public office has been the increase of power for Southern Democrats. Since the party in control heads all standing committees, Southern Democrats, by virtue of their seniority, have used their dominance of those committees to stifle civil and economic rights legislation.[66] Reactionary racial politics has long been common in the South. The White politician who was most virulently anti-Black usually received the most votes, and until 1965 Blacks were largely unable to vote in large numbers in the South.

Today, this type of racial politics exists on a national level. A man who campaigned on an anti-Black program in the 1972 presidential election is now the most popular candidate for the Democratic nomination for President for 1976.[67] He no longer campaigns on a pro-segregation platform but instead uses code words like law and order and antibusing. Since he has never retracted his past statements on race, most Whites can assume that his attitudes are still the same. The use of code words means that White people can vote to retain their racial privileges while claiming loftier motives of being anticrime and for neighborhood schools.

Religion

It was once said that 11 A.M. Sunday was the most segregated hour in America. That statement still holds true since most churches are organized along rigid racial lines. Despite its official position as the upholder of the society's moral values, the White church has been just as much a part of institutional racism as all the others. With the exception of certain religious groups, such as Quakers and Jews, organized religion has either participated in the colonial oppression of Blacks or failed to take any position against it. They originally furnished the ideology for slavery by their collaboration with the slaveholder's theory that slavery was necessary to convert the heathens to Christianity. During slavery, and afterward in the South, Blacks were not allowed in White churches although Klu Klux Klan meetings were permitted there.[68] The church's role in the colonization of Africa is succinctly expressed in the proverb, "When the missionaries arrived they had the Bible and Africans held the land. When they left, Africans had the Bible, and they had the land."

Sports

To the average sports fan, the field of athletics is surely an area of life where Blacks are blessed. It is commonly known that the top stars in the three major sports are Black and command high salaries. Statistically, Blacks also dominate professional sports, comprising half the basketball players, one-third of the football players, and 25 percent of those in baseball, but the racism in sports is revealed in another set of figures that show no Black head coaches in football, one in baseball, and only four out of seventeen head coach positions in basketball.[69] The number of Blacks in other auxiliary posts is comparatively low. What this amounts to is a tendency to exploit the Black athlete's skill in order to be competitive but to maintain White dominance in those areas where interpersonal relations are more important than technical skills. Edwards (1973) claims that Blacks may be regarded as physically superior to White athletes but intellectually inferior to Whites in general. Thus, in those positions requiring thinking and organizational ability, Whites hold a monopoly.[70]

Brower (1972) found that racial stereotypes played an important role in the positions played on professional football teams. Blacks were mostly represented in positions that required the natural abilities of speed and instinct while Whites dominated the positions that demanded high intellect, leadership, and tolerance for pressure. Almost all quarterbacks and centers are White while the majority of defensive ends, receivers, and kickoff returners are Black. It might be noted that the White positions pay better and have a greater longevity for those who play them.[71]

Among the other racial privileges Whites enjoy are dominance of second-string positions for players with marginal skills. The Black athlete on both amateur and professional teams has to possess superior skills and be a starter in order to stay on a team. Informal racial quotas exist for most professional teams and they can be maintained only by reserving second-string positions for Whites.[72] Another constant complaint of Black athletes is that they do not receive the lucrative income from endorsements of commercial products. In some instances, athletes virtually double their income from this source. But for a long time an unwritten rule on Madison Avenue was, "If a Black man peddles it regardless of who he is, Whites won't buy it."[73]

Welfare

Welfare is a favorite whipping boy of the politicians, another racist code word for voters, and one of the most effective instruments of colonial control ever devised. This system has managed to make many Blacks wards of the political state, dehumanize them, and tear families apart. It serves primarily to maintain the industrial reserve army of capitalism at the mere subsistence level and enforce social control of the Black population by colonial intermediaries euphemistically known as social workers. As in colonial societies it fosters a dependency in the native population and erodes ambition and the work ethic. The recipients of welfare have been subjected to the most dehumanizing practices such as invasion of privacy, sterilization, beaucratic intrusion into their sex lives, control over their children, and various facets of economic exploitation caused by their subject status.[74]

While these conditions may not have been the intentions of those who originally designed the welfare system, they have now become the objective result. Piven and Cloward (1971) list two chief functions of the welfare program: to restore order when mass unemployment leads to outbreaks of turmoil and to regulate labor. These regulative functions of welfare, they assert, are required by the chaotic nature of a capitalist economy. The first function serves to maintain the existing political-economic order. When families are dislocated by mass unemployment they may ultimately come to question the social order itself. To reestablish the system's legitimacy and authority a substitute system of social control must replace it, at least temporarily.[75]

In the process of regulating labor the welfare system gains control over its client population by distributing the resources men and women depend upon for survival. By giving vitally needed assistance, they enforce the work doctrine itself by the conditions they apply to the aid they give. Usually the employable poor are redirected into the work force by one of two means. They may work in the public sector such as the parks or sewage collection system. Or they may be contracted out to private employers who hire the poor and racial minorities. In the former instance, the welfare system incorporates surplus labor deriving from a declining state of the economy and in the latter case its policies are designed to overcome the poor fit between the labor market requirements and the characteristics of the labor force. The purposes these policies serve are chiefly economic: to maintain the stability of capitalism. However, they are couched in the moral terms of the Protestant ethic of work as marking the value of the individual.[76]

There is a clearcut link between the relief system and Black oppression. On a national level almost half the families receiving aid to dependent children are Black. Life on the whole is a constant ordeal for those in need of it. Most welfare recipients live at the bare subsistence level. In 1970, the average income of the more than four million men, women, and children on welfare was $1.15 per day.[77] The majority of Black families receiving welfare are headed by women. Remedies suggested by the government to restructure welfare into "workfare" are only subtle attempts to force several million Black welfare mothers to work—mostly at wretchedly paid, menial jobs no better than domestic servants.[78]

TOWARD A SOCIOLOGY OF RACISM

While racist attitudes permeate White America, on both the individual and institutional level, covertly and overtly, it becomes misleading to relate the oppressed condition of Blacks to what are essentially beliefs, ideas, and images. Racism is commonly defined as a belief in the inherent superiority of one race.[79] Discrimination, however, is a practice that treats people unequally. Although there is a correlation between the two, racism can be completely independent of discrimination. In the process of indicting racism for the oppressed condition of Blacks many forget who implements the racist practices of this society and why.

Racist ideas and practices emerged from the need to justify and perpetuate slavery. Once ideas are mobilized, they linger on for a time after the disappearance of the conditions that produced them.[80] White racism today exists in different social milieus and thus in a somewhat different form than a century ago. It survived after slavery for essentially the same reason that it was introduced under the slave system that developed from the seventeenth century on: for its convenience as an instrument of exploitation.

American society, despite its democratic facade, is controlled by three interlocking groups: the military, industrial, and political elites. C. Wright Mills (1959) called them the "power elite," in his book of the same name. His main thesis was that the leaders of the military, industrial, and political institutions coalesced to control American society because they had one common goal: the maintenance of capitalism.[81] White racism arose out of the needs of capitalism, it is a product of capitalism, and it cannot be understood without analyzing the advantages of racism to the capitalist class.[82]

Capitalism's leading features are private ownership of property and operation primarily for the private profit of the owners. According to Marx (1936), exploitation is built into capitalism as an economic system; whatever his wages may be under capitalism the worker is economically exploited. By the use of his labor the worker produces more than he is paid for by the capitalist for whom he works. This value is appropriated by the capitalist class in the form of profits and so the worker under capitalism is exploited.[83]

It was Marx's theory that the economic basis of a society determines its social structure as a whole as well as the psychology of the people within it. Political, religious, and legal institutions together with the ideas, the images, the ideologies by which men conceptualize the world in which they live are reflections of the economic basis of society.[84] While this theory may be necessary to explain the racist ideology and institutions of American society, it is not sufficient. White racism does not exist to the same extent in all capitalist societies and racism will not automatically end once capitalism ends. However, once capitalism ends, the forces that nurture racism will diminish. Racism currently is profitable, and eliminating the profit motive will enhance the chance that racism will wither away as a phenomenon on the American scene.

The actual practice of racial discrimination is carried out by the business class and its agents. While the overwhelming majority of Whites support political officials and institutions that perpetuate institutionally racist policies, they do not control the implementation of those policies—with several exceptions.

Racial discrimination in employment, for instance, is a manifest example of the industrialist's role in fostering the oppressed condition of Blacks. In certain instances, where labor unions control the hiring of workers in their industry, they are even more vigilant in excluding Black labor from their ranks. The landlords, realtors, and bankers direct the exclusion of Blacks from White neighborhoods with the strong moral support of most Whites. Racially segregated education and substandard education is the domain of the Boards of Education, a body dominated by businessmen. Politicians, whose role is central in legislating into law conditions of Black deprivation or failing to enact laws to alleviate them, are controlled by the wealthy members of this society through the financing of political campaigns for their election. The mass media, which disseminate racism through their channels, are directly supported by the captains of industry.

One might ask, How are the advantages of racism to the power elite weighed against the problems created by urban riots and Black militancy on college campuses? The answer can partly be found in the low wages paid Black workers. By relegating Blacks to what are called menial or Black men's jobs, they depress the wages paid for those occupational categories. The lower the Black worker's wage, the higher the profits. A similar tactic is used for females whereby clerical workers are paid less because it is a female occupation. Since this practice affects only a certain racial group, there is no protest from the White body politic, which sees itself as benefiting from this practice because the "better" jobs are reserved for White people.

The high unemployment rate of Black workers indicates their use as a reserve labor force, to be employed during times of industrial expansion, e.g., during wars. Despite their lower wages, the racism extant in American society allows for the superexploitation of the Black masses by ghetto merchants. Recent studies have revealed that Blacks are forced to pay higher prices for housing, that they are sold food of low quality at inflated prices; that they are charged exorbitant interest rates for loans, etc.[85] Such is the double penalty for being Black in White America—low wages and higher prices.

Discrimination in employment has other liabilities for Blacks, especially the young males. Because many Black youth could not find employment, they either volunteered or were drafted into military service all out of proportion to their number in the society. Over 45 percent of Black youth suffer from the twin evils of unemployment and underemployment. Curiously enough, they also constituted about the same proportion of the war casualties in Vietnam. Once a volunteer Army became a reality, there were massive increases in the number of Black soldiers.[86]

Such are the advantages that accrue to the business and military establishments from White racism and its extension into the area of employment. The political gains from racism were twofold: gaining political office on the basis of favoring racial segregation and winning political offices by being opposed to racism. Oddly, both the winners in this somewhat incompatible set of factors belong to the Democratic party. In the South, politicians were elected on how strongly anti-Black they appeared to be to their constituency. The primary bastion of White supremacist rule among the Southern Democrats derived in large part from the political disenfranchisement of the Black masses.[87]

In the Northern states, Democratic candidates usually took pro-civil rights positions. When the Democrats run in a presidential election, their voters are a coalition of Blacks, labor, liberals, and Southerners. After giving the Democrats their vote, Blacks stand by and watch the Democrats aid the White supremacists by giving them the chairmanship of key congressional committees. Recent trends indicate that the coalition of White supremacists and oppressed Blacks may be coming to an end.[88]

More and more, racist politics is spreading across the nation, although in a more subtle form than the White supremacy platform of the South. A platform of law and order is easily translated by most

Whites as meaning that Negroes must be kept in their place. While the 10 million or so votes that White supremacist George Wallace received in the 1968 presidential election were not enough to elect him, the law-and-order campaign of Richard Nixon assured him of victory. The subtle racist slogan of law and order has led to the contravention of long-established political customs as actors and policemen achieve political office without coming up through the ranks of their political party.

At the present time many of the traditional racial practices have changed. Through the militancy and independence of their struggle against racism, Blacks have eliminated the more harsh effects of racial subjugation. With the preoccupation of White Americans with the rising cost of living, and political corruption along with the cessation of ghetto rebellions and political marches and demonstrations, the concern of the majority group with race relations is at a low ebb. Those members of the power elite charged with maintaining racial harmony have apparently decided on a policy of neocolonialism for the Black community. Black leaders who are responsible to them and committed to working within the system are gradually replacing the White authority figures as leaders or members of the police force, military, prisons, welfare system, etc. No fundamental changes have been made in institutional values or functioning but the replacement of Whites with Blacks tends to undermine the resistance of Blacks to institutional oppression, especially those who viewed it solely as a racial issue.

The importance of studying sociology from a Black perspective is that it provides a conceptual framework from which to seek explanations of the plight of the Black community. Using the method of historical analysis, it is possible to understand the *psychosocial dimensions* as well as *politico-economic implications* of the oppressed condition of the Black masses. A relevant sociology of race should study not only the nature of social relations extant in human society but also economic and political factors. When this method is effectively applied to the solution of concrete problems in the Black community, then it will have served its purpose: to provide an identification of those concepts that point toward the ultimate goal of mobilizing the Black masses to seek their liberation from the colossus of American racism.

NOTES

1 Frances Merrill, *Society, Culture and Personality,* Prentice-Hall, Englewood Cliffs, N.J., 1961, chap. 1.
2 Douglas Davidson, "Black Culture and Liberal Sociology," *Berkeley Journal of Sociology,* pp. 164–183, 1969.
3 Harriet Martineau, *The Positive Philosophy of Auguste Comte,* Bell, London, 1896, p. 250.
4 C. Wright Mills, *The Marxists,* Dell, New York, 1962, pp. 37–38.
5 Karl Marx, *A Contribution to the Critique of Political Economy,* C. H. Kerr, Chicago, 1904, pp. 11–12.
6 John Hope Franklin, *From Slavery to Freedom,* Random House, New York, 1947, pp. 42–60.
7 Eric Williams, *Capitalism and Slavery,* University of North Carolina, Chapel Hill, 1944, pp. 19–20.
8 Williams, op. cit., pp. 7–9.
9 Walter Rodney, *How Europe Underdeveloped Africa,* Tanzania Publishing House, Dar-es-Salaam, 1972, pp. 103–106.
10 Basil Davidson, *The Lost Cities of Africa,* Little, Brown, Boston, 1959, p. 00.
11 Frank M. Snowden, Jr., *Blacks in Antiquity,* Harvard, Cambridge, Mass., 1970.
12 Ina Carinne Brown, *Race Relations in a Democracy,* Harper & Row, New York, 1949, p. 34.
13 Snowden, op. cit., chap. 8.
14 Stanley Elkins, *Slavery: A Problem in American Institutional and Intellectual Life,* University of Chicago, Chicago, 1968, pp. 52–74.
15 Kenneth Stampp, *The Peculiar Institution: Slavery in the Ante-Bellum South,* Knopf, New York, 1956, chap. 5.
16 Williams, op. cit., pp. 19–20.
17 William K. Tabb, *The Political Economy of the Ghetto,* Norton, New York, 1970, p. 25.
18 Harold Woodman, "The Profitability of Slavery," *Journal of Southern History,* vol. 29, pp. 303–325, August 1963.
19 M. F. Ashley Montagu, *Man's Most Dangerous Myth: The Fallacy of Race,* World, New York, 1964, p. 8.
20 Thomas F. Gossett, *Race: The History of an Idea in America,* Southern Methodist, Dallas, 1963.
21 Williams, op. cit., pp. 19–20.
22 Alfred Conrad and John R. Meyer, *The Economics of Slavery,* Aldine, Chicago, 1964, chap. 3.
23 Stampp, loc. cit.
24 Herbert Aptheker, *American Negro Slave Revolts,* International Publishers, New York, 1963, p. 162.

25 Woodman, loc. cit.
26 Benjamin Quarles, *The Negro in the Civil War*, Little, Brown, Boston, 1953.
27 W. E. B. DuBois, *Black Reconstruction*, Russell and Russell, New York, 1962.
28 Ibid.
29 Pietre, Van Den Berghe, *Race and Racism*, Wiley, New York, 1967, pp. 87–88.
30 Theodore Wilson, *The Black Code of the South*, University of Alabama, 1965.
31 Franklin, op. cit., p. 327.
32 C. Van Woodward, *The Strange Career of Jim Crow*, Oxford, New York, 1955, pp. 67–109.
33 Paul Lewinson, *Race, Class and Party, A History of Negro Suffrage and White Politics in the South*, Grossett and Dunlap, New York, 1965.
34 Idus Newly, *The Development of Segregationist Thought*, Dorsey, Homewood, Ill., 1968.
35 C. Gunnar Myrdal, *An American Dilemma*, Harper & Row, New York, 1962, pp. 182–204.
36 Oliver Cox, *Caste, Class, and Race*, Doubleday, Garden City, N.Y., 1948, p. 330.
37 W. E. B. DuBois, *Dusk of Dawn*, Harcourt and Brace, New York, 1940, pp. 170–172.
38 *Report of the National Advisory Commission on Civil Disorders*, Bantam, New York, 1968, pp. 407–409.
39 Stokeley Carmichael and Charles Hamilton, *Black Power: The Politics of Liberation in America*, Random House, New York, 1967, p. 4.
40 Henry Allen Bullock, *A History of Negro Education in the South*, Praeger, New York, 1970, pp. 1–35.
41 Christopher Jencks, et al., *Inequality*, Basic, New York, 1972, pp. 253–265.
42 Estelle Fuchs, "How Teachers Learn to Help Children Fail," *Transaction*, vol. 5, pp. 45–54, September 1968.
43 Kenneth Clark, *Dark Ghetto*, Harper Torchbooks, New York, 1965, pp. 126–127.
44 Walter E. Schafer, Carol Olesa, and Kenneth Polk, "Programmed for Social Class. Tracking in High School," *Transaction*, vol. 7, pp. 39–46, October 1970.
45 Charles V. Hamilton, "Race and Education: A Search for Legitimacy," *Harvard Educational Review*, vol. 28, pp. 669–684, Fall 1968.

46 Eldridge Cleaver, "Education and Revolution," *The Black Scholar,* vol. 1, p. 46, November 1969.

47 Alfred S. Arkley, "Integration and Political Growth," paper presented at the American Political Science Association Meeting, New York, 1973.

48 James C. Coleman et al., *Equality of Educational Opportunity,* U. S. Office of Education, Washington, 1966, p. 273.

49 "Blacks Say Integration Cost Jobs," *The Washington Post,* p. A-17, June 3, 1973.

50 Sterling A. Brown, "Negro Characters as Seen by White Authors," *Journal of Negro Education,* vol. 2, pp. 179–203, April 1933.

51 Thomas R. Cripps, "The Death of Rastus: Negroes in American Films Since 1945," *Phylon,* vol. 28, pp. 267–275, Fall 1967.

52 Alvin Poussaint, "Blaxploitation Movies—Cheap Thrills That Degrade Blacks," *Psychology Today,* vol. 7, pp. 22–23, February 1974.

53 Charles Allen, "In Defense of Bad Black Movies," *The Black Scholar,* vol. 4, pp. 62–63, November–December 1972.

54 Les Brown, *The Business Behind the Box,* Harcourt Brace Jovanovich, New York, 1971, pp. 218–219.

55 Ibid, pp. 60–61.

56 Pamela Douglas, "Black Television: Avenue of Power," *The Black Scholar,* vol. 5, p. 26, September 1973.

57 Marvin E. Perry, "The Colonial Analogy and Economic Development," *The Black Scholar,* vol. 5, pp. 37–42, February 1974.

58 David Caplovitz, *The Poor Pay More,* The Free Press, New York, 1963.

59 Robert W. Mullen, *Blacks in America's Wars,* Pathfinder, New York, 1973.

60 Clyde Taylor (ed.), *Vietnam and Black America,* Doubleday, Garden City, N.Y., 1973.

61 Paul T. Murray, "Blacks and the Draft: A History of Institutional Racism," *Journal of Black Studies,* vol. 2, pp. 57–76, September 1971.

62 Wallace Terry, II, "Bringing the War Home," *The Black Scholar,* vol. 2, pp. 6–19, November 1970.

63 Michael Getler, "Blacks and the U.S. Army," *San Francisco Sunday Examiner and Chronicle,* This World Section, p. 16, September 2, 1973.

64 Lewis M. Steel, "Nine Men in Black Who Think White," in Barry N. Schwartz and Robert Disch (eds.), *White Racism,* Dell, New York, 1970, pp. 362–372.

65 Derrick A. Bell, Jr., *Race, Racism and American Law,* Little, Brown, Boston, 1973.

66 Chuck Stone, *Black Political Power in America*, Dell, New York, 1968, pp. 42–81.
67 "Wallace Leads Poll of Demos," *San Francisco Chronicle*, March 31, 1975, p. 7.
68 Kenneth Stampp, *The Peculiar Institution*, op cit., p. 158.
69 Leonard Koppett, "Blacks as Managers: It's Still a Question of Qualification," *The New York Times*, p. 21, October 27, 1973.
70 Harry Edwards, "The Black Athlete: 20th Century Gladiators for White America," *Psychology Today*, vol. 7, p. 52, November 1973.
71 Jonathan Brower, "The Racial Basis of the Divison of Labor, Among Players in the National Football League as a Function of Racial Stereotypes," paper presented at the Pacific Sociological Association Meetings, Portland, Ore., April 1972.
72 Aaron Rosenblatt, "Negroes in Baseball. The Failure of Success," *Transaction*, vol. 4, pp. 51–53, September 1967.
73 Harry Edwards, *The Revolt of the Black Athelete*, The Free Press, New York, 1969, pp. 15–28.
74 Richard M. Elman, *The Poorhouse State, The American Way of Life on Public Assistance*, Pantheon, New York, 1966, pp. 3–28.
75 Frances Fox Piven and Richard A. Cloward, *Regulating the Poor. The Functions of Public Welfare*, Vintage, New York, 1971, chap. 1.
76 Ibid.
77 U.S. Dept. of Health, Education and Welfare, Social and Rehabilitation Service, National Center for Social Statistics, "Public Assistance Statistics," December, 1970, p. 7.
78 Robert Staples, "Public Policy and the Changing Status of Black Families," *The Family Coordinator*, vol. 22, pp. 345–353, July 1973.
79 Henry P. Fairchild, *Dictionary of Sociology*, Littlefield, Adams, Totona, N.J. 1965, p. 246.
80 One of the best discussions on the sociology of knowledge is in Robert Merton, *Social Theory and Social Structure*, The Free Press, Glencoe, Ill., 1957, chaps. 12–14.
81 C. Wright Mills, *The Power Elite*, Oxford, New York, 1959.
82 Allen, op. cit., p. 37.
83 Karl Marx, *Capital*, Modern Library, New York, 1936, chap. 32.
84 Karl Marx, *The German Ideology*, Progress Publishers, Moscow, 1964, p. 39.
85 David Caplovitz, *The Poor Pay More*, The Free Press, New York, 1959, pp. 137–154.
86 Robert Staples, "Black Mercenaries in Vietnam," *Liberator*, vol. 8, pp. 10–11, February 1968.
87 Stone, op. cit., pp. 65–66.
88 Allen, op. cit., pp. 274–284.

SUGGESTED READING LIST

Carmichael, Stokeley and Charles Hamilton: *Black Power: The Politics of Liberation in America,* Random House, New York, 1967.

Davidson, Basil: *The African Slave Trade,* Little, Brown, Boston, 1961.

Fogel, Robert W. and Stanley L. Engerman: *Time on the Cross: The Economics of American Negro Slavery,* Little, Brown, Boston, 1974.

Franklin, John Hope: *From Slavery to Freedom,* Random House, New York, 1947.

Franklin, Raymon S. and Solomon Resnik: *The Political Economy of Racism,* Holt, Rinehart and Winston, New York, 1973.

Genovese, Eugene D.: *Roll, Jordan, Roll: The World the Slaves Made,* Pantheon, New York, 1974.

Gossett, Thomas F.: *Race: The History of an Idea in America,* Southern Methodist, Dallas, 1963.

Montagu, M. F. Ashley: *Man's Most Dangerous Myth: The Fallacy of Race,* World, New York, 1964.

Mullen, Robert W.: *Blacks in America's Wars,* Pathfinder, New York, 1973.

Myrdal, Gunnar: *An American Dilemma,* Harper & Row, New York, 1962.

Piven, Frances Fox and Richard A. Cloward: *Regulating the Poor: The Functions of Public Welfare,* Vintage, New York, 1971.

Rodney, Walter: *How Europe Underdeveloped Africa,* Howard, Washington, 1974.

Snowden, Frank M., Jr.: *Blacks in Antiquity,* Harvard, Cambridge, Mass., 1970.

Tabb, William K.: *The Political Economy of the Ghetto,* Norton, New York, 1970.

Taylor, Clyde (ed.): *Vietnam and Black America,* Doubleday, Garden City, N.Y., 1973.

Van Den Berghe, Pierre: *Race and Racism,* Wiley, New York, 1967.

Van Woodward, C.: *The Strange Career of Jim Crow,* Oxford, New York, 1955.

Willhelm, Sidney M.: *Who Needs the Negro,* Schenkman, Cambridge, Mass., 1970.

Williams, Chancellor: *The Destruction of Black Civilization: Great Issues of a Race from 4500 B.C. to 2000 A.D.,* Third World, Chicago, 1974.

Williams, Eric: *Capitalism and Slavery,* University of North Carolina, Chapel Hill, 1944.

Chapter 3

Black Culture
and Personality

THE NATURE OF BLACK CULTURE

When it comes to the question of Black cultural forms, we find that
there are no easy or definitive answers. This is one of the most
controversial and complex aspects of Black life to put into a Black
sociological framework. In this area the differing points of view include
the denial of a Black cultural existence; that it exists but is primarily
a pathological response to racial oppression; that the Afro-American
culture is an extension of cultural traditions found on the African
continent, etc. The purpose of this chapter is to critically evaluate
some of the theories of Black culture, point out internal variations in
Black cultural patterns, look at some of the social bases of Black
culture, and examine some of the cultural traits found in the Black
community. We will not attempt to sift out a theory of Black culture
because that is beyond the scope of this chapter. Our principal purpose
is to illustrate the social and political influences on Afro-American
cultural forms and provide a better understanding of the dynamics

and significance of Black cultural behavior and its influence on personality structures.

The one theory we reject outright is that Blacks lack a culture of their own. All available evidence indicates that this is a false assumption, if only because no group can exist without a culture. Those who have advanced such an argument have commonly defined culture in very ethnocentric or restricted terms.[1] We will use a fairly simple definition of culture that has intellectual validity among most social scientists: Black culture refers to a learned composite of specific ways of thinking, feeling, and acting that are peculiar to the members of that group and distinguishes it from other groups. What is important here is not a specific cultural trait, which may be found among other racial, ethnic, or socioeconomic categories, but the sum total of its cultural configuration. By using this precise definition we can categorically assert that there is a Black cultural reality.

Although in agreement with our belief that Blacks have a culture of their own, Blauner (1970) notes that advocates of a distinct Afro-American culture have failed to clearly specify the content and character of that culture.[2] This is a generally accurate charge that has yet to be corrected. One reason for this deficit in Black cultural literature is that the research simply does not exist. The study of cultural forms has traditionally been the province of anthropologists. There is a very small pool of Black anthropologists, and many White scholars in this field of study have been so concerned with depicting Afro-Americans as culturally deprived or finding a pathological culture that they have defaulted in their scholarly responsibility to delineate the components of a Black cultural system.

Another problem with systematically describing Black cultural behavior is that it is a subjective, as well as an objective, observable phenomenon: Culture is the dynamic element in a social structure, an abstraction that is often expressed in thoughts and values. Hence, it is not always as measurable as other behavior. There can be a difference between what the researcher sees and what the subject of his study sees. Even the subject may act out the cultural patterns of his group without any conscious awareness of the reasons why. As Dr. Carl Word (1974), psychology professor at San Jose State University, sums up this process: "Black behavior is, in reality, an iceberg, whose tip represents all those elements taught by his [Black man's] culture, while the larger unseen portion contains all those habits acquired through imitation and observations."[3]

When considering what comprises the elements of a Black cultural system, the possession of values and norms are important in understanding the unique character of that system. The shared values of a group dictate what is considered good or bad and what the norms of conduct are in a given situation. A central value in Black life is that individuals should be spontaneous, natural, and authentic. This is often referred to as "soul," a feeling which most Blacks consider their exclusive property. Himes (1973) characterizes this term as meaning three things: spirituality, feeling, and spontaneity.[4] In sum it is a lifestyle characterized by a lack of restraint in dealing with people and life, being flexible in adapting to situations, and a free and impulsive approach to one's environment. A soulful lifestyle is something that is felt rather than practiced. This does not mean that it is an inherited trait, since it develops out of group experience and interaction, but it does make it difficult to capture in the traditional concepts and categories of social science.

Further confusion exists over the nature of Black culture because much of it is a fusion of other cultural elements. Cole (1970), for instance, observes that Black culture is composed of three components: that derived from mainstream America, similar cultural traits of other oppressed peoples, and behavior patterns that are uniquely found among Afro-Americans.[5] Davidson (1969) makes the important point that it is the particular way in which such borrowed traits are handled that gives a culture its distinctive flavor.[6] The ability of Blacks to improvise upon, or remold, mainstream traits to reflect their own values is an excellent example. Putting soul (i.e., deep feeling) into songs created by Whites is exemplified by Aretha Franklin singing gospel or Ray Charles performing country and western music. Murray (1970) comments that Black women are often able to do things with wigs and hair colors that could hardly have been envisaged by the White people who manufacture them.[7] The same can be said of clothes and other mainstream artifacts.

A separate Black culture has emerged and retained its distinctive character because members of that group have their greatest proximity to and interaction with one another. While we will examine other sources of the Black cultural system, it mainly derives from the shared experiences of Black people. Whatever other alternative sources exist, it is the fact that Blacks constitute a separate community which represents a symbolic environment. Each Black person is born into a community where he will be exposed to role models and behavioral expectations that he will ultimately internalize and incorporate into his own behavior pattern. It becomes a symbolic environment because the meanings attached to gestures are mutually shared and reinforced. For example, a man's linguistic expression such as the "rap," is reciprocated by his female audience, which responds appropriately. In certain communities, when one Black person passes another it is expected that they will exchange a friendly greeting or perhaps a soul handshake even though they do not know each other. This is the symbolic nature of much of the Black world and cannot be transferred to other cultures. Such an expression of mutually shared cultural traits also helps to build a bond of racial solidarity.

Such cultural traits, however, are not transmitted in the same way or acquired by all members of the Black community. There is no uniform Black culture to which all members of this group subscribe. No matter what source of Black culture is accepted by students of this subject, the Black response has differed according to certain norms, statuses, and areas that divide the Black population. We must also acknowledge that culture is not a static process for any group. It is an ongoing process that is continuously being changed by the mobility and actions of its members. Furthermore, some individuals, by virtue of their particular circumstances and outlook, will accept or learn only some parts of the culture and reject other aspects.

It is through socialization, i.e., the process by which the norms of a group are transmitted to the individual member, that the individual acquires a culture. Internalization of a group's norms and values is usually synonymous with learning and adapting to its culture. While this is regarded as the primary source of culture for individual participants, the process differs somewhat for Blacks. In most societies adults, usually parents, are the main cultural mediators. Among Blacks, the younger children are frequently placed in the care of older siblings and playmates. In this context the peer group is often creating or communicating the cultural content. Within the peer group the Black child may acquire his language skills, role models, moral standards, and code of conduct. This does not mean that the child has little interaction with adults. He is in greater communication with the adult world than his White, middle-class counterpart because of his involvement in adult activities.

Because the Black child is more likely to grow up in an extended family setting, there are a number of adult relatives and friends around to transmit the culture he will join. These adults also serve as models for his behavior. Through the process of imitating these adult role models, he begins to unconsciously acquire the content of his culture. Unlike many of his White counterparts, he is included in the social world of adults. Much of Black fraternization is confined to the household and the child is allowed to participate in social activities. Because the adult figures present may represent three generations, the child may assimilate the culture of many years of the Black experience.

VARIATIONS IN BLACK CULTURAL PATTERNS

Social Class

The assumption is commonly made that the bearers of Black culture are the lower class and that the middle class has acquired the values of the majority culture.[8] Such an assumption can be quite misleading for several reasons. Most members of the Black middle class are recent arrivals from the lower class and their different lifestyles are often due to pragmatic adaptations to mainstream culture in order to conserve their meager economic gains. White society demands that those in white-collar occupations conform to middle-class Anglo-Saxon norms. Hence, many middle-class Blacks relate to Black culture in a very secretive manner. Hare (1965) cites a case where he went to a party of the Black bourgeoisie and found that a stack of long-playing symphonic records was the main musical fare. Underneath the stack he found a Little Richard record which he played and which brought the party to life.[9]

Even if the Black middle class is not relating to what is regarded as lower-class Black culture, they do not necessarily share the cultural lifestyle of middle-income Whites. Frazier (1957) once claimed that "there have been only two vital cultural traditions in the United States: the Black folk culture and the genteel tradition of mulattoes

who assimilated the morals and manners of the slaveholding aris-
tocracy."[10] In the nineteenth century this latter group constituted
the Black middle class of its time. But the culture of which Frazier
speaks was only an imitation of upper-class White culture. However,
due to its separate existence the Black middle class can be said to have
a culture of its own, which is a variant of lower-class Black culture.
Frazier describes much of this culture in his classic study of the Black
bourgeoisie but misinterprets the significance of its behavior.

Some of the Black bourgeoisie's behavior patterns reflect Black
values. For example, the number of Black social clubs and parties was
seen by Frazier as an attempt to imitate White lifestyles. But, we
could just as easily view this emphasis on partying and socializing
as the expression of the Black value of communalism. Matthews (1972)
claims that the institution of partying and Black recreation generally
tends to consolidate Black family and Black community.[11] The
orientation is toward group activity and interaction—not individual
pursuits. In a contemporary sense the Black middle class is the group
that Valentine (1971) believes is shaping an emergent Afro-American
culture influenced by Black nationalism[12] as a revitalization movement.
As Murray (1970) has observed, "Certainly the Black masses don't
go around theorizing about culture, identity and hair texture."[13]

Region

In the United States different sections of the country often represent
semiautonomous cultural systems. Despite the assumption of a mainstream culture in this country there are considerable variations by
ethnicity, religion, class, etc. Regional sectors can form cultures because they comprise the physical boundaries in which individuals live
and interact. Hence, they come to share certain characteristics and
values because of the common modalities of living in the same geographical space. A similar regional variation in Black culture can be
found in two different areas: the urban North and rural South.

Among some of the cultural differences found in the South are
the centers of social life, clothing styles, language use, folklore, the
cultural heroes, etc. In the South, for instance, the church and fraternal halls are more often the center of social life whereas it is the
streets, poolrooms, and schools in the North. Some of these differences
can be traced to age since the rural South is older than the urban

North. Soul food is more often served as a steady diet in the South than in the North where one may have to go to restaurants that specialize in that type of food. Although pimps and hustlers are regarded as lower-class cultural heroes, such role models are not as prevalent nor as admired in the South. The flashy, flamboyant clothing styles associated with Blacks is more of a Northern, urban trait than in the South where a dressy Black person may still provoke suspicion and hostility.[14]

Sex Roles

Cultural differences by sex-role affiliation might appropriately be attributed to differences in sex-role expectations. Our concern here is the unusual role of cultural transmitters carried out by the two sexes in the Black community. A major difference is that Black males are the creators of much of their culture rather than having it transmitted by a female parent. One reason for this is that a major source of Black cultural transmission is ghetto street life. It is primarily males who congregate on street corners, in poolrooms, and other social centers where they learn the content of Black male culture and are exposed to the dominant role models. The rich vocabulary of Blacks is also largely a male creation. Folb (1973) has noted that "the more complex speech events in the ghetto are usually the province of male adults."[15] An interesting departure from conventional sex-role patterns is the clothing styles of Black males. In mainstream culture it has usually been the females whose dress has shown the most diversity while the clothing of males has almost been uniform. Yet, a major news magazine reports that among fashion designers Black men are considered the trend setters.[17]

Age

Cultural differences by age grades are probably greater than ever. A number of factors account for this generational break in cultural values. Many parents, exposed to child-rearing literature, raised their children in a different manner than the way in which they were socialized. The emergence of a youth culture is more prominent than in other years. In the case of Black youth it is partly because they are growing up in different environments than their parents, much of their culture is transmitted in the peer group, and there are alternative socializing forces in the form of television, movies, and the schools.

The generational cultural differences are often reflected in regional differences. Many of the older Black families remain in the South and the extended family unit has greater control over the youth in its community. One of the age differences expressed in cultural form is respect for the elders. Among rural Southern Blacks, older Blacks were respected and admired leaders of the community. But, Poussaint (1974) has observed that Black Northern youth increasingly show arrogance and an inflated sense of superiority in their relationship with adults.[17] Part of this trend can be accounted for by the confrontation of Black youth militancy with the more conservative orientation of older Blacks. However, some of it must be credited with the decline of the extended family in Northern ghettos and the less significant role of elders in that setting.

Other age-cultural differences also exist in the area of the family, religion, dance music, etc. As we mentioned earlier, culture is constantly being refashioned by the action of its participants. There is the feeling in some quarters that current changes in Black youth culture is not progressive, that the emphasis on drugs, sexual exploitation, and individualism is contrary to traditional Black values. This may well be true but it is also among Black youth that we find a very conscious orientation toward its African heritage, a willingness to struggle militantly against racism and economic exploitation, and a pride in being Black.

SOURCES OF BLACK CULTURE

For those who believe in the existence of a distinctive Black culture, the question inevitably arises as what the source of that culture is. The most reasonable answer is that Black culture derives from a number of diverse forces and it would be difficult to trace it to one source. Surely, a history of three hundred years of slavery and oppression has left its mark on Black behavior. The socialization process is an important mechanism for transmitting the content of a culture to its youth. Within the socialization process the imitation and modeling effects of role models and behavior tend to subtly convey cultural content. The other source of Afro-American culture is the African heritage that has been retained in part over time and space.

African Survivals

This is a controversial theory that states Blacks in the diaspora have retained many of the cultural traits they brought over from the African continent. Primarily associated with the late anthropologist, Melville Herskovits, it begs the question of how it was maintained and in what form. The Herskovits answer (1941) was that some Africanisms were retained by New World Blacks because they were practiced in secret, traits such as voodoo. As to the form in which they are exhibited, he claims they were often distinguished as a combination of cultural elements that had been integrated to form one cultural complex. This is the process of syncretism and is expressed in Afro-American music, language, customs, food, and religion. In the case of Afro-American social organization, many characteristics regarded as European were actually African in origin. The prevalence of female-headed households, common-law marriages, respect shown to elders are but a few examples.[18]

We will discuss some of the possible African survivals in Afro-American cultural traits in a later section. However, no matter how convenient it may be to believe that Afro-Americans are an African people in their cultural behavior, there is not sufficient evidence to reach such a conclusion. The retention of African features has a stronger case in some Caribbean and South American societies for reasons that are peculiar to them. But a group rarely is totally stripped of all its cultural heritage, especially when they live the kind of segregated existence of American Blacks. Blassingame (1972) provides us with a good evaluative yardstick for assessing Africanism in Afro-American culture with his statement that "whenever the elements of Black culture are more closely similar to African than European traits, we can be reasonably certain that we have identified African survivals."[19]

Oppression

It is difficult to ignore or deny the role of racial oppression in shaping Afro-American cultural forms. Culture is in part a way of adapting to one's environment and the primary adjustment Afro-Americans have been forced to make is to the practice of racial subjugation. A major problem in crediting oppression with some influence on culture is the use made of its validity by some social scientists. The culture-of-poverty theory is but one example of how the oppressed are blamed for their response to their oppression.[20] But not all cultural adaptations to oppression is negative. Moreover, some cultural forms that stem originally from reactions to oppression may lose their meaning to its participants and become a positive feature of its culture over a period of time. An excellent example is "soul food," which was originally a diet based on the poverty of Blacks. Henceforth, the creativity and imagination in cooking such food has made it delicious eating to Blacks, even those who can afford more expensive cuisine.

A number of Black cultural elements can be traced originally to the practice of racism. Blauner (1970) even asserts that "American racism was the key condition that encouraged a Black culture."[21] We know that certain features of Afro-American culture are reflections of their oppressed conditions. Spirituals, jazz, Black arts, and other cultural traits are all recognition of, or protest against, a Black existence in a basically hostile environment. Cole (1970) even regards a part of soul as "long suffering and weariness with racism and poverty."[22] Another scholar who stresses the positive influence of oppression on Black culture is Vincent Harding.[23] Among the side effects of being racially oppressed is the Black development of the gift of compassion. According to him, Blacks who have experienced racial subjugation and humiliation have developed a capacity to identify and sympathize with the dispossessed throughout the world.

Slavery

With the exception of those who are proponents of the African survivals theory, slavery would be regarded as the original source of Black cultural forms that were developed in the United States. Since the Africans brought to this country represented different tribal cultures, the more uniform Afro-American culture had to evolve from a variety of cultural forms during the slavery era. Hence, the culture of the slaves combined features of their African heritage along with some elements of American culture. This process of culture reorganization was facilitated through the social organization of the slave community. The slave's primary environment was the slave quarters where he interacted with his fellow slaves. In that setting he created his own religion, songs, dances, and superstitions.[24] Out of this slave culture came a unique form of language, customs, beliefs, and ceremonies that serve as the basis of a distinct Afro-American cultural system. This cultural form is a blend of African traits, elements formed out of the slavery experience and American patterns.

THEORIES OF BLACK CULTURE

It is in the past treatment of Black culture as a form of pathology that White scholars (and some Black scholars) have demonstrated their own brand of racism. Few, whatever their views of the liberation of Blacks, have recognized any merit in Black cultural traditions. At best, they have argued that Blacks had no culture of their own. In examining and evaluating these theories of Black culture, it is necessary to note that few, if any, evolved out of a conscious effort to study Black cultural forms. Most were studies of Black life or aspects of it. Many were not undertaken by American anthropologists, who have historically studied Black groups outside the United States. As a result, the theories of Black culture view it mostly as a non-existent or negative phenomenon.

Cultural Deprivation

This theory, or its variant, argues that there is no such thing as a separate Black culture. Much of the remedial education for Black children was based on the premise that they were culturally deprived. The essential principle behind this theory is reflected in the often-quoted statement by two sociologists that "the Negro is an American and nothing else. He has no values and culture to guard and protect."[25] This particular view, which was held by many students of Black life, has two different meanings. It was advocated by those who sought to integrate Afro-Americans into mainstream society as equal members by illustrating their similarity with other Americans. Or, it was used in conjunction with the theory that Blacks had not fully or adequately acquired the necessary elements of American culture. Whatever the intention of the advocate the results were the same: Blacks were characterized as the only unassimilated group in American society to be without a distinct cultural contribution to this country.

This myth persisted despite the differences found in Black institutional and behavioral forms that could not be accounted for by class factors. Various alternative explanations rationalized these differences. Liebow (1966) suggested that Blacks have a "shadow culture" that reflects their inability to meet society's expectations. Thus, they develop a pale, distorted, and sometimes contradictory version of the dominant society's values.[26] A similar version is the value-stretch hypothesis of Rodman (1963). He claims that poor people share the general values of the society with members of other classes but in addition they have stretched these values, which help them to adjust to their deprived circumstances. As an example, legitimate childbirth is preferred but "illegitimate children born within an alternate marital union are normatively accepted."[27]

Only by explaining away racial differences as a forced response to oppression are the proponents of this theory able to deny the existence of a unique, distinct Black culture. Many see this as a necessary tactic in a society which believes that its culture is the most correct form of living. It could well be that a different set of values determines Black behavior but that those values would never be acceptable to White America, which believes its values are superior and to be adhered to by all members of the society. Some Americans, who are not ethnocentric, have become color-blind and insist that we are all human beings. Such a philosophy ignores the fact that humans organized into groups on the basis of common characteristics, who interact primarily with one another, have as the sum of their shared experience a common culture.

Black Culture as Pathology

Those who have not aligned themselves with the culturally deprived school of thought were most often inclined to believe that Blacks had a culture but that it was essentially a negative one. A slight variant of the cultural deprivation theory, it asserted that Black culture was "a pathological condition of the general American culture."[28] Commonly referred to as the culture of poverty, it is characterized as a response to poverty that results in specific traits such as female dominance, desire for immediate gratification, fatalism, and disorganization.[29] It often focuses on Black family organization and the values springing from the family environment as the major source of these negative traits. The studies of Rainwater (1970)[30] and Moynihan (1966)[31] in particular charged the Black family with being a major reason for racial inequality in American society.

The pathological model is not a theory employed only by racists opposed to Black advancement. In fact, it has been more common to White liberals and even some Marxists.[32] The basis of the model is that poverty breeds poverty, that the conditions imposed upon the poor account for these pathological cultural forms that keep them in impoverished circumstances. Poverty, then, becomes something transmitted from generation to generation because the values poor people possess are a deterrent to achieving upward mobility in the social structure. Among the criticisms of this approach are that many of the features associated with the culture of poverty—unemployment, substandard incomes, congested living conditions—are merely definitions of poverty itself, not of a distinct culture.[33] In essence, this theory is simply an attempt by apologists for internal colonialism to shift the responsibility for the conditions of racial and class oppression onto the oppressed themselves. It is an effort to rationalize why some Americans fail to achieve the culturally prescribed goals of the society.

Biculturation Model

This is an approach to Black culture commonly associated with DuBois. He saw Blacks as always relating to two sets of social forces, the social processes of American life and to their experiences as Black people in that setting. It was what he called a "double consciousness," the need to always see oneself on two different levels. According to DuBois (1965), "One ever feels his twoness—An American, a Negro; two souls, two thoughts, two unreconciled strivings; two warring ideas in one dark body."[34] The anthropologist, Charles Valentine (1971), chose this as a key concept for making sense out of ethnicity and related matters. Referring to it as "biculturation," he describes it as "the collective behavior and social life of the Black community which is composed of a distinctive set of Afro-American traits combined with Euro-American patterns." According to Valentine, the process of socializing Blacks into both cultural patterns begins at an early age, is a lifelong process, and has equal importance in the lives of most Afro-Americans.[35]

Although the concept of biculturation enables us to understand how Afro-Americans learn and practice both the majority culture and Black culture at the same time, it does have some drawbacks in

understanding the dynamics of Black cultural behavior. Giving relatively equal weight to both cultural forms can be questioned because
it also accords equal importance to the socializing agents for each
culture. Whereas the kinship and peer group socialize the Black child
into Afro-American folkways, mainstream culture is largely transmitted
through external agencies such as television and schools or in other
cultural settings. Moreover, much of mainstream culture is in conflict
with Afro-American culture and cannot be easily integrated without
some personality dislocation. The commitment to Euro-American
values that Valentine speaks of is not necessarily positive. Many of
the Euro-American values required for successful achievements—e.g.,
formality, materialism, individualism—may be seen as values lacking
in intrinsic merit. While Afro-Americans may engage in such cultural
practices, this should not be taken as a strong commitment to those
values requiring such behavior.

CULTURAL TRAITS

In delineating specific Black cultural traits, we are limited to the
meager research available and our personal observations. While ample
studies are available on Black music, folklore, and religion, we still
have a void in many other areas of Black cultural practices. Moreover,
these cultural forms do not exist among all Blacks and in every geographical region where Blacks are found. Nor, in some cases, are they
peculiar to Blacks in form but only in style and prevalence. The traits
to be described here, however, make up a Black cultural complex that
gives the group a sense of solidarity, a way of communicating, and a
feeling of group continuity. Whatever its origin the trait becomes
invested with a group judgment that it is a proper and right way
of acting.

CUSTOMS AND RITUALS

This is an expected mode of behavior that meets with group disapproval
if not performed in the appropriate context. Among Blacks, especially
in Southern and rural areas, it is expected that most people will visit
close friends and relatives. On these occasions the sharing of food
is a normative part of the visiting routine.[36] Church going is another

cultural value in Southern Black communities since the church may be the center of the community's social life. Most rituals peculiar to Blacks are carried out in this institutional setting. Black church services are seldom the same as in the White church (even in the same denomination). Funeral services maintain some similarity to African customs. After the deceased is buried, the mourners celebrate his journey home by dancing, singing, and drinking. The body remains open to the view of others in rural Baptist churches. A collection is often taken as the mourners file by the corpse as a form of mutual aid. A prayer band and the all-night prayer meeting constitute another form of unique religious worship.[37]

Among other Black customs and rituals to note is the practice of calling older Black women by their first names. A woman named Mrs. Beaulah Jones would commonly be referred to as "Miss Beaulah." A ritual that many Blacks engage in is the Black handshake, which has many variations. In predominantly White settings, it is expected that you will speak to all Black people you encounter on the streets whether they are known to you or not. Black women expect admiring glances and a quick rap from Black males which do not have the same insulting meaning as in the White community. The congregation of Black males on streetcorners, in taverns, and in barbershops is another Black custom. Lewis (1955) calls this practice public idling.[38] It is an important source of social interaction for same sex role groups.

ESTHETICS

Among the various fine arts that embody Black culture, music is the one form most related to its African origin. As in African societies, music plays a central role in Afro-American life. It is not an event for them but is integrated into their daily existence. Music, for Afro-Americans, is rarely responded to in a passive manner. Levine (1971) notes that unlike any other group in the United States, Blacks consider music a participant activity rather than primarily a performer-audience phenomenon.[39] A major difference, for instance, between Black and White parties, is that at White parties the participants sit around, talk, and listen to music while Blacks are dancing to it (even among older Blacks this is true). Afro-American music is also transmitted in the oral tradition of African societies rather than by notation as among Euro-Americans. As is true of most Afro-American cultures music is basically social and comes out of Black gatherings at church, work, and in the community.[40]

There appears to be little dispute over the African origin of much of Afro-American music. There are similarities in the approach to playing the notes or tones, a relationship between the verse form in both idioms and the call-and-response pattern found in the blues and spirituals.[41] Keil (1966) claims that falsetto singing stems directly from Africa where it is regarded as the very essence of masculine expression. The singing styles of Ray Charles or B. B. King are very similar to the falsetto techniques of a West African cabaret singer.[42] Whatever its origin, music reflects the experiences and culture of Afro-Americans. As Donald Byrd (1972) expresses it, "It is expressionism, emotionalism, spiritualism and imagery, it is form, content and the imposition of Black feeling on an Aryan culture."[43]

African parallels are also found in certain forms of Black dancing patterns. This is particularly true of the Black church and in some forms of jazz dance. In the church African survivals can be seen in the practice of hand clapping, foot tapping, and in the ritualistic leaps during church services.[44] As typical of other Black cultural forms, dance is a part of the expression of Black people in social settings. The sensual nature of African dances is often reflected in Afro-American dances where body movements are not restricted as was common of Euro-Americans. Kinney (1971) has called attention to the responsorial form of dancing found in West Africa where the men interrupt the movement of their women in a call-and-response manner. She also observes a similar pattern among mainland Blacks where the women interrupt the basic movements of their partners.[45]

Black literature and drama share little in common with their African counterparts. American writing differs from the Euro-American version, however, because it does not deal with the universality of the human condition. Rather, it is a protest against the conditions of Black life in the United States. A majority of Black writers are concerned with analyzing Black existence in a racist society. Most of their works are written for a Black audience who will understand the common experience they share. Jeffers (1971) claims that Black literature is the conscience of man because it is basically a moral literature, a protest against human wickedness and man's inhumanity to man.[46]

FASHION STYLES

One aspect of Black culture known to White America is the form of dress and personal adornment peculiar to this group. It is conveyed to them through on-the-street encounters, television shows, and certain entertainment events. It is the clothing styles of Black males that have drawn the most attention. According to *Newsweek* magazine, "Through their clothes Black men are celebrating their freedom, displaying their success, exercising their creativity and affirming their racial pride. And, among designers and manufacturers, the fashion conscious Black man is considered a trend-setter in men's styles for all races."[47] While Black dress is now the object of White admiration and imitation, it is not the recent phenomenon implied in the above statement. Almost twenty years ago, Hylan Lewis (1955) observed that gaucherie in dress and grooming was a distinctive feature among local Blacks in a small, rural Southern community.[48]

Not only is flamboyancy and improvisation in clothing not a recent Black practice but it seems to be a pronounced cultural trait in the Afro-American community. Few Blacks ever adopted the somewhat casual and sloppy dress of many White youth. Even Black women have been admired for the way in which their clothing is embellished and worn. Although the reason for this cultural trait is unclear, Murray (1970) does remind us that African culture places emphasis on design and stylization. He cites the example of masklike makeup, flamboyant tribal headwear, and other inventiveness found among Africans as indications that Black dress styles are a possible extension of an African tradition.[49]

FOOD AND FOOD HABITS

There are obvious differences in the kind of food Blacks eat and the way it is prepared. Commonly labeled soul food, it originated during the slavery era when the bondsmen were given the leftovers from the pig. It consists of such items as pigs' feet, hamhocks, chitterlings, neck bones, hog maws, and so on. Such food is consumed in other cultures (and even among contemporary Euro-Americans today), but its special flavor as prepared by Blacks makes it unique to them. Even when cooking typical American food such as chicken the method of preparation gives it a special flavor. One eating habit that distinguishes Blacks from White Americans is the practice of eating whenever they feel like it, gathering food from pots and dishes that are continually simmering on the kitchen stove. A similar habit exists in some parts of Africa where food is left on a fire in the middle of the village for members to sample.[50]

The eating of food is more than a satisfaction of a biological need for Afro-Americans. Meal consumption is a way of bringing people together in a communal way. It is another form of group interaction that indicates the group orientation of Blacks. Although one may observe that food enterprises are a large proportion of Black businesses, they cater mainly to unattached individuals rather than families. Families eat at home where they can interact with one another. Guests for dinner are those persons who happen to be in your home at the time food is ready. To refuse to eat while others are eating can be insulting to a Black host. In some Black communities invitations are never extended for dinner if you visit a person's home. It is assumed that you will share their meal with them.

INSTITUTIONS AND ROLES

The two major Black institutions, the church and the family, are discussed extensively in separate chapters. In the Black church, the role of the minister is different, and so is his style. The role of the Black church has been different from that of the White church. The Black family is likewise a contrast to its White counterpart. It is organized more along extended kinship lines with women performing roles that deviate from the White female's role performance. Children are reared in a different manner and by a larger number of kinsmen and non-kin. Sexual taboos are not as strict and there is greater candor in the expression of sexual interest among both sex-role groups. Class variations influence the performance of role tasks as the middle-class Afro-American family takes on more of the surface characteristics of the middle-class White family.

Among the salient cultural roles in the Black community are entertainers and hustlers. Keil (1966) labels them cultural heroes. These performers function as culture and opinion leaders. While Whites have political statesmen to articulate their values, Blacks rely on entertainers and atheletes to "tell it like it is." These performers are expected to embody the Black concept of soul, to evoke a collective response in their audiences by reminding them of their common identity as a people.[52] The hustler is a special type created out of ghetto living conditions. He is the person who possesses the skills of rapping, manipulation of the system, and evasion to make it in this world. The most successful hustler may be the pimp, numbers runner, or drug peddler. Hustling is not just a technique used by these types. It is found even among some Black college students who are interested in "getting over" rather than mastering a subject.

LANGUAGE AND COMMUNICATION

One of the essential ingredients in a cultural system is a distinct language and communication pattern. It is in this area that some research has been done and there is a general consensus on the existence of a separate Black language code. Disagreements do arise over its origin and value. As a form of communication language is the medium through which culture is organized. People who have a unique language also have a separate world view. Language is the primary conveyor of cultural attitudes toward people and events. Since the shared experiences of Blacks differ from Whites, the language they speak forms and reflects their cultural values. As Fanon (1967) points out, "A man who has a language consequently possesses the world expressed and implied by that language."[53]

The origin and nature of what is called Black English remains in dispute. Some linguists have contended that it is nothing more than a direct descent from British dialect which the newly arrived slaves mastered in order to communicate with their masters and fellow bondsmen.[54] Contrary to this opinion is the view of others that the slaves created their own language according to the basic syntax of their West African languages. Since the slaveholders would not permit them to speak in their native tongues, they borrowed from the English language and integrated its words to the rules of their own language.[55] Even today linguists have noted parallels in African and Afro-American usage. There are similarities in the vowel sounds where the vowels are generally shorter and more stable, the use of the habitual tense, expression of plural nouns and multiple negatives, and employment of one-gender pronouns. Seymour (1972) comments that only the legacy of West African languages can explain the regularity of such language habits among Black people in various parts of the Western Hemisphere.[56]

While some critics acknowledge that Afro-Americans have a different speech pattern than Euro-Americans, they often characterize it as a careless way of speaking standard English and, consequently, of little value. Linguists, however, have demonstrated that it is a rather rigidly constructed set of speech patterns with the same kind of specialization in sounds, structure, and vocabulary as any other dialect. Those who hold the former view have the power to punish the Black individual for his nonconformity to standard English rules. Employers and schools, in particular, exercise negative sanctions against those who fail to adhere to the rules of standard English. The schools, in particular, provide many opportunities for the White child to learn and creatively display his language while there are few chances for the Black child to creatively explore and exercise his language. Jordan (1973) sees the ability to use one's language as deriving from the political power one has to use, abuse, accept, or reject words according to the control you exercise in the society.[57]

Language is an important facet of Black life because it is an expression of one of its basic values. The oral tradition among Afro-Americans means that verbal facility is of high prestige. An Afro-American who displays a mastery of Black parlance is much admired. This accounts, in part, for the high status accorded pimps and preachers.[58] In the Black community, children grow up learning a variety of verbal games. One of the most common is called playing the dozens. This is a verbal contest where the emphasis is placed on exchanging insults most often directed at your opponent's mother or other kinsmen. Another verbal skill is rapping, which Kochman (1972) defines as "a fluent and lively way of talking generally characterized by a high degree of personal style through which the speaker intends to draw the audience's attention to himself or some feature of himself that he feels is attractive or prestigious with his audience."[59] The Black facility with words has gained the admiration of many Whites who incorporate some Black terms in their own vocabulary. In the transfer, however, many of the words lose their original meaning or Blacks have created new ones to take their place.

Other racial differences exist in communication patterns. La France and Mayo (1973) found that Blacks tend to look at a person when speaking to him and away when spoken to. With Whites it was just the reverse pattern.[60] It has been noted that the custom of avoiding eye contact when others are speaking is typical of West Africans. Although not unique to Blacks, touching is another form of communication not as common among White Anglo-Saxon types. Touching is a way of establishing trust and confidence in individuals. Among many White Americans it is indicative of a sexual approach and often leads to feelings of distrust.

FOLKLORE AND MYTHOLOGY

Afro-Americans are among the few ethnic groups in the United States to maintain a storytelling tradition that forms a part of its cultural complex. This practice of storytelling stems from the oral tradition of Blacks and serves to validate cultural rituals and institutions and maintain conformity to the expected patterns of behavior. Again, we find that the folk tale was an important cultural form in West Africa. Storytelling was a normal practice that involved acting, singing, and gestures. Animal stories were a particular favorite because Africans humanize animals, whom they perceive as human beings in disguise.[62] The folk tales of Southern slaves also included African animals such as lions, monkeys, and elephants. Among the freedmen, the rabbit and tortoise figured prominently in their folklore. A common theme to these animal stories was the ability of the weaker animal to outwit and defeat this stronger opponent.[63] Although Brer Rabbit is no longer a prominent figure in Black stories, particularly in the urban North, Hannerz (1969) has noted that Black stories of today still emphasize the ability of their characters to overcome their weaknesses and triumph.[64]

Another characteristic Black myth is a belief in folk cures and magic. In certain areas of the rural South, there is still a strong belief in folk remedies for illnesses. Instead of going to doctors many people use herbs to cure certain illnesses. For some illnesses, the "root man" uses magic to cast off the spell that brought about the illness. These practices are found mostly in the area of "baffling diseases, mental states and love or sex problems."[65] In urban Black communities there is a strong belief in signs of the Zodiac as a guide to certain kinds of behavior. While astrology is of current interest to many

Americans, this writer's observation has been that Blacks have a much stronger faith in it than White Americans. Even class differences among this group do not seem to vary the strength of their belief that there is a correlation between the signs of the moon and human behavior.

VALUES

The values of a group refer to what it defines as the desirable and undesirable from a set of options used to guide behavior. Since values are subjective and probably none are unique to Blacks or exist in the same degree among all of them, one can describe only the traits which in their intensity and prevalence seem to distinguish them from Anglo-Saxons. Listed below are some of them:

Mutual Aid

While Anglo-Saxon norms dictate individualism and competition, Blacks tend to believe that they should help anyone in need. They have faith in the spirit of cooperation rather than competition. This value is reflected in their views on poverty, welfare and the ill-fed, and their exchange network.

Compassion

A humanistic attitude toward people is a Black characteristic. This is reflected in their view that people are more important than property. Perhaps this view derives from their own status as an oppressed people but most Blacks believe that if they possessed the power of the Whites, they would never treat them as harshly as they have been treated. They feel that all humans have a right to dignity and freedom from oppression.

Adaptability

The ability to survive in a society which is basically hostile to them has been an important factor to Blacks and has meant the shifting of family roles when necessary. It has involved the masks many Blacks must wear when dealing with Whites. It includes the techniques of evasion, deceit, militancy, or whatever is necessary in order to cope with the changing conditions of race relations.

Racial Loyalty

Black people believe that no matter what your basic differences may be with fellow Blacks, you must stand together in a common cause. Whites are never to be thoroughly trusted or incorporated into the intimate life of the Black community. It means that right or wrong, a fellow Black must be supported in any confrontation with Whites.

Table 3-1 Comparison of Black and White Value Orientations

Value Orientations	White	Black
Time	An element in society by which the individual compulsively regulates his life. Punctuality is of highest priority.	Flexible adherence to schedules. What is happening now is important and one must adapt to ranges in time rather than fixed periods.
Emotions	To be under rigid control in order to maintain discipline and not reveal emotional weakness. To be very guarded in public settings and never to be fully released.	Expression of natural feelings in all settings, public and private. Spontaneity in response to events and gestures is common. Be uninhibited and loose in reactions to verbal and physical stimuli. Let your inner feelings show and exude warmth.
Money	To be frugal in its use, saved for future purposes. To be accumulated even when not needed in order to possess the value it has. Often used to control persons who have little of it and limited access to its acquisition.	Is to be used to further communalism. Money per se is not important, not the measure of human value. Wealth is consumptive rather than exploitative. How money is used is more important than its acquisition. Property is a collective asset, not an individual one.
Morals	Strongest ones relate to personal morals such as sexual behavior, belief in God, cleanliness, moderation in use of alcohol, tobacco, etc.	How you treat people is of highest priority. Helping people in need is an important moral. Abstaining from harm to people or groups. A belief in the dignity of your fellow humans.

Value Orientations	White	Black
Status	Based on your income, family background, cultural skills, amount of power over others, race, religion, sex, etc.	Stems from personal qualities such as courtesy, compassion, friendliness, and naturalness. Innovation and adaptability also admired.
Children	Are often extensions of the parents. Expected to achieve a status similar to or higher than the parents. Will be loved and supported if they conform to parental values. Love is withdrawn if they deviate from certain social norms. Obedience to parental authority highly valued.	Are seen as a value in themselves, to be nurtured as a dependent being and loved throughout life regardless of their achievements. Creativity and free expression are encouraged. Often regarded as equal members of the family structure.
Individualism	In human society each individual must make his own mark through competition for the prestige goals of his culture. The rewards of his victory in the competition are his alone, to be shared only with certain prescribed people (e.g., wife, children) over whom he has control. Those who have not achieved success or are without sufficient resources have only themselves to blame because of their inability to compete.	The concept of the individual is usually subordinate to a group orientation. It is the group that is important and the Black self is an incorporated part of the social group. Cooperation through collective efforts is the accepted means of achieving culturally prescribed goals.

BLACK CULTURE AND PERSONALITY DEVELOPMENT

Although it is often regarded as an individual trait, personality is also related to culture and social organization. While the individual may possess a unique personality due to the total complex of experiences that only he encounters, there is also a modal personality found in certain societies. This modal (i.e., average) personality will characterize a group that shares certain experiences in common and develops traits peculiar to it as a result of group interaction. A generally uniform way of responding to social stimuli reflects the influence of culture on personality. Hence, the personality of individuals is dificult to separate from the environmental forces to which they are subjected. Popper (1963) has even asserted that "Men—i.e., human minds, the needs, the hopes, fears and expectations, the motives and aspirations of human individuals—are, if anything, the product of life in society rather than its creators."[66]

When we turn to the relationship between Black culture and Black personalities, we find that there are so many controversies and very few definitive conclusions. The argument has ranged from one author's assertion that no Black person has avoided the maladaptive symptoms in basic self-identity that are associated with living in a society that regards him as inferior[67] to the claim by a social psychologist that most psychological research on the Black self-concept should be dismissed as irrelevant.[68] A more reasonable view is that of Erik Erikson (1967) who notes that we do not know enough about the relationship of positive and negative elements within the Black personality and within the Black community to realize what is negative or positive.[69]

Since Blacks live in an oppressive culture, it has historically been assumed that their identity and self-esteem have been severely damaged by what is called the "mark of oppression." The logic behind this theory is that a White-dominated society provides no possible basis for a healthy self-esteem and every reason for self-hatred. Racism has created in Blacks a sense of inferiority that has developed a basic Black personality which is a caricature of the corresponding White personality because Blacks must adapt to the same cultural goals as Whites but without the resources to achieve them. As examples of this mark of oppression, a number of studies can be cited which reveal Blacks to hold a more negative self-concept than Whites, to prefer White-associated traits (e.g., skin color, hair texture, etc.) to Black ones, and to be generally characterized by self-abnegation, apathy, hedonism, etc.[70]

Despite the lack of reliable research on the subject, it appears that some Blacks have suffered from the psychological effects of racial oppression and that counterinfluences in Black culture have maintained a healthy identity for many others. It is also possible that recent changes in Black life have elevated Black self-esteem to a new high. To deal first with the effects of oppression on Black personality, a prominent theory is that slavery and its legacy have molded a modal Black personality. A hypothesis closely associated with historian Stanley Elkins (1959), it contends that the experience of slavery brought about a sambolike childishness among the bondsmen. Such a pattern of slave-master dependency was an inevitable adjustment to the closed system of slavery in order to ensure their physical and psychic survival.[71]

The Elkins thesis is weak because it ignores numerous cases of slave resistance to their enforced bondage and it confuses Black coping techniques with the internalized attitudes that comprise a personality. Moreover, the theories about the psychological damage to Blacks from racial oppression have the consequence, if not the intent, of furnishing scientific credibility to White views of Black inferiority. Their theme is: Blacks were not initially born inferior, they have been made inferior by generations of harsh treatment. Black inferiority is seen as social rather than genetic in origin but the stigma of inferiority remains unchanged. Murray (1970) points out the elements in Black life which indicate that the concept of Black self-hatred across-the-board is "preposterous." Among them he cites the disdain in which Blacks have long held "poor white trash," their dislike for many aspects of the hillbilly lifestyle, a Black belief that Whiteness is synonymous with being square, and so on.[72]

We can probably accept the fact that some Blacks have evidenced self-hatred because of their socially inferior position. But, even in the older research studies there was often a sizable minority (sometimes a majority) who did not perform on the tests or answer questions in such a way as to indicate feelings of low self-esteem. Those exceptions were rarely explained by the researcher. Moreover, the findings of such studies lent themselves to interpretations other than the ones employed by the researcher.[73] As a result of different contemporary interpretations and the Black nationalist orientation, a large number of recent studies have shown Blacks to have a high self-esteem,[74] to minimize skin color in selecting marriage mates,[75] and to have lower rates in the area of suicide, mental illness, and alcoholism.[76]

THE COLONIAL PERSONALITY

Students of classical colonial societies maintain that the process of colonization begins with the destruction of the native's personality by uprooting his traditional social structure. When native culture is replaced by European culture this brings about a collective inferiority complex that maintains the native's dependency upon the colonizer.[77] The inferiority complex of colonized peoples derives from two processes. One is primarily economic wherein the native associates power, privilege, and status with being White. The second is the internalization of this feeling of inferiority as the native acquires feelings of self-hatred and finds himself in a position of insignificance in his own society. He develops an obsession with his individual worth and constantly questions whether he is equal to the colonizer.[78]

The psychology of racial oppression diverges from the classical Marxist notion of alienation as a result of class oppression. In a class-based society the worker becomes alienated because his work is not a source of self-fulfillment but a miserable denial of self.[79] Colonial societies—based on racial oppression—develop alienation in the native personality because he is dehumanized, reduced to the level of human property, and consequently feels anxious, insecure, and worthless.[80] An even more important distinction in the Marxist and colonial models is how the oppressed are liberated from their alienation. Marx saw the disappearance of this psychological appendage of capitalism in a restructured socialist society. But the advocates of the colonial model saw psychological liberation as springing from struggle itself, not national liberation. Memmi (1965) asserts that "the colonial condition cannot be adjusted to: like an iron collar, it can only be broken." Hence, if Blacks are to be freed from their psychological shackles, it must be a therapy of struggle.[81] For Fanon (1970), violence was the force to effect the decolonization of the native personality. It was the instrument to free him from his inferiority complex and from his despair in inaction; it makes him fearless and restores his self-respect.[82]

A similar process can be observed in the personality traits of some Afro-Americans. As they became involved in the Black liberation struggle, their values and self-concepts began to undergo certain changes. Cross (1971) has described a series of well-defined stages each Black person must go through in order to achieve a Black identity. In stage one, *preencounter,* he tends to think and act in a manner that degrades Blacks and sees all forms of White culture as a superior model. After going through three other intermediate stages, in the fifth stage, *internalization-commitment,* he uses both Western and non-Western referents to guide his values, thoughts, and acts. Other characteristics developed during this stage include (1) an inner security and satisfaction within himself, (2) great love and compassion for all oppressed people, and (3) active participation in the community for the purpose of making it better.[83]

COUNTERVAILING INFLUENCES ON BLACK PERSONALITY

Many of the assumptions about the mark of oppression on Black personality ignore the possibility that even in a colonial society the colonized peoples may draw upon resources to maintain a reasonably healthy identity. Although Blacks may suffer all sorts of ego-deflating experiences in the larger White-dominated society, they can also find satisfaction in other aspects of their life or even retreat into a belief in a utopian religion or a political belief.[84] Among some of these counteracting forces, we find:

Religion

For years the Blacks' belief in religion has served to fortify them against the psychologically destructive force of racism. As noted earlier, the Black church has acted as a tension-reduction mechanism more than a norm-setting mechanism. Its peculiar character has served as a defense against the hostile White world, given credence to the cultural heritage of Black people, validated their self-worth, and provided them with hope for the future. Although it also was an impediment to the Black struggle, its recent decline is believed to be a factor in the increase in mental disturbance among the Black population.

Reference Groups

In cases where Blacks have been characterized as having a low self-esteem it has been assumed that one reason is that Whites have served as the model or guide for their expected level of achievement. By comparison they would rank inferior in many areas. To the contrary, Afro-Americans, who have high levels of self-esteem, often value themselves positively because their self-concept is formed from the standpoint of their own culture. The status they have is based on the prestige values that have meaning in their world and not in mainstream society.

Values

When the values of the White majority are not shared, failure to achieve some culturally prescribed goals does not have to result in a negative self-concept. In recent years the values of Afro-Americans have diverged considerably from Euro-Americans. White values, in particular, have fallen in disfavor among Blacks and also in the White youth population. Hence, a different value orientation means that White cultural values cannot destroy the Afro-American personality via the process of dictating desirable behavior and goals while denying the means for fulfilling them.

Family

Traditional personality theory has long contended that a child's experiences in the family form his basic personality at an early age. While a number of scholars have asserted that the disorganized Black family structure produces a negative identity in the Black child, the influence of the Black family can also be seen as a positive source of identity for the developing child. Much of the literature referred to has concentrated on the poorest and most oppressed Black families and individuals.[85] Within the family the Black child can develop a self-concept that enables him to distinguish between who he is, what he is worth, and what the dominant White culture says about him. There are studies that reveal Black children to be high in resiliency and survival skills. Halpern (1973) attributes this to "(1) the love and security he enjoys early in life, (2) his inclusion in all the family's activities, (3) his early opportunity for the assumption of physical independence and responsibility, and (4) the security provided by the many mothering figures available to him."[86]

Group Identification

This is one of the most important elements in the formation of a healthy personality. To the extent that Blacks identify with their group, its heritage and values, there is a sense of peoplehood, solidarity, and "we" feeling that is transformed into a feeling of positive self-worth. This occurs through the kind of interaction among Blacks: they speak the same language, share the same affect, know the same people. They have a unity that is transmitted symbolically through the way they approach one another. Blacks are never strangers when they first meet because they have similar experiences, attitudes, and features. They know what to expect from one another and are united in a common bond of suffering. Racial awareness makes all of this possible. The Black nationalist movement, in particular, has provided an ideology to explain the low socioeconomic status of Afro-Americans. And now it is White society which is seen as decadent and White racism which is defined as a social problem.

NOTES

1   C. F. Elliot Liebow, *Tally's Corner,* Little, Brown, Boston, 1966, pp. 208–209.
2   Robert Blauner, "Black Culture: Myth or Reality," in Norman Whitten, Jr. and John Szwed (eds.), *Afro-American Anthropology,* The Free Press, New York, 1970, p. 362.
3   Dr. Carl Word, quoted in *Jet,* p. 30, July 1, 1974.
4   Joseph Himes, *Racial Conflict in American Society,* Charles E. Merrill, Columbus, Ohio, 1973, pp. 88–89.
5   Johnnetta B. Cole, "Culture: Negro, Black and Nigger," *The Black Scholar,* vol. 1, p. 41, June 1970.
6   Douglas Davidson, "Black Culture and Liberal Sociology," *Berkeley Journal of Sociology,* vol. 14, p. 170, 1969.
7   Albert Murray, *The Omni-Americans,* Outerbridge and Dienstfrey, New York, 1970, p. 49.
8   Bennett M. Berger, "Soul Searching: Review of *Urban Blues* by Charles Keil," *Transaction,* vol. 4, pp. 54–57, July 1967.
9   Nathan Hare, *The Black Anglo Saxons,* Marzani and Mansell, New York, 1965, p. 53–54.
10 E. Franklin Frazier, *The Black Bourgeoisie,* The Free Press, Glencoe, Ill., 1957, pp. 112–113.
11 Basil Matthews, Black Perspective, Black Family and Black Community, paper presented at the Annual Philosophy Conference, Morgan State College, p. 23, April 1972.
12 Charles A. Valentine, "Deficit, Difference and Bicultural Models of Afro-American Behavior," *Harvard Educational Review,* vol. 41, p. 141, May 1971.
13 Murray, op. cit., p. 91.
14 Albert Murray, *South to a Very Old Place,* McGraw-Hill, New York, 1972.

15 Edith Folb, "Rappin' in the Black Vernacular," *Human Behavior*, p. 19, August 1973.
16 "Black Is Beautiful and Chic," *Newsweek*, pp. 54–57, September 10, 1973.
17 Alvin Poussaint, "Blaxploitation Movies–Cheap Thrills That Degrade Blacks," *Psychology Today*, vol. 7, p. 98, February 1974.
18 Melville Herskovits, *The Myth of the Negro Past*, Harper, New York, 1941.
19 John Blassingame, *The Slave Community*, Oxford, New York, 1972, p. 18.
20 Charles A. Valentine, *Culture and Poverty: Critique and Counterproposals*, University of Chicago, Chicago, 1968, pp. 48–77.
21 Blauner, op. cit., p. 356.
22 Cole, op. cit., p. 42.
23 Vincent Harding, "The Gift of Blackness," *Kalallageto*. Quoted in Davidson, op. cit., p. 173.
24 Blassingame, op. cit. pp. 41–76.
25 Nathan Glazer and Daniel P. Moynihan, *Beyond the Melting Pot*, M.I.T., Cambridge, Mass., 1965, p. 53.
26 Liebow, op. cit., pp. 213–222.
27 Hyman Rodman, "The Lower-Class Value Stretch," *Social Forces*, vol. 62, pp. 205–215, December 1963.
28 Gunnar Myrdal, *An American Dilemma*, Harper & Row, New York, 1944, p. 928.
29 Valentine, *Culture and Poverty*, op. cit., p. 77.
30 Lee Rainwater, *Behind Ghetto Walls: Black Families in a Federal Slum*, Aldine, Chicago, 1970.
31 Daniel P. Moynihan, *The Negro Family: The Case for National Action*, U.S. Department of Labor, Government Printing Office, Washington, 1966.
32 C. F. Davidson, op. cit.
33 Carol B. Stack, *All Our Kin*, Harper & Row, New York, 1974, p. 23.
34 W. E. B. DuBois, *The Souls of Black Folk*, Avon, New York, 1965 edition, pp. 214–215.
35 Valentine, "Deficit, Difference and Bicultural Models . . . ," op. cit., pp. 143–144.
36 Stack, op. cit., pp. 90–107.
37 Hylan Lewis, *Blackways of Kent*, University of North Carolina, Chapel Hill, 1955, pp. 140–145.
38 Ibid., pp. 68–72.
39 Lawrence W. Levine, "The Concept of the New Negro and the

Realities of Black Culture," in Nathan Huggins et al. (eds.), *Key Issues in the Afro-American Experience*, Harcourt Brace Jovanovich, New York, 1971, pp. 134–135.

40 Murray, *The Omni-Americans*, p. 183.
41 Ralph H. Metcalfe, Jr., "The Western African Roots of Afro-American Music," *The Black Scholar*, vol. 1, pp. 16–25, June 1970.
42 Charles Keil, *Urban Blues*, University of Chicago, Chicago, 1966, p. 27.
43 Donald Byrd, "The Meaning of Black Music," *The Black Scholar*, vol. 3, p. 30, Summer 1972.
44 Katherine Dunham, "The Negro Dance," in Sterling Brown et al. (eds.) *The Negro Caravan*, Dryden, New York, 1941, pp. 991–1000.
45 Esi Sylvia Kinney, "Africanisms in Music and Dance of the Americas," in Rhoda L. Goldstein (ed.), *Black Life and Culture in the United States*, Crowell, 1971, p. 55.
46 Lance Jeffers, "Afro-American Literature: The Conscience of Man," *The Black Scholar*, vol. 2, pp. 47–53, January 1971.
47 *Newsweek*, op. cit., p. 54.
48 Lewis, op. cit., pp. 54–64.
49 Murray, *The Omni-Americans*, pp. 49–53.
50 "Culture: Exploring the Racial Gap," *Time*, p. 75, May 9, 1969.
51 Stack, op. cit., pp. 90–107.
52 Keil, op. cit., p. 20.
53 Frantz Fanon, *Black Skin-White Masks*, Grove, New York, 1967, p. 18.
54 R. McDavid, "American Social Dialects," *College English*, vol. 26, pp. 254–260, January 1965.
55 J. L. Dillard, *Black English: Its History and Usage in the United States*, Random House, New York, 1972.
56 Dorothy Z. Seymour, "Black Children, Black Language," *The Washington Post*, p. B5, June 25, 1972.
57 June Jordan, "Black English, The Politics of Translation," *School Library Journal*, pp. 21–24, May 15, 1973.
58 Folb, loc. cit.
59 Thomas Kochman, "Black English in the Classroom," in C. Cazden et al. (eds.), *The Function of Language in the Classroom*, New York Teachers College, New York, 1972, p. 32.
60 Marianne Lafrance and Clara Mayo, "Gaze Direction in Interracial Dyadic Communication," a paper presented at the Eastern Sociological Association, Washington, D.C., May 1973.
61 *Time*, loc, cit.
62 Ivan Vansertima, "African Linguistic and Mythological Structures

in the New World," in Goldstein, *Black Life and Culture in the United States,* op. cit., pp. 12–35.

63 Blassingame, op. cit., pp. 20–21.
64 Ulf Hannerz, *Soulside: Inquiries into Ghetto Culture and Community,* Columbia, New York, 1969, pp. 115–117.
65 Lewis, op. cit., pp. 74–78.
66 K. R. Popper, *The Open Society and Its Enemies,* 4th ed., Princeton, Princeton, N.J., 1963, p. 93.
67 Doris B. Mosby, "Toward a Theory of the Unique Personality of Blacks: A Psychocultural Assessment," in Reginald L. Jones (ed.), *Black Psychology,* Harper & Row, New York, 1972, p. 129.
68 Wade Nobles, "Psychological Research and the Black Self-Concept: A Critical Review," *Journal of Social Issues,* vol. 29, pp. 11–31, January 1973.
69 Erik H. Erikson, "The Concept of Identity in Race Relations: Notes and Queries," in Talcott Parsons and Kenneth B. Clark (eds.), *The Negro American,* Beacon, Boston, 1967, p. 237.
70 Abraham Kardiner and Lionel Ovesey, *The Mark of Oppression,* Meridian, New York, 1951.
71 Stanley Elkins, *Slavery: A Problem in American Institutional and Intellectual Life,* University of Chicago, Chicago, 1959, chap. 3.
72 Murray, *The Omni-Americans,* p. 48.
73 Nobles, loc. cit.
74 William L. Yancey, et al., "Social Position and Self-Evaluation: The Relative Importance of Race," *American Journal of Sociology,* vol. 78, pp. 338–359, September 1972.
75 J. Richard Udry et al., "Skin Color, Status and Mate Selection," *American Journal of Sociology,* vol. 76, 722–733, January 1971.
76 John McCarthy and William L. Yancey, "Uncle Tom and Mr. Charlie: Metaphysical Pathos in the Study of Racism and Personal Disorganization, *American Journal of Sociology,* vol. 76, pp. 648–672, January 1971.
77 O. Mannioni, *Prospero and Caliban: The Psychology of Colonization,* Praeger, New York, 1964.
78 Fanon, op cit., p. 11.
79 T. B. Bottomore and Maximilien Rubel (eds.), *Karl Marx: Selected Writings,* Pelican, New York, 1961, pp. 176–178.
80 Fanon, op. cit., p. 51.
81 Albert Memmi, *The Colonizer and the Colonized,* Beacon, Boston, 1965, p. 28.
82 Dennis Forsythe, "Frantz Fanon: Black Theoretician," *The Black Scholar,* vol. 1, pp. 2–10, March 1970.

83   William E. Cross, Jr., "Toward a Psychology of Black Liberation,"
     in Vernon Dixon and Badi Foster (eds.), *Beyond Black or White*,
     Little, Brown, Boston, 1971, pp. 95–109.
84   Leonard Bloom, *The Social Psychology of Race Relations*, Schenk-
     man, Cambridge, Mass., 1972, pp. 81–84.
85   Edward J. Barnes, "The Black Community as the Source of Posi-
     tive Self-Concept for Black Children: A Theoretical Perspective,"
     in Reginald L. Jones (ed.), *Black Psychology*, Harper & Row, New
     York, 1972, pp. 166–192.
86   Florence Halpern, *Survival: Black/White*, Pergamon, New York,
     1973, p. 66.

SUGGESTED READING LIST

Brewer, J. Mason: *American Negro Folklore*, Quadrangle, New York,
1974.

Cole, Johnetta B.: "Culture: Negro, Black and Nigger," *The Black
Scholar*, vol. 1, p. 41, June 1970.

Davidson, Douglas: "Black Culture and Liberal Sociology," *Berkeley
Journal of Sociology*, vol. 14, p. 170, 1969.

Dillard, J. L.: *Black English: Its History and Usage in the United States*,
Random House, New York, 1972.

DuBois, W. E. B.: *The Souls of Black Folk*, Avon, New York, 1965
edition.

Fanon, Frantz: *Black Skin, White Masks*, Grove, New York, 1967.

Goldstein, Rhoda L.: *Black Life and Culture in the United States*,
Crowell, New York, 1971.

Herskovits, Melville: *The Myth of the Negro Past*, Harper, New York,
1941.

Lewis, Hylan: *Blackways of Kent*, University of North Carolina, Chapel
Hill, 1955.

Murray, Albert: *The Omni-Americans*, Outerbridge and Dienstfrey,
New York, 1970.

Suttles, Gerald D.: *The Social Order of the Slum: Ethnicity and Territory in the Inner City*, University of Chicago, Chicago, 1968.

Thomas, Alexander and Samuel Sillen: *Racism and Psychiatry*, Brunner/
Mazel, New York, 1972.

Valentine, Charles A.: *Culture and Poverty: Critique and Counterproposals*, University of Chicago, Chicago, 1968.

Whitten, Norman, Jr. and John Szwed: *Afro-American Anthropology*,
The Free Press, New York, 1970.

Institutions in
the Black Community

Institutions have been set up by all societies to enable a group to deal with its basic problems and adjust to its social, economic, and geographical conditions. We might define institutions as clearly defined units with roles and structures organized for the purpose of task fulfillment and the satisfaction of human needs. In White society that description would be more appropriate than in the Black community. Although Whites do not have total democratic participation in running their institutions, as America's egalitarian ideology would presume, they do have more input and control over them than does the Black community.[1]

A marked feature of institutions in the Black community is that they are externally derived and controlled by individuals outside the community. With the possible exception of two institutions, the family and the church, they are shaped by the colonial power structure in order to meet its needs rather than the needs of the community. The imposition of White control over Black institutions defines the limits in which they function. In this chapter we will not examine the church and family since they have been comparatively unaffected by White values and dominance. Our central purpose here is to assess the effectiveness and inadequacy of Black institutions as a result of White dominance over their structure and functioning.

BLACK INSTITUTIONS IN THE BLACK COMMUNITY

In examining these institutions it is incumbent upon us to recognize that all institutions related to Blacks function partly to maintain White oppression and partly to cater to the authentic needs of Blacks. Hence, there is a duality of functions for Black institutions which we must acknowledge in any evaluation of them. The church and family have both been positive institutions in meeting the needs of Blacks while political and economic institutions have been weighted toward the negative end of the spectrum.

Education

Only among the Black colleges do Blacks have any amount of control over their educational institutions. These colleges developed shortly before the Civil War and were founded by groups of religious denominations and wealthy White Northerners. Originally their purpose was to train missionaries and teachers, mainly for duty in this country. There are now approximately 111 Black colleges, and they are located primarily in Southern and border states. Until recently the majority of Black college graduates came from these schools, and they still enroll 44 percent of all Black college students.[2]

There is some disagreement over the historical functions of these colleges. It is quite clear that they furnished a "education" or at least the proper credentials to many poor Blacks who would not have otherwise received a degree. Others claim that they were established by Whites to protect their class and race interests. Earl Conrad (1967) asserts that their purpose was not only to teach the freedmen how to read and write but also, by providing learning in the form of the Bible, to temper this teaching, perhaps to moderate the freedman as well as free him.[3]

Whatever their intentions, the Black colleges turned out to be an effective mechanism of colonial control. By educating Blacks separately in poorly financed, badly run colleges, they gave Whites the advantage of achieving the higher status jobs by virtue of having attended a higher quality school so that they never had to compete for positions with Blacks who were ipso facto less capable. The main function of these Black colleges was to recruit a small number of natives into the elite class. Not only were they given some semblance of an educational program, but they also received indoctrination into the values of the colonizer.

Several observers of Black colleges have noted that they are mere caricatures of White universities. Instead of reflecting the culture from which their students came, they were exposed to ultra-American middle-class White values and standards. Jencks and Riesman (1969) write that "far from fighting to preserve a separate subculture as other ethnic cultures did, the Negro colleges were militantly opposed to almost everything which made Negroes different from Whites."[4] A former professor at one of these colleges charges that "they do immeasurably more harm than good, serving the racist society by gulling students into believing that they are receiving a good education while in fact they are being trained to be good niggers."[5]

Their failure to meet Black needs becomes slightly more understandable when it is revealed that only 6 of the approximate 111 Black colleges are controlled by Blacks. The rest are financed by White philanthropists, dominated by White boards of trustees, and were initially administered by White presidents and largely staffed by White faculty. Almost all of them now have Black presidents and a few have a Black majority on the faculty. But, as Jencks and Riesman note, the Black administrators who run these schools serve White interests and values even more than the White trustees and faculty.[6] Over 50 of these colleges are publicly supported and indirectly controlled by Southern Dixiecrats, either through appointment by the Board of Regents or via control over their budget.[7]

One result of the segregation of Black students in their own colleges has been the organization of a community of resistance against racial oppression. These colleges were the breeding grounds for student movements such as sit-ins, Black power, and Pan-Africanism during the sixties and seventies.[8] In classical Marxist terms, the concentration of a class of oppressed peoples tends to elevate their level of political consciousness. Most Black college students were from the working class and began to identify with their class of origin rather than acquiring the bourgeois values and aspirations for which they were being programmed. The Black administrators of these colleges, acting on behalf of the colonial ruling class, had subjected them to surveillance, harassment, and expulsion for their involvement in these racial struggles.[9] Some Black colleges, such as Howard University, began to reflect the class and racial interests of their student body. Moreover, these schools remain the primary source of employment for Black academicians.

Media

Most of the media in the Black community are White-dominated with the exception of the publishing industry and, to a limited extent, radio and recording. The Black press has a mixed history of accomplishment. In the main it has served as a protest organ for Black people and has mirrored their values and interests. Recently we have witnessed a decline in its relevance to Black people and a corresponding loss in its circulation and readership. Historically, its efforts have been heroic since it carries out two functions: reporting news and stimulating racial solidarity. It had its origin in 1827 when John Russuarm and Samuel Carnish published a weekly paper called *Freedom's Journal.* The expressed purpose of the Black press has been to protest injustices to Blacks. Many Black leaders have also been editors including Frederick Douglas, W. E. B. DuBois, and others.[10]

There are approximately 225 Black-oriented newspapers in the United States along with 65 such magazines. Only three of the newspapers are dailies, and the highest circulation for the largest is 70,000. The paper with the highest circulation is the noncommercial weekly *Muhammed Speaks,* published by the Nation of Islam, which has a circulation of 600,000 weekly; *The Black Panther* paper is second with sales of a 100,000 issues each week. Unlike White newspapers, the Black press tends to be largely dependent on circulation rather than advertising revenues. With the exception of the largest two, most of the Black newspapers have been declining in influence and circulation.[11]

Black newspapers are failing for a number of reasons. One of them is the lack of advertising revenue to take up the slack caused by a decline in circulation. According to the President of the National Newspaper Publishers Association, the largest Black press organization in America, the 100 largest White advertising agencies placed less than one-half of 190 of their ads in the Black press.[12] However, it has been its independence from White advertisers that has permitted Black newspapers to serve as the voice of the Black masses. It is feared that their tone of protest would be muted if they had to worry about losing the support of White advertisers. Some, for instance, have questioned the cozy relationship the Black press has with Gulf Oil, a major investor in three Portuguese colonial possessions in Africa. The president of that corporation has remarked that "Gulf Oil has always had a friend in the Black press."[13]

Another major problem of the Black press is its lack of relevance to the Black population, particularly the militant youth group. Most of the Black papers are owned by elderly men who have not changed their periodicals in the last twenty years, while the Black community has undergone significant changes. Some of these newspapers have dropped their attacks on White racism and spend most of their space on depreciating Black militants. Large numbers of them are tied to the Democratic and Republican parties, which has made it difficult for them to challenge contemporary issues of war, the environment, racist politics, etc. A few Black newspapers contain information on all aspects of racist oppression but the majority remain wedded to the past and the dream of assimilation into the colonial world.[14]

In the magazine publishing industry, one company virtually monopolizes the field. The Johnson Publishing Company of Chicago publishes four magazines, *Ebony, Jet, Black World,* and *Black Stars* with a total circulation of almost two million. Two other companies have a fairly large circulation but one is inserted into Sunday newspapers in Black neighborhoods and the other is owned by Whites.[15] Two Johnson Company magazines do not differ significantly from White-oriented periodicals except for the racial slant. The other pair are significant for their large readership and political content.

Ebony has the largest circulation, over a million, of any Black-oriented magazine sold on newstands. It also has its share of detractors for an earlier use of skin-bleaching creams and hair-straightener ads. Some have criticized it for the emphasis on success stories and its middle-class orientation. Yet, it continues to increase its circulation because it has remained a spokesman for Black liberation and has kept pace with the changing Black mood. While Black newspapers have expended much energy on attacking Black militants, *Ebony* has printed favorable stories about them and even opened up its pages to militant Black writers. The sister publication of *Ebony, Black World,* probably reflects the views of radical Blacks as well as any other Black publication. Its scholarly content, causing a low circulation, has forced the publisher to subsidize it with profits from his other magazines.

Another medium in the Black community is radio. Approximately 360 out of 7,000 radio stations are Black-oriented but a mere 19 are actually owned by Blacks. Many of the White owners of Black radio are Southerners, some of whom have become millionaires through their control of the Black communications media. In most of these stations, the personnel are Black except at the top positions.[16] One consequence of White ownership of Black-oriented stations has been their occasional decision to reorient their programming. In a few cases the majority of the Black staff have been dismissed because the White owner decided to change his program content to reach a different type of White audience.

A number of people are unhappy with what is generally called soul radio. One complaint is that rhythm and blues is played to the almost total exclusion of other Black musical expression. They feel that soul radio should reflect the cultural diversity and wide spectrum of Black tastes. Another scholar charges soul music with being politically neutral and hypnotic. Like alcohol and drugs it is a psychological depressant and hallucinatory, which releases the inhibitions and retards the thinking process.[17]

The concept of soul radio is basically no different from that of Top 40 White radio. Both are glib, move at double time clips, and shout their commercial message in auctioneer fashion. The difference is mainly in style. Even the news read on Black-oriented stations comes from the wire services and relates little to Black problems.[18] As one Black leader observes, these soul stations produce programs of the lowest caliber, looking for the lowest common denominator in the Black community, and offering content lacking in any social concern for real public service and the needs of the total Black community.[19]

Leadership Institutions

Black leadership represents a variety of philosophies and interests. As a result they have been under constant attack by some segments of the Black community. Veteran observers have remarked on what they call "ritual condemnation of Black leadership."[20] A common charge is that they represent the class interests of the Black bourgeoisie. Until recently an upper-class status almost automatically gave a Black the role of race leader. Since most of the Black leaders were from the higher stratum of the Black community, they were often alienated from the Black masses and regarded with suspicion.[21]

More often Black leaders were created by the colonial power structure to keep the masses in check. The best one could get out of them were token concessions that the ruling class would tolerate in order to maintain social order. Many Black leaders are far more concerned with their own gains than with the plight of the masses. They function to serve their own individual interests rather than the needs of the group. It is a common strategy of colonial powers to use native leaders as puppets and fronts for the colonial administration. As a reward for their conduct, they are often given favors and impressive-sounding but commonly meaningless posts.[22]

The effectiveness of Black leadership institutions can best be assessed by evaluating their relationship to the needs of the Black masses. Among the leading groups are:

The National Association for the Advancement of Colored People (NAACP) This is the forerunner of all civil rights organizations. Founded in 1909 to work for full legal equality for Afro-Americans, it is the oldest and still has the largest membership of all Black leadership organizations. Its means have been largely confined to working through the courts to seek development and enforcement of laws guaranteeing civil rights for Blacks.[23] Until 1955 the Black protest movement was centered in this organization, but growing disenchantment with its legal approach, which depended on the colonial power structure to reform itself, brought about a gradual but steady decline in its membership and influence.[24] It had an essentially middle-class outlook that eroded any working class base it had. In recent years it has become increasingly dependent on government grants, which were given for such purposes as an ROTC recruitment program.[25]

The Urban League This is a social work organization that is interracial in character and whose purpose is to find jobs and housing and increase educational opportunities of Blacks.[26] The success of this organization is mixed because of its strategy of wrangling concessions from the colonial ruling class through conciliatory techniques. Much of its financing comes from federal grants and the United Fund. Its Board of Directors is largely composed of the top members of business and industry. The past director often said he believed it more important for him to meet with powerful men in corporate boardrooms than standing on a Harlem street corner and talking with the Black masses.[27] At present it has taken on a more nationalistic character but it is a bourgeois nationalism in the form of developing a program of Black capitalism.[28]

Congress of Racial Equality CORE was originally a direct action group which used tactics of nonviolent sit-ins, freedom rides, and protest demonstration to eliminate racial barriers, in jobs, housing, and public facilities. The membership had a large number of Whites during that period. It never really had a strong base in the Black community because many of its goals had only symbolic meanings for the Black middle class and meant little or nothing to the masses. For example, its demonstrations against Black exclusion in White suburbs was irrelevant to the Black working class. Even if they were allowed to move out of the ghetto, they could not afford it.[29]

After the mid-sixties CORE took a nationalist position and became an all-Black organization. Unlike the Urban League it adopted a revolutionary rhetoric along with its conversion to a bourgeois nationalist program. The Chairman of CORE, Roy Innis, developed what he named the "Economic Theory of Nationhood," which called for Black control of all economic, political, and social institutions in Black communities for the purpose of economic development of these communities.[30] Operating under the slogan "Black power is Black business," CORE entered into a number of ventures, some financed by government and the foundations, to develop a Black economic structure.[30] Allen (1970) argues convincingly that, in reality, what this group's leaders are doing is tying the Black communities more firmly into the Structure of American corporate capitalism. In essence they are using the cloak of nationalism to transfer the oppressive instrument of White colonial domination into their hands and further their own interests as a class.[31]

Nation of Islam (Black Muslims) This group has its roots deeply entrenched in the Black community, at least in terms of recruitment and ideology. It is a religious organization with a political ideology that exhorts Blacks to repudiate the White religions and culture and form a separate nation in some part of the United States. Much of the recruitment of members is done in the prisons and ghettos, where this group seeks out the uneducated, unskilled, downtrodden Black underclass.[32] The Muslim organization appeals to two different types: nationalists and self-help. The former are attracted by the militant stance of the group and its emphasis on Black Nationhood. The latter come into the organization because of its emphasis on hard work and rigid personal morality.[33]

There is general agreement among most students of Black Muslim history that this group ranks among the most effective Black leadership organizations of all time. It has brought into its organizational fold those Blacks who were unreachable by other means and made of them dedicated members of the Black liberation movement. While doing this they have, through rigidly enforced discipline, amassed a huge amount of capital which they have gained from their various business enterprises. Moreover, most of this money has been used to build hospitals, schools, and mosques. A major criticism of this group is its lack of community involvement. Members isolate themselves in their organization and refuse to relate to many issues involving the Black community.[34] Another criticism has been directed at the lack of a clearcut political ideology and a heavy reliance on a countertheory of White evilness that is as simplistic and irrational as White theories about Black inferiority.

The Black Panther Party This group originated in Oakland, California in 1966 and played a leading role in the Black nationalist movement until 1972. It was an all-Black political party that adhered to a Marxist-Leninist ideology. Large numbers of Black youth from the underclass were attracted by its revolutionary program of armed defense and armed struggle against White domination and Imperialism. During the turbulent period of the late sixties and early seventies its leaders and members engaged in a number of confrontations with the police, which resulted in imprisonment, exile, or death for a significant proportion of the organization. Eventually weakened by internal strife and political repression, they turned to what was labeled community involvement.[35]

This community involvement offered a remarkable contrast to their past activities of organizing the Black community around armed struggle and armed defense. One of the most curious turnabouts was the Panthers' embrace of Black capitalism. The reasoning for their reevaluation of Black capitalists was that they too were victims of White corporate capitalism and needed to have their positive qualities cultivated. The Panthers determined their positive qualities according to whether they contributed sufficiently to the Panthers' survival programs. As a reward to those concerned Black businessmen, they often carried ads in the Black Panther newspaper encouraging Blacks to buy their products.[36]

A few other changes in the new Panther orientation was their involvement in the church and politics. They changed their attitude toward the Black church because of Minister Huey Newton's belief that once the party stepped outside of the church they were isolated from things the community was involved in.[37] Another transformation of this group was its entry into conventional politics. In 1973, the Chairman of the Party, Bobby Seale, ran for the office of Mayor in Oakland. He ran as a Democratic candidate and was quoted as saying his goal was "to turn Oakland into an all-American city."[38] After losing the election he turned his attention to reforming the local Democratic party and making it the Panthers' power base. A general consensus among Panther party watchers is that they are now pursuing a more modest and reformist program with a genuine revolution now only a distant vision.

Political Institutions

These governmental structures supposedly exist to serve their citizens and protect their boundaries from revolution or conquest. In the case of Blacks they have acted primarily as an instrument of colonial domination. Afro-Americans have been victims of a systematic subjugation under colonial rule in which the political state has been the chief executioner. Lerone Bennett (1968) charges that Blacks have carried out the dual roles of a political pawn within the political system while acting as a pressure force outside it. His thesis is that generally Blacks have been forced to act outside the political system because it has largely been unresponsive to their needs.[39] Another behavioral scientist writes that not only have Blacks been denied their political rights but as human beings they live outside the sphere of White American in dispersed colonial settlements throughout the United States.[40]

Politics has been irrelevant to Blacks throughout their history in this country. Although they arrived here in 1619 the right to vote was not granted them until the passage of the Fourteenth Amendment in 1865. During the reconstruction era, many White Southerners were disenfranchised and Blacks were elected to public office. Between 1870 and 1877 twenty Black congressmen and two Black senators served as public representatives from the South. These men were elected to those posts with the aid of the radical Republicans from the North and it was their interests they served, not their Black constituency. In the main they were alienated from the sentiments of the Black masses.[41] As a result of political compromises made between Northern White politicians and Southern capitalists, Blacks were soon stripped of their voting rights by a series of disenfranchising codes along with the violence against them by the Klu Klux Klan and other White groups. They did not regain that right until another seventy years had passed.[42]

There was almost total Black exclusion from electoral politics until the thirties. The first Black congressman outside the South achieved public office in 1928 and during the thirties Blacks were elected to state legislatures and city councils in a number of Northern and border states. With the emergence of the Roosevelt Administration Blacks defected in large numbers to the Democratic party and became loyal members of a coalition composed of White Southerners, trade unionists, and liberals. There were some minor gains from their participation in this party in the form of government-subsidized jobs, welfare, and social security. Whatever else they have received from Democratic administrations has come from mass struggles independent of that political party.[43]

The Black Vote   Both Black and White politicians have manipulated the Black vote. Despite claims to the contrary, it rarely has been that valued because of Blacks' allegiance to the Democratic party and blind loyalty to whatever Black candidate runs for a political office.

Since the days of the New Deal the Democratic party has had them in its hip-pocket and has taken their vote for granted. Because the opposition Republican party has the reputation of representing big business interests, and in recent years has relied heavily on racist appeals, Blacks have felt they had no real alternatives in political candidates on the national level.

During the sixties Blacks began to gain considerably more voting strength. With the passage of the Voting Rights Act in 1965, Blacks regained the franchise in the South. More significantly, as a result of changing demographic and social trends, Blacks became majorities or large minorities in a number of American cities. This domination, numerically, of urban centers enabled them to elect Blacks as mayors and to posts on city councils and boards of education. Some of the greatest gains were in the South where there are now many elected Black officials who fill posts ranging from police chief to mayor.[44] These political gains, however, only reflect the trend toward indirect colonial rule since a considerable amount of White control is exercised over Black political leadership and some of those Black politicians put their individual ambitions over group needs.

Black Politicians The Black politician who operates in the political arena faces a number of problems if he tries to serve his constituency. If he cooperates with those Whites who have political and economic power, only enough concessions to keep the natives under control will be made. To act against them is often to be rendered ineffective in achieving any gains at all. Banfield and Wilson (1963) point this out in their observation that "those who are elected generally find it necessary to be politicians first and Negroes second. If they are to stay in office, they must soft pedal the racial issues that are of most concern to Negroes as Negroes."[45]

Baron (1968) explained how this process worked in the city of Chicago. First, White leaders favored those Blacks who had totally identified with the traditional values and goals of White institutions without regard to their meaning to Blacks. Those who insisted on representing the interests of Blacks were isolated. They were infrequently consulted on critical questions, rarely appointed to important committees, and on key votes would find themselves voting with a small minority and occasionally alone. In the Democratic party machine, Blacks received fewer patronage positions and political favors than Whites. Additionally, they had to avoid the central organization on such critical issues as urban renewal and the schools.[46]

One consequence of this dilemma is the emergence of Black politicians as favor-seeking vassals and pawns of White political leaders who control the real political power. This has led to the pitiful situation of a group of Southern Black mayors meeting with arch-segregationist George Wallace and presenting him with a key to the city. Their explanation for their hospitality to a man who once vowed to keep Blacks out of the state's universities, shouting "segregation today, segregation tomorrow, segregation forever," was that "if we are going to be remembered as effective administrators and politicians we have to adopt the kind of postures necessary to deal with those folks in power."[47]

Some Blacks have not been deceived by their political representatives. A group of researchers reported that in the ghetto the political machinery is no better off than the other Black institutions. Their survey of Black political workers verified the ineffectiveness of Black politics. Although pressured by their constituency for better public services, the political workers found themselves unable to respond satisfactorily. When they were asked how the community viewed their city representatives, a majority said they considered them "part of the city government which must be asked continually and repeatedly in order to get things done."[48]

It is in the election of mayors of large cities that Blacks have achieved their most significant electoral victories. These mayors fall into three categories:

Small-Town and Ceremonial Mayors   A number of Black men have achieved this position in small towns and medium-sized cities. In small Southern towns, with populations under 25,000, these men are often elected by Black majorities. They are commonly community leaders serving in part-time positions that require full-time devotion. Their constituency is usually poor and they must rely on federal aid programs for community development projects.[49] The ceremonial mayor's function is largely limited to being a goodwill ambassador for his community. He has almost no power to effect change in his town. His constituency may be in either the South or North and often consists primarily of Whites. Since he yields no real political power, they may select him as a symbol of racial progress. Examples of these cities are Cincinatti, Ohio and Highland Park, Michigan.

Black-Power Mayor This is the politician who is elected to his post by the city's Black majority. He has greater freedom to cater to Black nationalist sentiment since he has little need for White votes. Often he runs for office in opposition to the party machine and colonial establishment. The two most common examples are Newark, New Jersey and Gary, Indiana where Blacks were almost solely responsible for their victories. Once in office, however, they find that the power of the office of Mayor is more apparent than real. An often quoted statement of this problem comes from Mayor Hatcher of Gary, Indiana:

> There is much talk about Black control of the ghetto. What does that mean? I am Mayor of a city of roughly 90,000 Black people but we do not control the possibilities of jobs for them, of money for their schools or state-funded social services. These things are in the hands of the United States Steel Corporation and the County Department of Welfare of the State of Indiana. Will the poor in Gary's worst slums be helped because the pawnshop owner is Black, not white?[50]

As more Blacks take over the rein of city government, they will find that little has been gained in terms of real power. Piven and Cloward (1968) report that local government has been considerably weakened since the peak of the ethnic political machines. While the federal government receives two-thirds of all tax monies, the local governments collect only 7 percent. This weakened tax base reveals the great vulnerability of localities to the national centralized power. Another threat to Black political control of the cities is the formation of metropolitan government, which includes suburban areas as voting districts. Both these trends will lighten the impact of Black voting power on American politics and political priorities.[51]

Coalition Mayors These are men elected to office in cities with sizable Black populations but not enough to make up a voting majority. Hence, these men develop a strategy that can form a loosely organized coalition of Black and White voters to give them a margin of victory. The basic element in this strategy is to get as many Blacks registered to vote as possible. Their support of a Black candidate is taken for granted despite his stand on the issues. Then, enough White votes must be captured by assuring them that he is a candidate of all the people and will not represent any special interest groups nor will he participate in any nationalist actions. Sometimes he will even condemn Black militants as extremists and promise greater support for the police force.[52]

This strategy has been successful in Cleveland and Los Angeles with Detroit and Atlanta having a similar situation. In the case of Los Angeles and Cleveland, the Black candidates ran against White candidates generally regarded as ineffective in running their cities. Both men received the support of influential businessmen and the mass media. Their expectation, which turned out to be correct, was that the only thing that would change would be the mayor's skin color. Even with this support, however, it is worth noting that none of those Black candidates for mayor has received a majority of White votes. A majority of Whites are still not ready to accept a Black man in that position. Only a 90 percent Black vote for these men has put them into office.

The case of Carl Stokes, Mayor of Cleveland, is illustrative of what happens when a Black mayor takes office. The first 10 appointments he made were 80 percent White. Although Blacks had complained of police abuse, he appointed a hardliner as police chief in order to appease Whites and show he was not soft on crime. The police force was increased by half and he called out the National Guard to crush the rebellions of the Black community in 1968. After serving three years as Mayor 70 percent of Black housing was still classified as substandard and only 20 of the city's 180 schools passed health and safety inspection that year. Despite the need for social services more than 60 percent of the city's budget was allocated to the police.[53]

Although the Black mayor of Los Angeles received fewer than half of the White votes cast, he claimed a victory for the American system. According to Tom Bradley:

> I believe for the young people it has great significance. Far too many have been turned off by the political process. Some opted

to do nothing. I lived in the system. I believed in it. This election showed that if they are willing to work hard enough, prepare well enough, it is also possible for them to dream as I have dreamed.[54]

The Black congressmen have not fared much better in their ability to effect change on behalf of the Black population. Due to nationalist sentiment, they have organized into a Black Caucus to address themselves to the issues of concern to Blacks. Yet, most of them remain wedded to the Democratic party and pursue their personal ambitions of rising into the upper ranks of its heirarchy. For instance, they have completely ignored Black positions of anti-Zionism and antibusing when formulating their own position. There is only one Black senator, and his orientation toward Blacks is reflected in his biographer's statement that he is a man first, an American second and a Negro third.[55]

With such political leadership to follow, it is no surprise to find that a greater percentage of eligible Black voters stay away from the polls on election day than eligible White voters.[56] Corresponding to this Black voter apathy are the survey findings that show over half the Blacks interviewed do not believe elected officials can be trusted. Young and well-educated Blacks believe that the political system as it is presently structured will not be responsive to them. A general consensus is that Black political leadership appears to be out of touch with much of the Black community.[57] The only reasonable conclusion that can be reached is that they are serving different masters and interests. Black political institutions in their current stage only presage the indirect colonial control of the masses.

Economic Institutions

Economic institutions have never played a significant role in Black life although the myth of a Black business empire has existed for a number of years. Unlike other ethnic groups, Blacks never developed a strong merchant class that could supply its members with jobs, capital, and philanthropic donations to schools and charities. Ofari (1970) attributes this, in part, to the tradition of African communal practices where goods, services, and land were collectively shared. The idea of buying and selling or employing labor for the purpose of exploitation was alien to people of African descent.[58] Consequently, after slavery ended and Blacks were theoretically free to engage in private enterprise, not only did they lack a strong capitalist ethic but they did not possess any knowledge of business techniques or practices.

Some Blacks have engaged in commercial ventures since they arrived on these shores. Free Blacks owned property, a few owned slaves, others engaged in such enterprises as tailoring and clothing, newspapers, cooking, and livery stables. After emancipation the freedmen established themselves in banks, insurance companies, large farms, real estate, cosmetics, and small businesses that were service-oriented such as hairdressing and barbershops. Many of the larger businesses failed because of Black ignorance of business methods and poor management. The smaller commercial enterprises have always been marginal operations that seldom supported more than the proprietor and his family.[59]

A number of reasons account for the Black businessmen's failure to gain a strong toehold in the capitalist world. Foremost among them are the obstacles put in their way by White racism. They have generally been restricted to serving the impoverished Black market and rarely allowed to compete in the general market. White banks have refused to grant them credit and capital to start or expand any commercial enterprises. Thus they have never been allowed to maintain anything but marginal enterprises. Being confined to a clientele characterized by low income, high levels of employment, comparatively large debts, and few financial assets, they are forced to operate in an extremely bad business environment.[60] The enterprises that survived have been those that Whites would not open to Blacks such as insurance, mortuaries, barbershops, restaurants, etc. When White entrepreneurs realized a profit could be made by catering to this part of the Black market, they began to monopolize them too. Today, there are fewer Black-owned life insurance companies, banks, and hotels than there were in 1929.[61]

One common reason for Black business failure is poor management. A major factor here is that many Blacks who go into business do so simply because they cannot find decent employment and they start an enterprise with very little capital and a limited inventory. They tend to be the less capable Blacks because those who are poorly educated but bright will enter the underworld of the hustler and pimp. Others who have obtained a higher education go into the professions instead of business because they expect a higher rate of return.[62]

The lack of Black businesses appears strange considering the strength of the Black market. As a group they have an income higher than all but eight nations throughout the world with a yearly earned income of $55 billion. Yet in 1969, 163,000 Black-owned businesses had total receipts of only $4.5 billion and 151,996 employees.[63] This is best explained by economic colonialism, as Roy Innis points out:

> There is a striking similarity between so-called Black communities and underdeveloped countries. Both have always been oppressed. Almost always there is an unfavorable balance of trade with the oppressor or exploiter, both suffer from high unemployment, low income, scarce capital and we can point to a series of other similarities.[64]

One other similarity to the colonial countries is the lack of trust and confidence between Black merchants and their customers. Most Black businesses are owned by a single person because of the lack of confidence Blacks have in one another. The customers complain of discourteous treatment, inflated prices, and the low quality of goods and services. Some of the Black merchants respond that Blacks expect more of them than White merchants, that they demand social services and credit, and fail to pay their bills on time. And, they charge that many Blacks prefer to trade with Whites than their own kind.[65] A fairly accurate assessment of this situation is that internal colonialism has created a tiny class of Black capitalists who tend to inept and who engage in shoddy business practices that are noticeable because they do not have the capital or expertise to finesse their unethical business procedures in the same way as more wealthy White capitalists. Hence, the Black customer learns to be wary of them.

Despite this obvious failure of Black business, the Nixon Administration's main program for dealing with Black poverty was the development of Black capitalism. There was no Black involvement in the formulation of this program, except for a few members of the Black bourgeoisie, and it lacked any strong community support. After some four years in operation trying to help Blacks start their own businesses and secure loans more easily, the Black share of the nation's businesses was still less than 4 percent and these firms have less than 1 percent of all business receipts. A major error was the emphasis on small businesses, which have a high mortality rate in general and especially within the Black community. One survey in Chicago revealed that 80 percent of the Black-owned firms started in 1972 failed by the end of the year.[66] Under the Ford Administration, no substantial changes have occurred and Black businessmen have suffered the most from the present economic recession.

There were many illusions created by the establishment of a Black capitalism program. A noted Black economist, Andrew Brimmer (1969), estimates that even if Black businesses created by this program were successful, only 550,000-775,000 additional jobs would be created by 1980, representing a mere 7 percent maximum percent of the projected Black labor force at that time.[67] Another authority has commented that if the Black consumer market becomes that attractive, large national corporations will move into it on a large scale and such competition will hardly favor the marginal Black business class. Indeed, some of the Black businesses operating in the ghetto now are wholly owned subsidiaries of the White parent company.[68]

The main objection to Black capitalism, however, is that it does not change the substance of economic exploitation. It only changes the skin color of the exploiting class in the hope that nationalist aspirations can be channeled into supporting the present politico-economic system. Fanon (1965) spoke to this indirect control of the natives when he wrote: "Seen through its eyes, its mission has nothing to do with transforming the nation; it consists prosaically, of being the transmission between the nation and . . . neocolonialism."[69]

BLACK CONTROL AND ALTERNATIVE INSTITUTIONS

Our examination of Black institutions reveals that they have been largely ineffective in producing positive change on behalf of the Black masses. They have suffered under the weight of colonial control and were unable to represent Black interests even when they so desired. Putting Black figures in fundamentally colonial institutions does not seem to be the answer. In the words of Bill Strickland (1972), "The myth we must lay to rest is that American structures under White or Black control can produce the changes in material and moral life that Black people need."[70] The task before us is to build institutions anchored in the Black community that will function to support Black consciousness, further it, and defend it against all the attacks the powerful colonial power structure will direct against it.

The place to begin is in the political arena. Blacks must discard the politics of reliance on the two major parties, which have never responded to their needs. They need a national Black political party organized around a program of change and unity, a program arrived at objectively through nationwide discussions within Black communities. Such a program would coordinate efforts to achieve complete control over the Black community. Through the actions of such a party the school system can be centralized and new educational systems sponsored to train Black minds to seize control of their destiny. It can establish cooperative efforts to control the resources within Black community and to divide its wealth according to the needs of each community.

Black leadership must respond to the imperatives of such a program, the right of people to have democratic control over their own lives and communities. They should not run for public office in order to further individual ambitions but to advance the interests of Black people. And, those interests can be furthered only by breaking with the two parties of economic exploitation and racism. Moreover, they should seek the help of the Black population in reconstructing the Black community. Community councils can be established to assist in policy decisions and administer the affairs of the Black nation. Such community participation can help prevent Michels' (1959) "iron law of oligarchy," where leaders seek to serve their own interests before the needs of the group they purport to represent.[71] The ultimate result of these suggestions should be institutional forms that really do satisfy basic human needs.

NOTES

1 Robert Blauner, *Racial Oppression in America,* Harper & Row, New York, 1972, pp. 65–70.
2 U.S. Dèpt. of Health, Education and Welfare, Office of Education, *Federal Agencies and Black Colleges,* Government Printing Office, Washington, 1972, pp. 82–85.
3 Earl Conrad, *The Invention of the Negro,* Eriksson, New York, 1967, p. 153.
4 Christopher Jencks, and David Riesman, *The Academic Revolution,* Doubleday, Garden City, N.Y., 1969, p. 425.
5 Ann Jones, *Uncle Tom's Campus,* Praeger, New York, 1973, pp. 210–212.

6 Jencks and Riesman, op. cit., p. 424.
7 Ibid., p. 433.
8 Harry Edwards, *Black Students,* The Free Press, New York, 1970, pp. 17–25.
9 Howard Zinn, *SNCC: The New Abolitionists,* Beacon, Boston, 1964, pp. 235–236.
10 Ronald E. Wolseley, *The Black Press, U.S.A.,* Iowa State, Ames, Iowa, 1971, pp. 17–29.
11 Ibid, pp. 9–16.
12 Carlton Goodlett, "Black Press Lighting Road to Freedom," *Dawn,* p. 15, January–February, 1974.
13 Francis B. Ward, "The Black Press in Crisis," *The Black Scholar,* vol. 5, p. 36, September 1973.
14 Baxter Smith, "Issues Facing the Black Press," *The Militant,* p. 14, February 1, 1974.
15 Wolseley, op. cit., pp. 117–119.
16 The Congressional Black Caucus, "A Position on the Mass Communications Media," paper presented at Harvard University, April 5, 6, and 7, 1972, p. 8.
17 J. K. Obatala, "Soul Music in Africa," *The Black Scholar,* vol. 2, p. 12, February 1971.
18 Hollie I. West, "Black Radio," *The Washington Post,* p. L-1, January 28, 1973.
19 The Congressional Black Caucus, loc. cit.
20 Gunnar Myrdal, *An American Dilemma,* Harper, New York, 1944, p. 731.
21 E. V. Essien-Udom, *Black Nationalism,* University of Chicago, Chicago, 1962, pp. 16–17.
22 Robert L. Allen, *Black Awakening in Capitalist America,* Doubleday, Garden City, N.Y., 1970, p. 11.
23 Charles Flint Kellog, *NAACP: A History of the National Association for the Advancement of Colored People,* 1909–1920, John Hopkins, Baltimore, 1967.
24 Louis Lomax, "The Negro Revolt Against Negro Leaders," *Harper's,* p. 47, June 1960.
25 "Wilkins Ouster Story Is Totally Erroneous," *The Los Angeles Sentinal,* p. A3, January 31, 1974.
26 Whitney Young, *To Be Equal,* McGraw-Hill, New York, 1964, pp. 26–31.
27 "C. F. Whitney Young. He Was A Doer," *Newsweek,* p. 29, March 22, 1971.

28 Allen, op. cit., p. 211.
29 Auguste Meier and Eliot Rudwick, *C.O.R.E.: A Study in the Civil Rights Movement, 1942–1968,* Oxford, New York, 1973, p. 184.
30 Allen, op. cit., pp. 185–186.
31 Ibid, p. 191.
32 Essien-Udom, op. cit., pp. 201–231.
33 John Howard, "The Making of a Black Muslim," *Transaction,* vol. 3, pp. 15–21, December 1966.
34 George Breitman (ed.), *Malcolm X Speaks,* Grove, New York, 1966, p. 171.
35 Earl Anthony, *Picking Up the Gun,* Dial, New York, 1970.
36 Ross K. Baker, "The Transformation of the Panthers," *The Washington Post,* p. B1–2, February 13, 1972.
37 Baker, loc. cit.
38 "And a New Bobby," *Newsweek,* p. 30, April 2, 1972.
39 Lerone Bennett, Jr., "The Politics of the Outsider," *Negro Digest,* p. 57, July 1968.
40 Leslie B. McLemore, "Toward a Theory of Black Politics—The Black and Ethnic Models Revisited," *Journal of Black Studies,* vol. 2, p. 324, March 1972.
41 Chuck Stone, *Black Political Power in America,* Delta, New York, 1970, chap. 3.
42 C. Vann Woodward, *The Strange Career of Jim Crow,* Oxford, New York, 1955, pp. 105–106, 141–143.
43 Stone, op. cit., pp. 58–81.
44 "The Black Political Gain in the South," *The San Francisco Chronicle,* p. 8, February 4, 1974.
45 Edward C. Banfield and James Q. Wilson, *City Politics,* Harvard and M.I.T., Cambridge, Mass., 1963, p. 293.
46 Harold Baron, "Black Powerlessness in Chicago," *Transaction,* vol. 6, pp. 27–33, November 1968.
47 "Southern Mayors Deal with Realities," *Jet,* p. 20, December 6, 1973.
48 David Baesel et al., "White Institutions and Black Rage," *Transaction,* vol. 6, p. 29, March 1969.
49 "The South's Black Mayors and Their Heavy Burden," *San Francisco Sunday Examiner and Chronicle,* This World Section, p. 24, December 9, 1973.
50 Quoted in Allen, op. cit., p. 139.
51 Francis Fox Piven and Richard A. Cloward, "What Chance for Black Power," *New Republic,* p. 23, March 30, 1968.
52 Jeffrey K. Hadden, "The Making of the Negro Mayors 1967," *Transaction,* vol. 5, pp. 21–30, January–February, 1968.

53 James M. Naughton, "Mayor Stokes: The First Hundred Days," *The New York Times Magazine,* p. 26, February 25, 1968; Dunan Williams, "Why Democrats Can't Solve Problems Facing Cleveland's Black Community," *The Militant,* p. 18, August 3, 1973.

54 "Tom Bradley: A Personal Victory," *The Washington Post,* May 31, 1973, p. A8.

55 John Henry Cutler, *Ed Brooke: Biography of a Senator,* Bobbs-Merrill, New York, 1972, p. 3.

56 "Black Voting Percentage Drops Lower than Whites," *Jet,* p. 30, December 13, 1973.

57 David O. Sears, "Black Attitudes Toward the Political System in the Aftermath of the Watts Insurrection," *Midwest Journal of Political Science,* vol. 4, pp. 315–344, November 1969.

58 Earl Ofari, *The Myth of Black Capitalism,* Monthly Review, New York, 1970, p. 10.

59 Lerone Bennett, Jr., "The Quest for Economic Security," *Ebony,* pp. 66–78, February 1974.

60 Andrew F. Brimmer, "Economic Integration and the Progress of the Negro Community," *Ebony,* vol. 25, pp. 118–121, August 1970.

61 Dempsey Travis, "Can Black Builders and Bankers Survive?" *The Black Scholar,* vol. 5, p. 28, February 1974.

62 Marvin E. Perry, "The Colonial Analogy and Economic Development," *The Black Scholar,* vol. 5, p. 41, February 1974.

63 Bureau of the Census, U.S. Department of Commerce, *Minority, Owned Businesses,* 1969, Washington, U.S. Government Printing Office, August 1971, p. MB-1, Table B.

64 The American Assembly, *Black Economic Development,* Prentice-Hall, Englewood Cliffs, N.J., 1969, p. 53.

65 St. Clair Drake and Horace Cayton, *Black Metropolis,* Harcourt, Brace, New York, 1945, pp. 439–449.

66 "Black Capitalism—Mostly an Empty Promise," *Time,* p. 58–59, July 9, 1973.

67 Andrew Brimmer, "Economic Potential of Black Capitalism," address before the American Economic Association, New York, December 29, 1969.

68 Martin Rein, "Social Stability and Black Capitalism," *Transaction,* vol. 6, p. 4, June 1969.

69 Frantz Fanon, *The Wretched of the Earth,* Grove, New York, 1965, p. 125.

70 Bill Strickland, "The Crisis and Challenge of Black Politics," address before the African and African-American Studies Conference at Atlanta University, Atlanta, December 8, 1972.

71   Robert Michels, *Political Parties*, Dover, New York, 1959, pp. 400–403.

SUGGESTED READING LIST

Allen, Robert L.: *Black Awakening in Capitalist America*, Doubleday, Garden City, N.Y., 1970.

Anthony, Earl: *Picking Up the Gun*, Dial, New York, 1970.

Blackwell, James: *The Black Community: Diversity and Unity*, Dodd, Mead, New York, 1975.

Bullock, Henry Allen: *A History of Negro Education in the South*, Praeger, New York, 1970.

Clark, Kenneth: *Dark Ghetto*, Harper Torchbooks, New York, 1965.

Drake, St. Clair, and Horace Cayton: *Black Metropolis*, Harcourt, Brace, New York, 1945.

Essien-Udom, Essien Udosen: *Black Nationalism*, University of Chicago, Chicago, 1962.

Jones, Ann: *Uncle Tom's Campus*, Praeger, New York, 1973.

McGrath, Earl J.: *The Predominantly Negro Colleges and Universities in Transition*, Columbia, New York, 1965.

Meier, Auguste and Eliot Rudwick: *C.O.R.E.: A Study in the Civil Rights Movement, 1942–1968*, Oxford, New York, 1973.

Ofari, Earl: *The Myth of Black Capitalism*, Monthly Review, New York, 1970.

Perry, Marvin E.: "The Colonial Analogy and Economic Development," *The Black Scholar*, vol. 5, pp. 37–42, February 1974.

Stone, Chuck: *Black Political Power in America*, Delta, New York, 1970.

Tabb, William K.: *The Political Economy of the Ghetto*, Norton, New York, 1970.

Walton, Hanes, Jr.: *Black Political Parties*, The Free Press, New York, 1972.

Walton, Hanes, Jr.: *Black Politics*, Lippincott, Philadelphia, 1972.

Wilson, James Q.: *Negro Politics*, The Free Press, Glencoe, Ill., 1960.

Wolseley, Ronald E.: *The Black Press, U.S.A.*, Iowa State, Ames, Iowa, 1971.

The Black Family

As the United States' largest visible minority, the Black population has been the subject of extensive study by behavioral scientists. Its family life, which has been of particular concern, has some unique characteristics because of a history that is uncharacteristic of other ethnic groups. There are four traits of the Black group that distinguish it from other immigrants to the United States. These differences are cultural in the sense that (1) Blacks came from a country with norms and values that were dissimilar to the American way of life; (2) they were composed of many different tribes, each with its own languages, cultures, and traditions; (3) in the beginning, they came without females, and, most importantly; (4) they came in bondage.[1]

Historically Black family life has been studied from the aspect of its problems. While the study of White families has been biased toward the middle-class family, the reverse has been true in the investigation of Black family patterns. Until recently almost all studies of Black family life have concentrated on the lower-income stratum of the group, while ignoring middle-class families or even "stable" poor Black families. Moreover, the deviation of Black families from middle-class norms has led to the definition of them as "pathological." Such labels ignore the possibility that while a group's family forms may not fit into the normative model, it may have its own functional organization to meet the needs of that group.[2]

One purpose of this description of the Black family lifestyle is to demonstrate how it is organized to meet the functional prerequisites of the Black community. Additionally, the forces that Black families encounter, which create the existence of large numbers of "problem" families, must be carefully examined. Out of this systematic analysis of Black family adaptations may come a new understanding of the Black family in contemporary American society.

THE PRESLAVERY PERIOD

There are several historical periods of interest in evaluating Black family life in the United States. One is the precolonial era on the African continent where the Black American population originated. The basis of African family life was the kinship group, which was bound together by blood ties and the common interest of corporate functions. Within each village, there were elaborate legal codes and court systems that regulated the marital and family behavior of individual members. The philosophy of family life was based on humanitarianism, mutual aid, and community participation. Although no two tribes in Africa were the same, the continent was generally humane in its treatment of the individual and the creation of meaningful roles for everyone.[3]

In African communities, marriage was not merely a matter between individuals, but the concern of all family members. A woman, for instance, was not just a man's wife, but "the wife of the family." As a result of this community control of marriages, the dissolution of a marriage was a severe action and used only as a last resort. Most marriages involved a payment by the husband's family to compensate the bride's family for the loss of her services and to guarantee good treatment. This was not the purchase of a woman who became her husband's property. After marriage, a woman remained a member of her own family, since they retained a sincere interest in her well-being.[4]

Regardless of the meaningful role of women in precolonial Africa, the authority pattern in the family was patriarchal. This male control was based not so much on benign dominance, but on the reverence attached to the man's role as protector and provider for the family. He had to perform the heavy manual labor and make the decisions. Only if he successfully carried out his responsibilities would respect and admiration be accorded him. On certain days, the wife and children would bestow as much respect upon him as subjects would a king. If it was a fete day, his sons-in-law and daughters would be there to present him with some small gifts. They would pay him their reverences, bring him a pipe, and then go into another room where they all ate together with their mother.[5]

Children in African societies were considered symbols of the continuity of life. During their formative years, children enjoyed a carefree life. Until they reached the age of nine or ten, they had no responsibilities, but then they began to learn their role requirements and responsibilities to the tribe. The boys would build small huts and hunt fierce game. Girls would play house and care for their babies (often a younger sister). When they reached the age of fifteen, they were considered adults and almost ready to begin families of thier own.[6]

The structure and function of the Black family was radically changed under the system of slavery. What did not change, however, was the importance of the family to African people in the New World. While the nature of marriage and family patterns was no longer under the control of the kinship group, it nevertheless managed to sustain the individual in the face of the many destructive forces he was to encounter in American society.

THE SLAVE FAMILY

Originally, Blacks came to the American continent as indentured servants, along with Whites from Europe who shared the same status. During this period, 1619–1640, race played a significant, but not central, role in the social relations between Black and White indentured servants. They worked together as equals, and even intermarriage between the two groups was tolerated. However, the development of large tobacco and cotton plantations created the need for a huge, cheap labor force, and Black slavery was substituted for White servitude. Although Whites were enslaved at one point in time, Englishmen began to use Blacks exclusively, since they presented so few of the difficulties encountered with Whites. Because of their color, Blacks could be more easily apprehended and could be handled with more rigid methods of discipline, which subjected them to a moral and spiritual degradation that was unacceptable to members of the White population.[7]

Slavery had its greatest impact on the family life of the Blacks. Most of the slaves who came in the beginning were males. The Black female population was not equal to the number of males until 1840. As a result, sex relations between Black slaves and indentured White women was fairly extensive. Some of the interracial relationships were more than casual contacts and ended in marriage. The frequency of miscegenation between male slaves and free White women grew to the extent that laws were passed to prevent any further increase. Before the alarm over the incidence of miscegenation, male slaves were encouraged to mate with White women since the children from such unions were also slaves, thereby increasing the property of the slavemaster.[8]

In attempting to get an accurate description of the family life of slaves, one has to sift through a conflicting array of opinions on the subject. Reliable empirical facts are few, and speculation has been rampant in the absence of data. However, certain aspects of the slave's family life are undisputed. Slaves were not allowed to enter into binding contractual relationships. Since marraige is basically a legal relationship which imposes obligations on both parties and exacts penalties for their violation, there was no legal basis to any marriage between two individuals in bondage. Slave marriages were regulated at the discretion of the slavemaster. As a result, some marriages were initiated by slaveowners and just as easily dissolved.[9]

Hence, there were numerous cases where the slaveowner ordered slave women to marry men of his choosing after they reached the age of puberty. Owners preferred a marriage between slaves on the same plantation, since the primary reason for slave unions was the breeding of children who would become future slaves. Children born to a slave woman on a different plantation were looked upon by the slaveholder as wasting his man's seed. Yet, many slaves who were

allowed to get married preferred women from a neighboring plantation. This allowed them to avoid witnessing the many assaults on slave
women that occurred. Sometimes, the matter was resolved by the
sale of one of the parties to the other owner.[10]

Historians are divided on the question of how many slave families
were involuntarily separated by their owners. Despite the slaveholder's
commitment to maintaining the slave families intact, the intervening
events of a slaveholder's death, his bankruptcy, or lack of capital
made the forceable sale of some slave's spouse or child inevitable. In
instances where the slavemaster was indifferent to the fate of slave
families, he would still keep them together simply to enforce plantation discipline. A married slave who was concerned about his wife
and children, it was believed, was less inclined to rebel or escape than
would a nonmarried slave. Whatever their reasoning, the few available
records show that slaveowners did not separate the majority of their
slave couples.

This does not mean that the slave family had a great deal of
stability. While there are examples of some families living together
for forty years or more, most slave unions were dissolved by personal
choice, death, or the sale of one partner by the master. Although
individual families might not have remained together for long periods
of time, the institution of the family was an important asset in the
perilous era of slavery. Despite the prevalent theories about the destruction of the family under slavery, it was one of the most important survival mechanisms for African people held in bondage.[11]

In their state of involuntary servitude, the slaves began to form
a new sense of family. Whereas, in African society, the family was
based on the system of kinship within the tribe, under slavery it was
the community of slaves into which the individual found his identity.
Tribal affiliation was reorganized to encompass those individuals bound
together by the commonality of their Blackness and their enslavement.
It was in this context that many of the traditional functions of the
family were carried out and the former philosophical principle of
survival of the tribe held fast.[12]

In the slave quarters, Black families did exist as functioning
institutions and as models for others. The slave narratives provide us
with some indication of the importance of family relations under
slavery. It was in the family that the slave received affection,

companionship, love, and empathy. Through the family, he learned how to avoid punishment, to cooperate with his fellow slaves, and to retain some semblance of his self-esteem. The socialization of the slave child was another important function for the slave parents. They could cushion the shock of bondage for him, inculcate in him values different from those the masters attempted to teach him, and represent another frame of reference for his self-esteem besides the master.[13]

Much has been written about the elimination of the male's traditional functions under the slave system. It is true that he was often relegated to working in the fields and siring children, rather than providing economic maintenance or physical protection for his family. Yet, the father's role was not as insignificant as presumed. Ex-slaves often spoke of their affection for their fathers and the pain of separation. Although he could not perform many of the functions traditionally assigned to fathers, there were other ways he could acquire respect from his family. Where possible, he could add to the family's meager rations of food by hunting and fishing. Or, he could gain the approval of his family and fellow bondsmen by making furniture for the cabin or building partitions between cabins that contained more than one family.[14]

It was the male slaves' inability to protect his wife from the physical and sexual abuse of the master that most pained him. Yet, as a matter of survival, few tried, since the consequences were often fatal. But it is significant that tales of their intervention occur frequently in the slave narratives. There is one story of a slave who could no longer tolerate the humiliation of his wife's sexual abuse by the master before his eyes. He choked him to death with the knowledge that it meant his death. He said he knew it was death, but it was death anyhow, so he just killed him.[15]

Slave children learned many valuable lessons from their parents. Some taught them submission as a way of avoiding pain, suffering, and death. However, they were not taught categorical obedience. Rather, they were frequently instructed to fight the master when their relatives were in danger. One example was W. H. Robinson's father who told him, "I want you to die in defense of your mother."[16] Some parents taught the child pride in his African heritage. One student related how his father often boasted that he had a pure strain of Black blood in his veins and could trace his ancestors back to the very heart of Africa.[17]

The importance of the family is underlined by the numerous cases of fugitive slaves who had run away in an effort to find mates who had been sold to another owner. In most cases, these couples were bound together by affection, not morality or a contractual agreement. These bonds were just as strong, even when there was no legal marriage. As Matthews (1972)[18] has noted, the valid African marriage does not need any kind of ceremonial sanction external to the domestic consent, no bride price and no ceremony, sacred or secular. Yet, slaves had a reverence for the legal marriage and the protection the law afforded. Bibb (1972) states that "there are no class of people in the United States who so highly appreciate the legality of marriage as those persons who have been held and treated as property."[19]

Slavery in the United States is frequently compared with the same institution in South America, where it was considered more humane. It was the Spanish Slave Code and the Catholic Church in Latin America that provided safeguards for the slave's person, his family, and his worth as a human being. These two forces supposedly led to the encouragement of manumission and stable marriages among free and slave Blacks.[20] This polarity of the two slave systems in North and South America does not hold up under close examination. There was considerable variation among the Latin American nations in their use and treatment of slaves. In some Latin societies, there was very humane treatment of slaves and, in others, inhumane treatment.[21] As for the Spanish Slave Code, it was not only unenforced, but never promulgated in any of the Spanish Caribbean colonies. Moreover, some of the measures encouraging marriage among the slaves in South America were designed to hold the slaves to the plantation estates with family ties.[22]

One aspect of Black family life frequently ignored during the slave era is the free Black family. This group, which numbered about half a million, was primarily composed of the descendants of the original Black indentured servants and the mulatto offspring of slaveholders. For this minority of Black families, the assimilation and acculturation process was relatively less difficult. They imitated the White world as closely as possible. Because they had opportunities for education, owning property, and skilled occupations, their family life was fairly stable. Some of them even owned slaves, although the majority of Black slaveholders were former slaves who had purchased their wives or children. It is among this group that the Black middle-class was originally formed.[23]

AFTER EMANCIPATION

An indication of the importance attached to the family by the bonds-man was the number of freed slaves searching for family members from whom they had been separated. Some had been apart for as long as thirty years. The means used to reunite families ranged from placing ads in Black newspapers to the trek of one ex-slave who walked 600 miles during a two-month stretch. Many of the slaves who had co-habited together made plans for a legal marriage with the knowledge that they no longer faced the possibility of eventual exploitation and separation.[24]

There has been a prevailing notion that the experience of slavery weakened the value of marriage as an institution among Afro-Ameri-cans. Yet, the slaves married in record numbers when the right for a freedman to marry was created by governmental decree. A legal marriage was a status symbol, and weddings were events of great gaiety. In a careful examination of census data and marriage licenses for the period after 1860, Gutman (1973)[25] found the typical house-hold everywhere was a simple nuclear family headed by an adult male. Further evidence that Black people were successful in forming a biparental family structure are the data showing that 90 percent of all Black children were born in wedlock by the year 1917.[26]

The strong family orientation of the freedman was observed by many students of the reconstruction era. One newspaper reported a Black group's petition to the state of North Carolina asking for the right "to work with the assurance of good faith and fair treatment, to educate their children, to sanctify the family relation, to reunite scattered families, and to provide for the orphan and infirm."[27] Children were of special value to the freed slaves whose memories were fresh with the history of their offspring being sold away. After slavery, the slave-born generation of freedmen cherished their children all the more and devoted their lives to providing them with land and an education.

It was during the late nineteenth century that the strong role of women emerged. Males preferred their wives to remain at home, since a working woman was considered a mark of slavery. But, during a period described as "the most explicitly racist era of American history,"[28] Black men found it very difficult to obtain jobs and, in some instances, found work only as strikebreakers. Thus, the official organ of the African Methodist Episcopal Church exhorted Black families to teach their daughters not to avoid work, since many of them would marry men who would not make more than an average of 75 cents a day.[29] In 1900 approximately 41 percent of Black women were in the labor force, compared with 16 percent of White women.[30]

What was important, then, was not whether the husband or wife worked, but the family's will to survive in an era when Blacks were systematically deprived of educational and work opportunities. Despite these obstacles, Black families achieved a level of stability based on role integration. Males shared equally in the rearing of children, women participated in the defense of the family. As Nobles (1974)[31] comments, a system where the family disintegrates due to the loss of one member would be in opposition to the traditional principle of unity which defined the African family.

This principle was to be tested during the period of the great Black migration from the rural areas of the South to the cities of the North. The rise of Black illegitimacy and female-headed households are concomitants of twentieth-century urban ghettos. A subsequent doubling of those phenomena strongly indicate that the condition of many lower-class Black families is a function of the economic contingencies of industrial America.[32] Unlike the European immigrants before them, Blacks were disadvantaged by the hard lines of Northern segregation along racial lines. Furthermore, families in cities are more vulnerable to disruptions because of the traumatizing experiences of urbanization, the reduction of family functions, and the loss of extended family supports. Inasmuch as racial discrimination against Blacks in the South was at a higher level, they were less likely to retreat from the more vulnerable conditions of urban poverty in the North than White migrants from the South.[33]

In the transition from Africa to the American continent, there can be no doubt that African culture was not retained in any pure form. Blacks lacked the autonomy to maintain their cultural traditions under the severe pressures to take on American standards of behavior. Yet, there are surviving Africanisms reflected in Black speech patterns, esthetics, folklore, and religion.[34] Blacks have preserved aspects of their old culture that have a direct relevance to their new lives. And, out of the common experiences they have shared, they have forged a new culture, which is uniquely Afro-American. The elements of that culture are still to be found in their family life.

THE MODERN BLACK FAMILY

Demographic Characteristics

Most Black families adhere to the nuclear family model. In 1972, approximately two-thirds of Black families had both the husband and wife present. A significantly larger percentage of Black households were headed by a female than in White families. While White families had a woman head in 9 percent of all such families, 30 percent of Black families were headed by a woman. Moreover, this was an increase of 8 percent from the last decade. This large number of female-headed households is mostly a result of socioeconomic forces. As the level of income rises, so does the number of male-headed families. At the upper income level of $15,000 and over, the percentage of male-headed households is comparable to that for White families. If we combine families reconstituted by a second marriage with those never broken, 69 percent of Black children live in families with both a father and mother present.[35]

One of the most significant changes in the period 1960–1970 was the decline in the Black birth rate. In 1968 it reached its lowest level in the past twenty-five years. However, the White birth rate declined even more rapidly (29 percent versus 32 percent), and the total birth rate of 3.13 children per Black woman is still higher than that of 2.37 for White women. This differential is influenced by a number of factors including regional variations, rural-urban differences, and, most importantly, socioeconomic levels. In 1967 Black women in the South had more children than those who lived in the North, and the birth rate of urban Black women was lower than that of Black women in rural areas. Significantly, middle-class Blacks have the lowest fertility rate of almost every demographic category in the United States, whereas middle-class Catholics and Mormons have the highest. College-educated Black women actually have a lower birth rate than college-educated White women.[36]

One of the more significant events of the last decade was the steady decline in the out-of-wedlock births to Black women, while the illegitimacy rate among Whites has shown a steady rise. According to the 1971 census, the illegitimacy rate among Whites went from 9.2 to 13.2 (per 1,000 unmarried women 14–44 years old) between 1960 and 1968, while the rate among Blacks decreased from 98.3 to 86.6 during the same time span. Some of this racial difference in the illegitimacy rate increase can be attributed to the more frequent, and effective, use of contraceptives and abortions among Black women. One study found that Black women received about 25 percent of all the legal abortions performed in hospitals nationwide.[37] However, the White illegitimacy rate has been underestimated in the past because of unreported abortions, falsification of medical records, and shotgun weddings.[38]

As noted earlier, about 30 percent of Black families are headed by women. About 60 percent of these families have incomes below the official poverty level, despite the fact that 60 percent of the women who are heads of Black households work (most of them full time). Over 10 percent of this group were unemployed in the year 1971, and slightly less than 50 percent received welfare assistance.[39] These female-headed households included widowed and single women, women whose husbands were in the armed forces or otherwise away from home involuntarily, as well as those separated from their husbands through divorce or marital discord. The majority of these female-headed households came about through separation or divorce, while a quarter of them involved widows, and 20 percent were never married.[40]

Social Structure

It is generally acknowledged that the Black kinship network is more extensive and cohesive than kinship bonds among the White population. The validity of this assumption is borne out by the census data which show that a larger proportion of Black families take relatives into their households. Billingsley (1968)[41] divides these families into three general categories. They include (1) the "incipient-extended family," composed of a husband and wife who are childless and take in other relatives; (2) the "simple extended family," a married couple with children who have other relatives living with them; and (3) the "attentuated extended family," a household composed of a single, abandoned, legally separated, divorced, or widowed spouse living with his or her own children, who takes additional relatives into the home. According to the 1970 census, the attentuated family is the most common with 48 percent of families headed by elderly women taking in relatives under 18. The proportion of White families is only 10 percent. In the incipient-extended family category, 13 percent of Black couples took in relatives under 18, compared with only 3 percent of White couples.[42]

There is some disagreement on the reason for the stronger kinship bonds among Black families. Adams (1970)[43] has suggested that minority status tends to strengthen kin ties because of a need for mutual aid and survival in a hostile environment. Others have attributed it to the individual's general distrust of neighbors and neighborhoods, the prevalence of large female-headed households receiving public assistance, and the high rate of residential mobility which make long-term friendships difficult.[44] In opposition to the above theories is the argument by Matthews (1972)[45] and Nobles (1974)[46] that contemporary Black kinship patterns are but a variant of the extended family system found in African societies.

Matthews (1972)[47] advances the proposition that Afro-Americans are relating to their African heritage when they function as members of a corporate group. The individual in the Black community, he says, is always relating to the remainder of the total Black community. In fact, Black togetherness is at the heart of Black social organization. The Black extended family is the functional unit of the Black community. Nobles (1974)[48] states that the Black family socializes its members to see no real distinction between the personal self and other members of the family. They are both the same. The individual's identity is always the group's identity, and families function according to this philosophical orientation.

Whatever the source of Black kinship bonds, they provide a very valuable service to Black families. A number of studies have revealed that kinsmen help one another with financial aid, child care, advice, and other forms of mutual aid.[49] Another important function of kinship groups is to enhance the emotional relationships within the kinship network and beyond. They perform this function by the high frequency of social interaction they have with one another. Hays and Mindel (1973)[50] found Black families interacted with more of their extended kin in almost every category of kinship than did White families. In the Podell study[51] welfare mothers were shown to have a high frequency of interaction with relatives. Most of them had relatives living nearby, and they were in regular contact with friends and relatives in the neighborhood.

With the possible exception of elderly parents, Black families rely more heavily on extended kin than White families. The range of the kin network is extensive and includes parents, siblings, cousins, aunts, uncles, etc. A unique feature is the inclusion of nonblood relatives who are referred to and regarded as kinsmen: Among lower-class Black males, for instance, males who are unrelated to one another "go for" brothers and interact on that fraternal basis. Usually, this is a special friendship in which the normal claims, obligations, and loyalties of the kin relationship are operative.[52] These parakinship ties seem to be a facilitating and validating agent of Black life in the United States.

Within the Black nuclear family, there is a fluid interchanging of roles. This role flexibility is assumed to have emerged out of the economic imperatives of Black life. Although family theorists have stated that men carry out instrumental (i.e., economic support) functions in the family and women are assigned expressive (i.e., domestic and emotional) functions, Billingsley (1968)[53] noted that these tasks were interchanged by Black husbands and wives. It was not at all uncommon for Black males to engage in expressive functions in regard to the maintenance of family solidarity and to assist in child rearing and household tasks.[54] The instrumental role of many Black women is well known. A large number of working Black wives help to keep many Black families in the middle-class category, or at least out of poverty. Even Black youth participate in family affairs by caring for younger siblings and occasionally working to supplement the family income.[55]

One finds no special status or authority associated with roles in the Black family. Contrary to theories about the Black matriarchy and the dominance of women, most research supports the fact that an equalitarian pattern typifies most Black families.[56] In a succinct summary of authority patterns in the Black family, Hill (1972) states: "The husbands in most Black families are actively involved in decision making and the performance of household tasks that are expected of them. And, most wives, while strong, are not dominant matriarchs, but share with their husbands the making of family decisions—even in the low-income Black families."[57]

The myth of the Black matriarchy has been reinforced by the failure of many students of Black family life to distinguish between the terms *dominant* and *strong*. While the Black woman has needed to be strong in order for the Black family to survive, she has not necessarily been dominant.[58] In fact, she has not had the resources to impose her authority on many Black males in the society. The husband in most Black families is the primary breadwinner. Even in lower-class Black families, the wife's income is only a small part of the total family income. In 85 percent of low-income Black families, the husband's income is higher than the wife's.[59]

Social Class and Style of Life

When it comes to describing social classes and lifestyles among the Black population, the task is made difficult for a number of reasons. Among them is the fact that social class is an analytical concept that is neither (1) universally accepted in the social sciences, (2) conceived in precisely the same way by all students of social stratification, nor (3) commonly designated by the same label.[60] This difficulty is magnified when attempting to delineate the Black class structure. Among the difficulties encountered is the massive amount of mobility in the Black middle-class structure, with a fairly large number of upwardly mobile Blacks. Another is the number of middle-class Blacks who want to preserve their cultural traditions and thus adopt values and lifestyles which are commonly associated with the lower class.[61]

If income and educational levels are used, approximately 30 percent of Black families would be in the middle-class category. The rest would fall in some level of the lower-class stratum, with only a negligible number in the upper-class group. In 1970, about 28 percent of Black families had an income over $10,000. About 38 percent of Black families in the North and West had incomes greater than $10,000.

Over 50 percent of Blacks, 25 to 29 years old, had completed high school in 1971. About 20 percent of young Blacks are presently enrolled in college. Most of these Black members of the middle class will have a very recent origin from the lower-class group.[62]

However, the concept of social class refers to more than a person's educational and income levels. It is measured just as well by cultural values and behavioral patterns, i.e., a class lifestyle. Bernard (1966)[63] divides Black families into two strands: the "acculturated" and "externally adapted." The former term describes those Blacks who have internalized Western norms and the latter, those Blacks who have adapted to these norms superficially. It is this writer's belief that most middle-class Blacks belong in the externally adapted group. Instead of internalizing White values, most new members of the Black middle class have adopted certain middle-class practices as a strategy for obtaining a decent life.

The paucity of research on middle-class Black families does not provide much data for this assumption,[64] but if one examines the dynamics of middle-class Black behavior, a certain pattern emerges. For example, the sexual behavior of upwardly mobile Black females is more conservative because a premarital pregnancy can mean dropping out of school and ruining one's chances of gaining entrance into the middle class.[65] When the middle-class Black female becomes pregnant before marriage, she is more likely to get an abortion than her lower-class counterpart.[66] Middle-class Black families have a significantly lower family size than low-income Black families, not because they place less value on children, but because they perceive a very direct link between low income and large families. These class differences in marital and familial behavior among Blacks reflect pragmatic choices, not different values.

The best example of middle-class Blacks' refusal to internalize Western values can be seen in their consumption patterns. Frazier (1962)[67] described their lack of regard for the Protestant ethic, which emphasizes the measure of human value by thrift, wealth, accumulation of capital, etc. In fact, Frazier's main thesis was that they had not internalized "genuine" middle-class values. The fallacy in his thesis was that he failed to relate this trait to the African heritage and philosophy. African people are not a money-oriented group. Money qua money is not important. Once the basic necessities are supplied, wealth is to be consumed, not saved. The crucial standard of the individual is not his wealth, but feeling for his fellow man.[68] One notes that Black conspicuous consumption is usually oriented toward the group's approval. In recent years, the imitation of White values has declined in favor of a more Black lifestyle, and social events are geared to obtain money to support Black causes.

Within the lower-class group there are a variety of Black families. One finds a strong belief in hard work and the value of education. A recent study revealed that poor Black youth who have grown up in welfare families have a more positive attitude toward the desirability and necessity of work than the children of the White middle class.[69] In another study, a slightly larger number of Black workers expressed a desire to take a job as a car washer rather than go on welfare, even if the pay for the two sources of income was the same.[70] A number of studies have documented the strong desire of lower-income Black families to have their children attain a higher educational level than they have.[71] One result of this parental support is that 75 percent of Blacks enrolled in college are from families in which the head had no college education.[72]

THE FAMILY LIFE CYCLE

Courtship and Marriage

Studies on Black dating and sexual patterns are few and unreliable.[73] As with the research on other areas of Black family life, the focus has been on problems allegedly resulting from the different dating styles of Afro-Americans. Thus, one rarely finds a study of Black sexuality that does not associate that aspect of Black behavior with the problems of illegitimacy, female-headed households, and welfare dependency. The sexual relationship of Blacks is rarely, if ever, investigated as an element of the normal functioning of Black families. The intricate meaning and emotional dynamics of the Black sexual relationship are seldom captured in most Black family studies.[74]

Heterosexual relationships develop at an early age in the communal setting of Black social relationships, and children participate in the high life activities of adults.[75] This is a time of feasting, drinking, and dancing. Even very young children are often matched with members of the opposite sex at this time. Males and females learn to interact with one another on the romantic level usually associated with the postadolescent stage for Whites. Hence, one study of Black students aged ten to seventeen found that half or more of the males and females at all ages claimed to have a boy/girl friend, to have participated in kissing games, and to have been in love.[76]

Within the same sex peer group, Black males and females are socialized into their future pattern of sex-role interaction. Males learn the technique of rapping, a linguistic pattern designed to convince the female that he is worthy of her interest and further used as a verbal prelude to more intimate activity. The female acquires the ability to discriminate between men who are with it and learns how to unmask a weak rap. When the male petitions her for sex, she may accept if interested or if she has other motivations. Whether she agrees to participate in premarital sexual activity will not be founded on the morality of such behavior, but on the practical consequences (pregnancy) which may ensue.[77]

This lack of moral emphasis on sexual behavior will be in opposition to the teachings of her parents. Most Black parents (usually the mother) urge their daughters to remain chaste until an adult—not until marriage. They are rarely told that premarital coitus is sinful, but that sex relations before marriage can result in pregnancy. The Black female's reference group, however, is her peers, and they are more supportive of the philosophy that losing one's virginity is a declaration of maturity, of womanhood. Those who refuse to indulge are often subordinating peer group approval to their desire for upward mobility (that is, premarital pregnancy can mean dropping out of school and forgoing further education). Yet, they do not condemn others who decide to participate in premarital sex, even when their decision is to refrain.[78]

Perforce, much dating behavior among Blacks is ipso facto sexual behavior.[79] In fact, among most Black youth, there is no such thing as the dating pattern found among the White middle class. Young people meet in their neighborhoods and schools and soon begin to go out with one another. Sexual involvement may begin shortly afterward.[80] In their recent investigation of Black females aged fifteen to nineteen, Zelnik and Kantner (1972)[81] reported that, by the age of nineteen, over 80 percent of their Black subjects had engaged in premarital intercourse. However, while the proportion of comparable White nonvirgins was lower, it was that group which had sex more frequently and with more sexual partners.

While Black women have an intrinsic appreciation for the sexual relationship, it is laden with an emotional meaning for them. Once sex has taken place, the intensity of the emotional relationship begins. As her association with her sexual partner becomes routinized, the emotional aspect is increased, and the male is ultimately expected to limit his close relationships with other women.[82] In the Zelnik and Kantner (1972) study,[83] over 60 percent of their subjects said their relations had been confined to a single partner. Half of the nonvirgins said they intended to marry the male. The Reiss (1964)[84] comparison of Black and White premarital sexual standards revealed that, although relatively permissive, Blacks are not generally promiscuous—they tend to require affectionate relations as a basis for sexual behavior.

Most Black women desire a stable, enduring relationship—ultimately marriage. This feeling is not always reciprocated by Black males.[85] Many Black men apparently evade the institution altogether; a fairly large proportion of them (13.8) never marry at all.[86] Traditionally, males have been less oriented toward marriage and the domestic responsibilities it entails. In the case of the Black male, his reluctance to marry is reinforced by the unhappy marriages around him and the abundance of women available for companionship in his environment. For the Black female desirous of marriage, these facts of Black life all work to her disadvantage.

When it comes to finding a compatible mate, she faces a number of obstacles. One of the biggest hurdles is the excess number of Black women vis-à-vis Black men. In the age group over fourteen, there are approximately a million more Black females than males listed by the United States Census.[87] Although the actual number of Black males is higher due to their underenumeration in the census, the number of Black men available to Black women for marriage is really fewer than the census figures would indicate. This low number of eligible Black males is due to their higher rate of mortality, incarceration, homosexuality, and intermarriage.[88] Once all these factors are considered, there may be as many as two million Black females without a male counterpart. This fact is particularly important when the reasons are sought for the large number of female-headed households in the Black community. There is simply no way of establishing a monogamous, two-parent household for many Black women within a racially endogamous marriage.

Still, most Black women maintain an ideal concept of the man they would like to marry. This idealistic standard of mate selection, however, must often be subordinated to the realities they encounter. In the lower-class group, a woman frequently will settle for a man who will work when he is able to find employment, avoid excessive gambling, drinking, and extramarital affairs, provide for the children, and treat her with respect. Even these simple desires cannot be met by many lower-class Black husbands who are unable to find work and retreat into psychologically destructive behavior such as alcoholism, physical abuse of their wife, etc.[89]

The middle-class Black woman has a slightly better chance of fulfilling her desires for a compatible mate. She is likely to require economic stability, emotional and sexual satisfaction, and male participation in child rearing. One aspect of White marriages is conspicuously missing—Black women do not expect their husbands to support them in the style of the pampered wife who remains at home. Both Black men and women are in agreement that she will work after marriage. And, it has been found that the wife's employment does not pose a threat to the Black male's self-image. Black males are more likely to believe that the wife has a right to a career of her own than White males. The dual employment of both spouses is often necessary to approach the living standards of White couples with only the husband working. It also reflects the partnership of Black men and women that has existed for centuries as part of their African heritage.[90]

Even in the middle class, however, marriage has proven to be a fragile institution for Blacks. While marriages are dissolving in record numbers for all racial groups, it has been particularly high for Blacks. In the last decade, the annual divorce rate has risen 75 percent. For White women between the ages of twenty-seven to thirty-two, the probability of their marriages ending in divorce is one in three. For comparable Black women, the chances are one in two. In 1971, 20 percent of married Black women were separated or divorced, compared with 6 percent of similar White women.[91]

The problems of being Black in a racist society have their ramifications in the marriage arena. It seems quite evident that whatever difficulties lower-class Black spouses have in their interpersonal relations are compounded by both the problems of poverty and racism. The middle-class Black marriage is threatened less by poverty than by the shortage of Black males, particularly in terms of educational background. There are approximately 85 college-educated Black males available for marriage to every 100 Black female college graduates. Many Black college women—especially those at Black institutions—remain single.[92] Others may marry men with less education, and this type of hypogamous marriage has a greater statistical probability of ending in divorce.[93] One result of the male shortage in the Black middle class has been the tendency of women seeking educated, high-status Black professional men to pursue men who are married as fair game. This type of female competition becomes a direct assault on a man's marriage and increases the risk of divorce.[94] Such demographic pressures do not pose as great a threat to White marriages.

Another factor contributing to the shortage of educated Black males is the tendency of males in the middle class to date and marry White women, while White males are less involved with Black women.[95] In the most recent period, there has been a discernible increase in interracial dating and marriage. Public opinion polls support the notion that there is a growing tolerance of interracial marriage by both Blacks and Whites.[96] The common belief is that most interracial marriages involve a Black male and White female, and some studies document this in an examination of marriage records.[97] However, until 1970 there were reported 51,000 known interracial marriages, and they were about evenly divided between Black men and Black women as the non-White spouse. One reason for the belief that most interracial marriages involve Black men and White women is that they are more visible. The marriages of Black women to White husbands may go unnoticed because they are more likely to take place in rural settings, suburbs, and outside the country. In 1970 the intermarriage rate of Black males to White females was double the rate of Black females.[98]

The growing trend toward interracial marriages has occurred in the midst of a large movement of Black youth toward Black nationalism and separatism. A good part of this paradox can be explained by the entrance of many Blacks into previously all-White settings such as the predominantly White university, where they meet and associate with Whites as equals. Much larger numbers of Blacks and Whites date but do not marry. Most Blacks have other Blacks as their first preference for dating and marriage.[99] It is estimated that fewer than 5 percent of the Black population are interracially married. Although there are studies showing interracial marriages to be more stable than intraracial unions,[100] one sees indications that the external pressures against such marriages, along with the difficulties of marriage in general, pose a threat to the continued stability of many such unions.

Whereas certain problems exist in Black marriages, high separation and divorce rates are not necessarily a valid measure of the stability and functionality of Black families. What is important is whether they meet their functional obligations. There are many female-headed households, for instance, that socialize their children into successful adult roles. The biggest problem they face is the economic and employment discrimination against women, which hinders their ability to sustain a decent life for them and their children.[101] In this endeavor, they frequently have the support of a Black male who may not be the legal husband/father. Schulz (1969)[102] has reported that the lower-class Black male contributes to the welfare of his woman more than is commonly acknowledged and plays an important role as a substitute father to her children.

Childhood and Child Rearing

One of the most popular images of Black women is that of "Mammy," the devoted, affectionate nursemaids of White children. This motherly image of Black women probably has some basis in fact. Motherhood has historically been an important role for Black women, even more meaningful than their role as wives.[103] In the colonial period of Africa, missionaries often observed and reported the unusual devotion of the African mother to her child. The slave mother also developed a deep love for, and impenetrable bond to, her children.[104] It would appear that the bond between the Black mother and her child is deeply rooted in the African heritage and philosophy that place a special value on children because they represent the continuity of life.[105]

Many studies have conveyed a negative image of the Black mother because she does not conform to middle-class modes of child rearing.

Yet, Black mothers have fulfilled the function of socializing their children into the multiple roles they must perform in this society. They prepare them to take on not only the appropriate sex and age roles, but a racial role as well. Children must be socialized to deal with the daily realities of White racism. Black females are encouraged to be independent rather than passive individuals because many of them will carry family and economic responsibilities along.[106] Taking on adult responsibilities is something many Black children learn early. They may be given the care of a younger sibling, and some will have to find work while still in the adolescent stage. The strong character structure of Black children was noted by child psychiatrist Robert Coles (1964)[107] as he observed their comportment under the pressures of school integration in the South during a very volatile era.

The Black mother's child rearing techniques are geared to prepare her children for a kind of existence that is alien to middle-class White youngsters. Moreover, many White middle-class socialization patterns may not be that desirable for the psychological growth of the child. The casual upbringing of Black children may produce a much healthier personality than the status anxieties associated with some rigid middle-class child-rearing practices.[108] Using threats of the withdrawal of love if the child fails to measure up to the parent's standards is much more common among White parents than Black parents of any class stratum. One result of the Black child's anxiety-free upbringing is a strong closeness to his parents.[109]

While Black parents are more likely to use physical, rather than verbal, punishment to enforce discipline than White parents, this technique is often buttressed by the love they express for their children. Moreover, as Billingsley (1969)[110] has noted: "Even among the lowest social classes in the Black community, families give the children better care than is generally recognized, and often the care is better than that given by white families in similar social circumstances." One indication of this care is found in the statistics which show that child neglect and abuse are much more common in White families than in Black families. Black children, for instance, are underrepresented in institutions for dependent and neglected children.[111]

The most undesirable aspect of the Black child's socialization is reputed to be the inculcation of a negative self-identity.[112] A plethora of studies have found that the Black child has a low self-esteem because of his Blackness and the fact that many children grow up in homes without a male model. A number of studies are emerging which are in opposition to the theories of low self-esteem among Blacks. McCarthy and Yancey (1971)[113] reviewed the literature on Black self-esteem, found much of it invalid, and concluded that Blacks are less likely to suffer from low self-esteem because they belong to a solidary group with an ideology that explains their lowly position.

In a replication of some of the earlier studies on Black children's drawings, a pair of researchers reported that the current emphasis on Black culture had led to a significant change in the characteristics of those drawings. When Black children were asked to draw features that they most admired and wished were characteristic of themselves, most of their figures resembled other Black people.[114] In another investigation it was discovered that even Black children from a separated or never-married family did not have a lower self-esteem than Black children from other families, and Black children as a group did not have lower self-esteem than White children as a group.[115]

One factor behind the high self-esteem of the Black child is the relationship with his parents, who are not nearly as alienated from their children as many White parents appear to be. When Scanzoni (1971)[116] attempted to measure who the Black child identified with, both males and females identified with their parents and wanted to be like them. Although there was more of a positive identification with the mother, especially by the females, the father was the male figure most admired by the children of both sexes. Outside of the family, children of both sexes were inclined to select a male as the person they most respected.

The Aged

Extensive data on the Black elderly are not available. Based on what we presently know, the older Black person is not as likely to live with one of his children as are the White aged. In most cases, the grandmothers are more likely to take children into their own households than to be taken into the household of their kinfolk. About half (48 percent) of elderly Black women have other related children living with them—in contrast to only 10 percent of similar White families.[117] This is but one more indication of the strong cohesiveness and prevalent concern for one another within Black families.

Because they live longer than Black men, widowhood comes at an earlier age for Black women. In 1970, over two-thirds of aged Black women were widows in comparison to 54 percent of similar White women. They were also more likely to be widowed than were Black males (32 percent) or white males (17 percent).[118] Due to a history of gross discrimination against it, the Black aged family has a median income of only $3,222. Of those elderly Blacks living alone, about 75 percent had incomes of less than $2,000 in 1969. One result of this overwhelming poverty is that 26 percent of the elderly wives in Black families continue to work after reaching the age of 65. Only 15 percent of elderly White wives remain in the labor force past that age.[119]

The extended kin structure in the Black community manages to buttress the psychological isolation and poverty of the Black aged. Most of them have a significant amount of interaction with their children, especially an older daughter. Where there is no child present or in the vicinity, they can rely on secondary kin, such as siblings, cousins, and even "make-believe" kin.[120] In return, many Black grandmothers provide in-kind services, such as babysitting. Most aged Black parents desire to live independently of, but in close contact with, their children. Where their socioeconomic conditions permit, the adult children assist their elderly parents.[121]

CHANGE AND ADAPTATION

One of the most fluid institutions in American life is the family. Probably in no other sphere of our society have such rapid and profound changes taken place. While the changes are most significant for White Americans, Blacks, too, are influenced to some degree by the same forces. Among the most visible trends are the increase in sexual permissiveness, challenges to the traditional concept of a woman's role, more divorces, and reductions in the birth rate. Although Blacks are part and parcel of these dynamics, their different history and needs preclude any close convergence of their family lifestyle with that of White families.

There is considerable disagreement over whether a revolution in sexual behavior has occurred. Some argue that only the public acknowledgement of sexual behavior has changed, thus giving the appearance of *actual* changes in what people are doing sexually. Yet, it is impossible to refute the fact that the openness of sexual permissiveness reflects a revolution in attitudes. The most significant change is in the sexual liberation of White women. There are many indications that the double standard of sexual conduct is disappearing or being modified. This change in male attitudes about female sexuality has little effect on Black female sexuality, since Black women have rarely been subjected to the same sexual restrictions as White women.

Previously, the sexual liberation of Black women had been the source of White American stereotypes of Afro-Americans as morally loose. In reality, Black women escaped the fate of many White women who were condemned to premarital chastity and marital frigidity. The healthy attitudes Blacks have toward sex have aided them in avoiding some of the "deviant" sexual actions more common to Whites. One finds a much less incidence of mate swapping, homosexuality, transvestism, pornography, and incest in the Black population.[122] However, Blacks have shared in the general sexual freedom of Whites, especially the Black middle class. There is more of an acceptance of sexual cohabitation, different forms of sexual expression, out-of-wedlock births, etc., among the Black middle class today.

Much of the sexual revolution is caused by challenges to the traditional concept of a woman's role in society. White women are demanding equality in employment opportunities, legal rights, shared responsibility for raising children, and to be freed of the liabilities only women face in the United States. Few Black women are involved in the women's liberation movement because many of its demands seem irrelevant to their needs. They, particularly, cannot relate to White women who want to enter the labor force, cease being viewed as sex objects, or be freed from child care responsibilities. They also cannot relate to the view of marriage as an oppressive institution.

The demands of White women are not relevant to the reality of Black women. They have always been in the labor force, whether they wanted to or not. Black women have not been depicted as sex objects as much as they have been *used* as sex objects. Motherhood and marriage were two institutions denied them in the past. Because they had to work, many were deprived of time to enjoy their children. Marriage was a luxury many could not afford or the conditions of their lives would not provide. To the many Black women who are heading households, a husband would be a welcome figure.

However, many of the methods and goals of the women's liberation movement are of importance to Black women. Now that women are declaring their independence from the domination of men, there will be a greater acceptance of women heading families by themselves. Perhaps the society will then make provisions for eliminating some of the problems incurred by female-headed households, e.g., child care facilities. The demand for equal employment opportunities and an income parity for women in the same jobs as men is very important to Black women. It is Black women who are the most victimized by employment and income discrimination against females. They, who are most likely to be heads of households, will earn the low salaries paid women on the assumption that they do not have families to support.

The shortage of Black males available for marriage may force Black women to rethink the idea of a monogamous marriage that will last forever. There are simply not enough Black males around to permit fulfillment of this desire. Perhaps some convergence of White and Black marital patterns is possible. White women, too, face a shortage of five million males due to the higher infant mortality rate for White males. It appears that many White females have abandoned heterosexual relationships for the gay world. Black women, in the main, remain more committed to an exclusive male-female dyad. However, the continued failure of marriage to meet their emotional needs could bring about their willingness to consider more radical lifestyles than heretofore.

There is some indication of a homogenization of Black family lifestyles. This mass family pattern will not be based on the White middle-class nuclear family model. Rather, the increasing nativist sentiments among Black youth may culminate in a family system based on a combination of African and Afro-American cultural systems, which will transcend the class and regional variations that now exist. While White Americans are questioning whether the family as an institution can survive, Blacks may decide that it must become stronger and more relevant to their lives. As the Black youth of America, the group most imbued with the spirit of Black nationalism, becomes the majority of the Black population, the process of Africanizing the Black family may be accelerated. Whether this occurs or not will depend on whether the forces of racial integration and movement into the middle-class stratum lead Blacks in the direction of assimilation and acculturation or into the congealation of an Afro-American identity.

Internal Adaptations

The changes in the interior of the Black family, while ideologically in the direction of Pan-Africanism, are statistically in the direction of assimilation and acculturation. Examples of this phenomenon are seen in the diffusion of Blacks into predominantly White suburbs, the increase in interracial dating and marriage, higher incidences of suicide and mental illness, and a decline in the extended family pattern. However, these patterns reflect the variation in the Black community. What is surprising is that, given the pace of racial integration in American society, more Blacks have not become assimilated into the majority population's mode of behavior. The integration of the school systems, desegregation of suburbia, and greater access to knowledge of majority cultural norms through the mass media have provided, without precedent, opportunities for Black acculturation.

Instead, we find Blacks demanding separate facilities and organizations on White university campuses. Those Blacks who moved to the suburbs continue their social lives in the inner cities. While the extended family may not exist together in the same household, its functions of providing emotional solidarity and other kinds of assistance are still carried out. Moreover, the concept of the extended family is broadened to include all members of the Black community. These are among some of the internal adaptations made by the Black community to prevent the trend of racial integration from diluting its cultural unity.

In contrast to the demands of White women for emancipation from the passive role ascribed to the female gender, Black women are thinking of adopting the subordinate position of African women. Their contention is that the roles of men and women are different, not unequal. In some of the Black nationalist organizations, the women are placed in auxiliary groups, while the men take leadership roles. Much of this behavior is a reaction to the history of Black life in this country when Black women had the leadership of the family thrust upon them. Black men were not allowed to fulfill the ascribed male role functions. Hence, in some circles, it is now believed that Black women should step back and let Black men emerge as the leader of the family and the race.

Another most important adaptation under consideration is the adoption of polygyny as the Black marriage system. The assumption here is that there are not enough Black males to go around and that the sharing of husbands could stabilize Black marriages and provide certain legal benefits to women now deprived of them. At least two Black nationalist organizations are on record as advocating polygyny for the Black population. However, the number of Black polygynous marriages is infinitesimal since such marriages are illegal in this country, and thus no legal benefits can accrue to the second wife. Moreover, in African society, the practice of polygamy is closely related to the economic system, and people are socialized to accept it.

Problems and Prospects

The problems Black people face are essentially the same as for the past century. Those problems are not related to family stability, but the socioeconomic conditions that disrupt families. In general, the problems are poverty and racism. While the last decade has produced a decline in racial segregation and White stereotypes of Black inferiority, Blacks are still singled out for discriminatory treatment in every sphere of American life. Moreover, while Whites are in agreement about the racial discrimination Blacks are subjected to, any national effort to further remedy these racist practices has a low priority among White Americans.

A low socioeconomic status continues to plague many Black families. Whereas some Blacks have achieved a higher standard of living as a result of the civil rights movement, large numbers continue to live below the poverty level. A disproportionate number of these Blacks will be female heads of families. They will have more responsibilities and less income than any other group in American society. Yet, no effective programs are being proposed to meet the needs of a third of all Black families. The Family Assistance Program proposed will be most useful in enforcing mandatory work requirements for women who cannot find employment now, but even if they could find jobs, the child care facilities in the Black community are few and inadequate. Also, the persistence of employment and salary discrimination against women in general will continue to handicap Black women in their struggle to maintain a decent life for their families.

However, poverty is not the only reason for the high breakup rate of Black marriages. The increase in the Black divorce rate in recent years is due to sociopsychological factors as well. A primary cause is the independence of Black women. Marital stability among Whites in the past was based on the subordinate status of women. Once White women were emancipated from the economic domination of men, their divorce rate increased radically. Black women have been independent—economically and psychologically—for a much longer period to time. While there is nothing inherently wrong with the equality of sex roles in the family, when men are socialized to expect unchallenged leadership in family affairs, conflict is an incvitable result.

The increased rate of interracial marriages will continue because more Blacks and Whites will meet as peers. Some Black men will marry White women because the society's standards of beauty are still White. More Black women will marry White men because they can provide them with a greater amount of economic security and because they have become disenchanted with Black men. Whatever the reason, these marriages will face many obstacles. In an era of unabated White racism and Black nationalism, many interracial couples will become outcasts in both Black and White communities. The internal problems of marital conflict will be compounded by external pressures as well.

It is difficult to project the future of Black families because there are several parallel trends occurring at the same time. Many Blacks are entering the middle class as a result of higher education and increased opportunities. At the same time the future is dim for those Blacks in the underclass. The forces of automation and cybernation are rendering obsolete the labor of unskilled Black men who are in danger of becoming a permanent army of the unemployed. The status of Black women is in a state of flux. Some welcome the liberation forthcoming from male control, while others urge a regeneration of Black male leadership. Easier and cheaper access to contraceptives and abortions may mean a considerable decline in the Black birth rate. Simultaneously, many Blacks express concern with the implications of genocide in Black family limitation. Whatever the future of Black families, it is time to put to rest all the theories about Black family instability and give recognition to the crucial role of this institution in the Black struggle for survival.

NOTES

1 Andrew Billingsley, *Black Families in White America,* Prentice-Hall, Englewood Cliffs, N.J., 1968, pp. 37–38.
2 Andrew Billingsley, "Black Families and White Social Science," *Journal of Social Issues,* vol. 26, 127–142, November 1970.
3 A. R. Radcliffe-Brown and Darryl Forde, *African Systems of Kinship and Marriage,* Oxford, New York, 1967, pp. 1–13.
4 John Hope Franklin, *From Slavery to Freedom,* Knopf, New York, 1967, pp. 28–31.
5 E. Franklin Frazier, *The Negro Family in the United States,* University of Chicago, Chicago, 1939, p. 7.
6 Sheila Hobson, "The Black Family: Together in Every Sense," *Tuesday,* pp. 12-14, 28–32, April 1971.
7 Franklin, op. cit., pp. 48–49.
8 Frazier, The Negro Family. . . , pp. 17–18.
9 Kenneth Stampp, *The Peculiar Institution,* Vintage, New York, 1956, pp. 198–199.
10 John Blassingame, *The Slave Community,* Oxford, New York, 1972, pp. 86–87.
11 Ibid, pp. 77–103.
12 Wade Nobles, "African Root and American Fruit: The Black Family," *J. Social and Behavioral Sciences,* vol. 20, pp. 52–64, Spring 1974.
13 Robert H. Absug, "The Black Family During Reconstruction," in Nathan Huggins et al. (eds.), *Key Issues in the Afro-American Experience,* Harcourt Brace Jovanovich, New York, 1971, pp. 26–39.
14 Blassingame, op. cit., pp. 92–93.
15 Absug, op. cit., p. 29.
16 Blassingame, op. cit., p. 99.
17 Frazier, *The Negro Family. . . ,* p. 15.
18 Basil Matthews, "Black Perspective, Black Family, and Black Community," a paper delivered to the Annual Philosophy Conference, Baltimore, April 1972.
19 Cf. Bibb quoted in Blassingame, op. cit., p. 87.
20 Frank Tannenbaum, *Slave and Citizen,* Knopf, New York, 1947, p. 65.
21 Sidney Mintz, "Slavery and the Afro-American World," in John Szwed (ed.), *Black America,* Basic, New York, 1970, p. 37.
22 Gwendolyn Midlo Hall, "The Myth of Benevolent Spanish Slave Law," *Negro Digest,* pp. 31–38, February 1970.
23 Frazier, op. cit., pp. 142–163.

24 Absug, op. cit., pp. 32–33.
25 Herbert Gutman, cited in *Black Lines*, vol. 2, p. 16, Winter 1972.
26 Jessie Bernard, *Marriage and Family Among Negroes*, Prentice-Hall, Englewood Cliffs, N.J., 1966, p. 3.
27 Absug, op. cit., p. 34.
28 Elizabeth Miller, *The Negro in America: A Bibliography*, Harvard, Cambridge, Mass., 1966, pp. vii–vii.
29 Absug, op. cit., p. 39.
30 Rayford Logan, *The Betrayal of the Negro*, Collier, New York, 1965, p. 162.
31 Nobles, op. cit., p. 59.
32 Charles H. Anderson, *Towards a New Sociology*, Dorsey, Homewood, Ill., 1971, pp. 275–277.
33 William Yancey, "Going Down Home: Family Structure and the Urban Trap," *Social Science Quarterly*, vol. 52, pp. 893–906, March 1972.
34 Melville Herskovits, *The Myth of the Negro Past*, Beacon, Boston, 1958.
35 U.S. Bureau of the Census, *Current Population Reports: The Social and Economic Status of the Black Population in the United States, 1971*, ser. P-23, no. 42, 1972, p. 104.
36 Clyde Kiser and Myrna Frank, "Factors Associated with the Low Fertility of Non-White Women of College Attainment," *Milbank Memorial Fund Quarterly*, vol. 45, Little, Brown, Boston, pp. 427–449, October 1967; Leslie Aldridge Westoff and Charles Westoff, *From Now to Zero*, 1971, pp. 234–277.
37 U.S. Population Council, *Report on Abortions by Age and Race*, U.S. Population Council, Washington, 1972.
38 William Ryan, "Savage Discovery: The Moynihan Report," in Robert Staples (ed.), *The Black Family: Essays and Studies*, Wadsworth, Belmont, Calif., 1971, pp. 58–65.
39 Robert Hill, *The Strengths of Black Families*, Emerson-Hall, New York, 1972, pp. 13–14.
40 U.S. Bureau of the Census, *The Social and Economic Status . . .*, p. 101.
41 Billingsley, *Black Families in White America*, pp. 16–21.
42 U.S. Bureau of the Census, *Current Population Reports: School Enrollment, October, 1970: Population Characteristics*, ser. no. 222, 1970, p. 20.
43 Bert N. Adams, "Isolation, Function, and Beyond: American Kinship in the 1960's," *J. Marriage and the Family*, vol. 32, pp. 575–598, November 1970.

44 Joe R. Feagin, "The Kinship Ties of Negro Urbanites," *Social Science Quarterly,* vol. 49, pp. 660–665, December 1968; Jerome Stromberg, "Kinship and Friendship Among Lower-Class Negro Families," a paper presented at the Annual Meeting of the Society for the Study of Special Problems, San Francisco, June 1967.
45 Matthews, op. cit.
46 Nobles, op. cit.
47 Matthews, op. cit.
48 Nobles, op. cit., p. 61.
49 Feagin, op. cit.; William Hays and Charles Mindel, "Extended Kinship Relations in Black and White Families," *J. Marriage and the Family,* vol. 35, pp. 51–57, February 1973; Lawrence Podell, *Families on Welfare in New York City,* Center for the Study of Urban Problems, New York, n.d., pp. 38–39; Stromberg, op. cit.
50 Hays and Mindel, op. cit., p. 53.
51 Podell, op. cit.
52 Elliott Liebow, *Tally's Corner,* Little, Brown, Boston, 1966, pp. 161–207.
53 Billingsley, *Black Families in White America,* pp. 25–26.
54 Robert Stone, *Welfare and Working Families: Low Income Family Life Styles,* Lexington, Lexington, Mass., 1971.
55 Hill, *The Strengths of Black Families,* pp. 11–15.
56 Herbert Hyman and John S. Reed, "Black Matriarchy Reconsidered: Evidence from Secondary Analysis of Sample Surveys," *Public Opinion Quarterly,* vol. 33, pp. 346–354; Delores Mack, "Where the Black Matriarchy Theorists Went Wrong," *Psychology Today,* vol. 4, p. 24, January 1971; Russell Middleton and Snell Putney, "Dominance in Decisions in the Family: Race and Class Differences," *American Journal of Sociology,* vol. 29, pp. 605–609, May 1960.
57 Hill, *The Strengths of Black Families,* p. 20.
58 Joyce Ladner, *Tomorrow's Tomorrow: The Black Woman,* Doubleday, Garden City, N.Y., 1971, pp. 35–36.
59 Hill, *The Strengths of Black Families,* p. 13.
60 Harold Hodges, *Social Stratification,* Schenkman, Cambridge, Mass., 1964, pp. 12–13.
61 Sidney J. Kronus, *The Black Middle Class,* Merrill, Columbus, Ohio, 1971, pp. 19–39.
62 U.S. Bureau of the Census, *The Social and Economic Status . . . ,* pp. 31–33.
63 Bernard, op. cit., pp. 32–34.
64 Kronus, op. cit., pp. 13–17.

65 Ladner, *Tomorrow's Tomorrow . . .*, p. 202; Robert Staples, "The
    Sexuality of Black Women," *Sexual Behavior*, vol. 2, pp. 4–15,
    June 1972.
66 Paul Gebhard et al., *Pregnancy, Birth, and Abortion*, Harper, New
    York, 1958, p. 164.
67 E. Franklin Frazier, *Black Bourgeousie*, Collier, New York, 1962,
    pp. 146–149.
68 Matthews, op. cit., Albert Murray, *The Omni-Americans*, Outer-
    bridge and Diensterey, New York, 1970, pp. 94–96.
69 Leonard Goodwin, *Do the Poor Want to Work: A Socio-Psycho-
    logical Study of Work Orientations*, Brookings, Washington, 1972,
    pp. 53–69.
70 Curt Tausky and William J. Wilson, "Work Attachment Among
    Black Men," *Phylon*, vol. 32, pp. 23–30, Spring 1971.
71 Arthur Cosby, "Black-White Differences in Aspirations Among Deep
    South High School Students," *J. Negro Education*, vol. 40, pp. 17–
    21, Winter 1971; Edward E. Harris, "Personal and Parental In-
    fluences in College Attendance: Some Negro and White Differ-
    ences," *J. Negro Education*, vol. 39, pp. 305–313, Fall 1970;
    Michael Hindelang, "Educational and Occupational Aspirations
    Among Working Class Negro, Mexican-American and White Ele-
    mentary School Children," *J. Negro Education*, vol. 39, pp. 351–
    353, Fall 1970.
72 U.S. Bureau of the Census, *School Enrollment*, cited in Hill, op.
    cit. p. 53.
73 Robert Staples, "Towards a Sociology of the Black Family," *J.
    Marriage and the Family*, vol. 33, pp. 19–38, February 1971.
74 Clarence Rollo Turner, "Some Theoretical and Conceptual Con-
    siderations for Black Family Studies," *Black Lines*, vol. 2, pp. 13–
    28, Winter 1972.
75 Lee Rainwater, "The Crucible of Identity: The Lower-Class Negro
    Family," *Daedalus*, vol. 95, pp. 258–264, Winter 1966.
76 Carlfred Broderick, "Social Heterosexual Development Among
    Urban Negroes and Whites," *J. Marriage and the Family*, vol. 27,
    pp. 200–203, May 1966.
77 Ladner, *Tomorrow's Tomorrow . . .*, loc. cit.
78 Ibid.
79 Staples, "The Sexuality of Black Women," p. 4.
80 Bernard Rosenberg and Joseph Bensman, "Sexual Patterns in
    Three Ethnic Subcultures of an American Underclass," *Annals of
    the American Academy of Political and Social Science*, pp. 61–
    75, March 1968.

81 Melvin Zelnik and John Kantner, "Sexuality, Contraception, and Pregnancy Among Young Unwed Females in the United States," a paper prepared for the Commission on Population Growth and the American Future, May 1972.

82 Ladner, op. cit., pp. 203–204.

83 Zelnik and Kantner, op. cit.

84 Ira L. Reiss, "Premarital Sexual Permissiveness Among Negroes and Whites," *American Sociological Review,* vol. 29, pp. 688–698, October 1964.

85 Broderick, op. cit., p. 202.

86 U.S. Bureau of the Census, *Current Population Reports: Marital Status and Family Status,* no. 198, 1969, p. 20.

87 U.S. Bureau of the Census, *The Social and Economic Status . . . ,* p. 24.

88 Robert Staples, "The Myth of the Black Matriarchy," *The Black Scholar,* vol. 1, pp. 9–16, January–February 1970; Jacquelyn Jackson, "But Where Are the Men?" *The Black Scholar,* vol. 3, pp. 30–41, December 1971.

89 St. Clair Drake and Horace Cayton, *Black Metropolis,* University of Chicago, Chicago, 1945, p. 586; Rainwater, *Behind Ghetto Walls . . . ,* pp. 48–54.

90 Leland J. Axelson, "The Working Wife: Differences in Perception Among Negro and White Males," *J. Marriage and the Family,* vol. 32, pp. 457–464, August 1970.

91 U.S. Bureau of the Census, *The Social and Economic Status . . . ,* p. 101.

92 Alan E. Bayer, "College Impact on Marriage," *J. Marriage and the Family,* vol. 34, pp. 600–610, November 1972.

93 Robert Staples, *The Black Woman in America,* Nelson-Hall, Chicago, 1973, p. 115.

94 Irving Rosow and K. Daniel Rose, "Divorce Among Doctors," *J. Marriage and the Family,* vol. 34, pp. 587–599, November 1972.

95 Beth Day, *Sexual Life Between Blacks and Whites,* World, New York, 1972, pp. 103–120.

96 George Gallup, "Growing Tolerance Found Regarding Interracial, Interfaith Marriages," *The New York Times,* p. B51, November 19, 1972.

97 David Heer, "Negro-White Marriage in the United States," *J. Marriage and the Family,* vol. 28, pp. 262–273, August 1966; Thomas Monahan, "Are Interracial Marriages Really Less Stable?" *Social Forces,* vol. 48, pp. 461–473, June 1970.

98 David Heer, "The Prevalence of Black-White Marriage in the United States, 1960 and 1970," *J. Marriage and the Family*, vol. 36, pp. 246–259, May 1974.

99 Alvin Goins, "Ethnic and Class Preferences Among College Negroes," *J. Negro Education*, vol. 29, pp. 128–133, Spring 1960.

100 Joseph Golden, "Facilitating Factors in Negro-White Intermarriage," *Phylon*, vol. 20, pp. 273–284, Fall 1959, Monahan, loc. cit.

101 Sonia Pressman, "Job Discrimination and the Black Woman," *The Crisis*, pp. 103–108, March 1970.

102 David Schulz, "Variations in the Father Role in Complete Families of the Negro Lower Class," *Social Science Quarterly*, vol. 49, pp. 651–659, December 1969.

103 Robert Bell, "The Relative Importance of Mother and Wife Roles Among Negro Lower Class Women," in Robert Staples (ed.), *The Black Family: Essays and Studies*, Wadsworth, Belmont, Calif., 1971, pp. 248–256.

104 Joyce Ladner, "The Legacy of Black Womanhood," *Tuesday*, pp. 4–5, 18–20, April 1972.

105 Radcliffe-Brown and Forde, op. cit., pp. 72–82.

106 Ira Iscoe, Martha Williams, and Jerry Harvey, "Age Intelligence and Sex as Variables in the Conformity Behavior of Negro and White Children," *Child Development*, vol. 35, pp. 451–460, June 1964.

107 Robert Coles, "Children and Racial Demonstrations," *The American Scholar*, vol. 34, pp. 78–92, Winter 1964.

108 Arnold Green, "The Middle Class Male Child and Neurosis," *American Sociological Review*, vol. 11, pp. 31–41, February 1946.

109 David Nolle, "Changes in Black Sons and Daughters: A Panel Analysis of Black Adolescents' Orientation Toward Their Parents," *J. Marriage and the Family*, vol. 34, pp. 443–447, August 1972; John Scanzoni, *The Black Family In Modern Society*, Allyn & Bacon, Boston, 1971, pp. 102–151;

110 Andrew Billingsley, "Family Functioning in the Low-Income Black Community," *Social Casework*, vol. 50, pp. 563–672, December 1969.

111 U.S. Bureau of the Census, *Inmates of Institutions*, P.C.(2)3A, Table 31, 1960, p. 44.

112 Rainwater, *"The Crucible of Identity . . . ,"* pp. 258–264.

113 John McCarthy and William Yancey, "Uncle Tom and Mr. Charlie: Metaphysical Pathos in the Study of Racism and Personal

Disorganization," *American Journal of Sociology,* vol. 76, pp. 648–672, November 1971.

114 Wayne Dennis, "Racial Change in Negro Drawings," *J. Psychology,* vol. 69, pp. 129–130, May 1968; Jeanne Fish and Charlotte Larr, "A Decade of Change in Drawings by Black Children," unpublished manuscript, December 1971.

115 Morris Rosenburg and Roberta Simmons, *Black and White Self-Esteem: The Urban School Child,* American Sociological Association, Washington, July 1971, pp. 74–87.

116 Scanzoni, op. cit., pp. 104–111.

117 Robert Hill, "A Profile of the Black Aged," *The Los Angeles Sentinel,* p. A-14, October 7, 1971.

118 Jacquelyn Jackson, "Marital Life Among Older Black Couples," *The Family Coordinator,* vol. 21, pp. 21–28, January 1972.

119 Hill, "A Profile of the Black Aged," loc. cit.

120 Jacquelyn Jackson, "Comparative Life Styles and Family and Friend Relationships Among Older Black Women," *The Family Coordinator,* vol. 21, pp. 477–486, October 1972.

121 Jacquelyn Jackson, "Negro Aged Parents and Adult Children: Their Affective Relationships," *Varia,* vol. 2, pp. 1–14, Spring 1969.

122 Staples, "The Sexuality of Black Women," p. 11.

SUGGESTED READING LIST

Billingsley, Andrew: "Black Families and White Social Science," *Journal of Social Issues,* vol. 26, pp. 127–142, November 1970.

——: *Black Families in White America,* Prentice-Hall, Englewood Cliffs, N.J., 1968.

Billingsley, Andrew and Marilyn Greene: "Family Life Among the Free Black Population in the 18th Century, *Journal of Social and Behavioral Sciences,* vol. 20, pp. 1–18, Spring 1974.

Bims, Hamilton: "The Black Family: A Proud Reappraisal," *Ebony,* vol. 29, pp. 118–127, March 1974.

Davis, Angela: "Reflections on the Black Woman's Role in the Community of Slaves," *The Black Scholar,* vol. 2, December 1971.

Frazier, Franklin E.: *The Negro Family in the United States,* University of Chicago, Chicago, 1939.

Heer, David: "The Prevalence of Black-White Marriage in the United States, 1960 and 1970," *Journal of Marriage and the Family,* vol. 36, pp. 246–259, May 1974.

Hernton, Calvin, *Sex and Racism in America,* Doubleday, New York, 1965.

Hill, Robert, *The Strengths of Black Families,* Emerson-Hall, New York, 1972.

Ladner, Joyce: *Tomorrow's Tomorrow: The Black Woman,* Doubleday, Garden City, N.Y., 1971.

Lieberman, Leonard: "The Emerging Model of the Black Family," *International Journal of Sociology of the Family,* vol. 3, pp. 10–22, March 1973.

Liebow, Elliot: *Tally's Corner,* Little, Brown, Boston, 1966.

Nobles, Wade: "Africanity: Its Role in Black Families," *The Black Scholar,* vol. 5, pp. 10–17, June 1974.

Scanzoni, John: *The Black Family in Modern Society,* Allyn & Bacon, Boston, 1971.

Shimkin, Demitri B., Edith Shimkin, and Dennis Frate (eds.): *The Extended Family in Black Societies,* Mouton Publishers, The Hague, Netherlands, 1975.

Stack, Carol B.: *All Our Kin: Strategies for Survival in a Black Community,* Harper & Row, New York, 1974.

Staples, Robert: *The Black Family Essays and Studies,* Wadsworth, Belmont, Calif., 1971.

Staples, Robert: *The Black Woman in America,* Nelson-Hall, Chicago, 1973.

Staples, Robert: "The Myth of the Impotent Black Male," *The Black Scholar,* vol. 2, pp. 2–9, June 1971.

Staples, Robert: "Towards a Sociology of the Black Family: A Decade of Theory and Research," *Journal of Marriage and the Family,* vol. 33, pp. 19–38, February 1971.

Turner, Clarence Rollo: "Some Theoretical and Conceptual Considerations for Black Family Studies," *Black Lines,* vol. 2, pp. 13–28, Winter 1972.

Willie, Charles V. *A New Look at Black Families,* Prentice-Hall, Englewood Cliffs, N.J., 1974.

Chapter 6

Sociology of
Black Religion

Since sociology is considered a science, it does not investigate such questions as the existence of God or his influence on the empirical world. However, religion is a legitimate field of study because it is an institutional form that serves many functions in a number of societies. That is the legitimate concern of sociology, not whether religious behavior is rational or not but what purpose it serves in the total functioning of the social structure. The sociological view is that religion is a set of organized social and cultural activities which are in themselves neither stupid nor smart nor rational nor irrational.[1] Religion is no more irrational than any other form of symbolic behavior such as dress, customs, or ceremonies. Our focus of inquiry is on the practical consequences of religious belief and activity for Afro-Americans.

A number of students of Black religious behavior have asserted that Blacks throughout the world are a fundamentally religious people. Herskovits (1941) characterized their deep religious bent as overriding all other forms of social expression.[2] In the view of Dubois (1903), Blacks were religious beings by instinct and endowed with a deep emotional nature which naturally gravitates them toward the supernatural.[3] The historical and contemporary evidence indicates that religiosity is related to levels of social and cultural development. In some societies the church has dominated all other institutions while in others it has had relatively little significance. In Greece, Coulanges (1955) noted that religion was such a pervasive force it became a basic part of the Greek personality.[4]

While religion has played a central part in Afro-American life, it has by no means matched the Greek experience. If we measure religiosity by church attendance, two surveys—some forty years apart—show Blacks to be no more religious than Whites. Based on 1926 data Mays and Nicholson (1933) found that less than 60 percent of Blacks attended church and that White men actually had a higher rate of church attendance than Black males.[5] The Gallup polls during the years 1954-1968 disclosed that White Catholics had the highest church attendance rate with Black Protestants a distant second.[6] The five major Black denominations in the United States have approximately ten million adult members in addition to six million Sunday school members. Another million are probably members of predominantly White churches.[7]

However, the importance of Black religion cannot be measured solely in terms of body counts or various denominations. It is what Washington (1964) calls the Black folk religion that cuts across all other variables.[8] This folk religion binds Black people to a common history born and shaped out of suffering and oppression. As sociologists we must examine the forces that created the Black church and its unique role in Afro-American life.

Before analyzing the historical and cultural elements that shaped the Black church, we must understand the exact role it did play in the Black struggle for liberation. Scholars are not at all agreed on the role of the Black church. Opinions range from the statement of one Black minister who said: "If there had been no church, there would have been no civil rights movement today"[9] to the comment of a Black sociologist: "The indifference of the Negro church to current social issues and its emphasis on the values of a future life lent indirect but vital support to the [status quo] race patterns."[10] The conflicting opinions might be reconciled by the Engels' (1955) notion that where religious thought styles dominate an epoch, protest will be phrased in religious terms as well as the justifications for oppression and escapist fantasies.[11]

AFRICAN RELIGION

Because of the diversity of African religious forms, it is not possible to depict a typical form of religious activity. Probably a most uniform characteristic of African religion is the belief that there is no separation between the spiritual world and the individual's ongoing activities. Religious forces are believed to involve themselves in one's daily life. A supreme being, in some form or other, patterns the events that occur in the empirical world. Or, in other words, the compartmentalization which takes place in much of the Western world is absent.[12] Individuals are not allowed to separate the religious beliefs they adhere to on Sunday morning from, for instance, their business practices the rest of the week. African religious codes are integrated into the daily life of its adherents.

A common characterization of African religions is the concept of animism. This terms refers to a belief in spiritual beings and is usually applied to what are labeled "primitive societies." It is used in a negative sense because scholars have regarded it as ignorant superstitions and dark and cruel fetishism. As Mbiti (1969) has illustrated, African religions are neither simple nor all the same. He points out that the common belief that Africans worshiped nature and made idols of animals is very inaccurate. Although some animals such as lizards and snakes have an important status in African religious thought, they are only a few of the symbolic representations of man's relationship to a supreme being.[13]

Among the other characteristics of African religion was a belief in ancestral spirits. As with other aspects of the African religion, this belief structure was related to its social organization. The spirit that existed in a dead relative became a god after his death and looked after his family.[14] This belief system reaffirmed the African code of communalism by its emphasis on the care of the deceased person's family by his spirit long after his departure.

The cohesiveness of the African kinship group was illustrated by the elaborateness of funeral rites found throughout the African continent. Because a funeral was the climax of life, a tribal custom was to give the deceased person a funeral that symbolized their respect. Each member of the family participated by presenting gifts and engaging in some ritual incident to internment. This practice was a sacred obligation of the deceased's survivors and served to create a community of fraternal brotherhood through the collective sentiments of the dead person's surviving kinsmen about the symbolic meaning of his death.[15]

It is primarily the ethnocentrism of Western anthropologists and historians that has led them to depict African religions as a mass of superstitious beliefs derived from ignorance and a primitive level of development. African religions are no more illogical than Western religions, and neither can be subjected to empirical validation. As in Western societies, African religions are related to the survival of a people in a given epoch. As Durkheim (1947) has pointed out, it is not the special nature of religious conceptions that constitute its benign influence but the fact that the beliefs and practices are common to all the faithful, hence contributing to the construction of a moral community.[16]

RELIGION AND SLAVERY

Most of the Africans sold into slavery were non-Christians. In fact one of the initial justifications for enslaving them was to convert the "heathens." Despite this rationalization for the forced bondage of Africans, the slaveholders had some reservations about teaching them Christian religious thought through the Bible. This reluctance to acquainting slaves with the Bible was due in part to laws forbidding slaves to read and write. It was also based on the fear that knowledge of the Bible would instill in the slave ideas of human freedom and equality that were incompatable with the institution of slavery. After it was decided that it was legal and moral to be both a Christian and a slave, many slaveholders furnished religious instruction and a place of worship for their slaves, or at least did not interfere with missionary work among them.

Some slaveholders dropped their opposition to religious teachings when they realized that the Bible contained sufficient defense of slavery. Many of the most compliant slaves, they found, were those who read the Bible. Eventually, the slaveholders came to see supervised religion as one of the most effective means of social control. Stampp (1956) points out that the religious teachings the slave received gave divine approval to slavery in that failure to obey one's master was an offense against God. The obedient slave, they were taught, would get eternal salvation as a reward for faithful service.[18] Organized White religion gave strong support to the existence of slavery. In the last three decades before the Civil War the White church was one of the strongest allies of the proslavery element.[19]

As for the bondsmen, they had entered the New World with religious traditions they could not retain in their pure form. Needing an escape valve from the intolerable conditions of slavery and the barren life of the rural South, they formed what Frazier (1964) calls the "invisible institution of the Black church." The minister was usually just another slave who knew a little something about the Bible. He would preach to them in small gatherings about their own code of religion, which was different from the White one. These meetings were not supervised by Whites. Religious songs reflecting the slave's conception of the world and his other-world outlook were sung.[20]

While those religious activities seemed harmless enough, others were pursued for different purposes. Some religious meetings were used to plot escape strategies, and free Black churches served as stations on the underground railroad. The spirituals were employed to transmit coded messages to the congregation or to assist runaway slaves. More important, however, was the fact that many of the leaders of slave rebellions were Black preachers. The most significant slave insurrections were spearheaded by Black ministers such as Gabriel Prosser, Denmark Vesey, and Nat Turner. This led historian Liston Pope (1964) to conclude that the biblical teachings often inspired revolt among slaves and was illuminated particularly in insurrections and revolts in the period between 1800 and 1831.[21]

The tie between Black religious activity and slave revolts led to a number of restraints on their religious freedom, which between 1820 and 1860 was generally placed under White restraint and super-vision. The state of South Carolina passed one of the first legislative acts restricting Black religious services. In 1800 it passed a law for-bidding Blacks "even in company with white persons to meet together and assemble for the purpose of religious worship, either before the rising of the sun or after the going down of the same."[22] A number of Southern states simply outlawed all Black preachers. Slaves were allowed to meet by themselves only if a White minister led them or if a White man observed them. Eventually, most slaves were forced to attend the churches of their masters.[23]

Although Southern Whites feared that religious activity would cause their bondsmen to revolt, other students of this era point out that slave frustration was sublimated into emotionalism and their hopes were fixed on the afterworld. The spirituals, it is claimed, represented the slave's attempt to escape through song.[24] Even the ministers so feared by the slaveowners often preached obedience and faithfulness to their congregation. This was particularly true if the master allowed religious services on the plantation. Slave preachers taught their fellow bondsmen to be loyal to their masters and to endure the pains and problems of this world and to look forward to better things in the afterlife. Hamilton (1972) cites the case of one Black minister who was so skillful in this technique that other slaveholders sought his services for the pacification of their slaves.[25]

During this same period, what Frazier (1964) labeled the "institutional Black church" developed among free Blacks. It was first founded by a freed slave, Richard Allen. Allen had earlier preached sermons from the pulpit of a White church before an incident that occurred in 1787. Blacks were permitted to sit only in the gallery of this church, but by mistake Allen and Absalom Jones occupied the wrong side of the gallery and were literally dragged from their knees as they prayed. Subsequently they formed the Free African Society, which resulted in the founding of the first Black church, the "African Methodist Episcopal Church," in 1816 with Allen as the first Black bishop.[26] Allen, himself, was an intermediate type of Black minister who urged Blacks not to hold malice or ill will against the slaveholders, but he also preached that slavery was against God's will and that slaveowners would be punished by God.[27]

Most slaves—and free Blacks—had joined Baptist or Methodist churches. Historians and other social scientists are in disagreement on the reasons why. Frazier (1964) believed that the field slaves were drawn to these two denominations because they preached a simple doctrine of salvation through conversion in which a highly emotional experience was of primary importance. These two religious organizations provided the most effective way of unleashing contained emotions that the institution of slavery had created. Blacks could shout, sing, and receive an emotion-laden sermon from their pastor. When the first institutional Black church was to be formed, its founders argued over which form of worship—Baptist or Methodist—was more suited to the religious needs of Blacks. Most Blacks initially chose the Methodist church, but eventually most of them affiliated with the Baptists.[28]

AFRICAN RELIGIOUS SURVIVALS

Although sociologists such as Frazier assert that the religious myths and cults of Africa had no meaning whatever for Afro-Americans, it seems reasonable to assume that all remnants of the African religious heritage were not eradicated by the passage of time, physical distance, or the manner in which they were enslaved. In fact, Dubois (1898) claimed that the Black church was the only social institution among Blacks which started in Africa and survived slavery and that under the leadership of the priest and medicine man the church preserved the remnants of African tribal life. The Black church, he believed, had its roots in African soil and has preserved many functions of tribal organization. These functions are revealed in its religious activity, its social authority, and general guiding and coordinating work.[29]

Another view on the relationship between African and Afro-American religions is held by St. Clair Drake (1970). He believes there was a blending of African and European religious elements that created a creole religious culture. It contained elements of each nation with modifications and reinterpretations of materials from both sources. Once such a syncretic culture came into existence, those newly arrived Africans could be inducted into that culture and not face the same difficult adjustments as the original group. Drake also makes the important point that while Black preachers might have pacified the slaves with their exhortations to obey their masters and look to the afterworld for salvation, they were simultaneously developing group pride and self-respect by naming their churches "African" and painting a verbal picture of a glorious past.[30]

The most extensive investigation of African continuities in Afro-American religion was carried out by Herskovits (1933). He cites the following religious customs that can be traced to the African past: (1) spirit possession; (2) dancing with African steps and identical motor behavior; (3) singing that derives in manner, if not in actual form, directly from Africa; (4) references to crossing the River Jordan; (5) wakes; (6) shallow burials; (7) passing of small children over coffin; (8) inclusion of food and money in coffin; (9) fear of cursing; (10) improvisation of songs of ridicule.[31]

It was the retention of African religious values that guided the bondsmen's choice of religious denominations. Herskovits (1935) indicates that the newly arrived African slaves were attracted to the Baptist church because their form of religious worship was closely associated in the minds of the bondsmen with the familiar river cults in West Africa and especially since a large number of river cult priests had been enslaved.[32] Dubois (1903) was in basic agreement with the notion that Black attraction to the Baptist faith was due to the mystic character of Africans. It was the visible rite of baptism that appealed so strongly to the new slaves.[33]

Scholars are in greater agreement over the African link to Afro-American spirituals although some have claimed that the slaves were taught spirituals by their owners or that spirituals were merely imitations of European folk songs.[34] Southern (1972) defines Black spirituals as the religious musical expression of Black people and distinguishes it from the gospel song, which is the invention of a single personality who provides a definitive version of his song by writing it in musical notation or by making a recording of it. In contrast, the spiritual exists for a long time in oral tradition, the original author may not be known, and the song is reshaped over a number of years to the point where it bears no resemblance to its original form.[35]

Even Frazier (1964) admitted that the spirituals reveal some continuity with the African background, especially in the Afro-American shout songs. These types of songs are called by this name because they are sung while Black worshippers are engaged in what might be called a holy dance.[36] They may be seen as an elemental religious expression among Afro-Americans. Southern also found that spiritual songs are in the African tradition with their emphasis on antiphonal performance, a loud strident vocal quality, and bodily movement during the singing. What has happened, she notes, is that because over the years Blacks have forgotten the African text of their songs they substituted the words in English and altered original melodies in the process of oral transmission.[37]

The important role of the minister and his preaching style are considered another link to the African past. In response to the question of where Afro-American ministers got their preaching style, Mitchell (1970) replied that there is good reason to believe that African culture influenced all Black preachers to use a musical and pleasing voice, with or without moaning or chanting. As an example he cites the use of imagery to project some practical maxim of morality—in this case employing the parable of an eagle teaching her newly fledged offspring to fly. The technique of using animal figures to convey great truths is typical in African religious services. Another pattern traceable to African culture is the call-and-response form of interaction between pastor and congregation. This is a form of worship where the congregation talks back to the preacher.[38]

Black ministers, or priests, have been one of the most distinctive and charismatic personalities in Black life. Dubois (1903) asserted that the chief remaining trait of African religious traditions among the Afro-Americans was the priest or medicine man. To the slaves he represented the healer of the sick, the interpreter of the unknown, the supernatural avenger of wrong, and the one individual who expressed the longing, disappointment, and resentment of a stolen and oppressed people.[39] What better person, asks Herskovits (1941), to lead a resistance to slavery than the Black preacher? Who else had the sanction to assure supernatural support to his followers and convince them to rebel against their condition by his assurance that the powers of their ancestors were aiding them in their struggle for freedom?[40]

There are a number of other Afro-American worship practices that appear to have their roots in Africa. The elaborateness of the death ceremonies among Blacks is one of them. Providing mutual aid, supporting one another in time of sickness, and giving benefits to the widows and fatherless children are other examples of the African communal spirit. Judging an act as sinful by its consequences, not the act itself, fits in well with the elaborate codes of African societies. Yet, there are critics who contend that what appear to be African survivals in the United States are actually chance occurrences. Few, however, question the vestige of Africanisms in Caribbean religious forms.

In certain areas of the Caribbean and South America, there are religious beliefs and practices that are markedly African, involving as they do spirits that have obvious African names, spirits of whom it is believed take possession of the faithful during rituals. Haiti and Brazil are two cases in point. In both countries the Blacks are often baptized Catholics and many elements of Catholicism have been fused with African elements. Black priests and priestesses occupy a high revered status because it is believed that they control rain and war and the smelting of iron. Another set of gods are believed to enter their bodies and transform them into oracles, soothsayers, and diviners. The names of the gods are African as are the names of specific rituals, the titles of the participants in the ritual, etc. What Africans regard as the *guju* man, West Indians call the *obeah* man and he performs the functions of allaying anxiety, assuring good luck, and confounding enemies.[41]

A common religious practice that is traced to the African past is voodoo (or vodu). The voodoo ceremony originated with the Ewe Tribe and consists of the use of charms or fetishes for the purpose of bewitching others or shielding oneself from harm. Adherents of voodoo believe in one supreme God and find in him the same kind of inspiration others find in the God of the so-called civilized religions. While it has been characterized as a supreme form of irrational superstition, it is in essence a religion of the masses, explaining for them the nature of the world in which they live and how they can protect themselves from the omnipresent evil from which they wish to be delivered.[42]

According to Wilmore (1973), voodoo has always been adaptive to the anti-White feelings of oppressed Black people. Wherever it is found, he claims, one can expect a militant, religiously inspired rejection of White values and White control. This certainly seemed to be the case in the armed struggle in Haiti. James (1963) reports:

> The rising was . . . a thoroughly prepared and organized mass movement . . . voodoo was the medium of the conspiracy. In spite of all the prohibitions, the slaves had travelled miles to sing and dance and practice the rites and talk; and, now since the revolution (in France) to hear the political news and make their plans. Boukman, a Papaloi, or High Priest, a gigantic Negro, was the leader.

> Boukman gave the last instructions and after voodo incanta-
> tions . . . stimulated his followers by a prayer spoken in creole. . . .
> Our God who is good to us order us to avenge our wrongs. He will
> direct our arms and aid us. Throw away the symbol of the God
> of the whites who has so often caused us to weep, and listen to
> the voice of liberty, which speaks in the hearts of all us.[43]

African religious forms are more distinct in Caribbean and South
American Black cults because of the different nature of slavery in
those areas. It seems that such cults are also more common in countries
with a strong Catholic background. Herskovits (1937) suggests two
reasons: (1) Catholic theology and ritual were not as compatible
with the slave's religious needs and (2) the Catholic belief in many
saints could be more easily fused with African belief systems of
polytheism (many gods).[44] South American slavery did not have
a obliterating effect on the African's family life and cultural traditions.
For example, African or African-derived languages are still spoken
in some parts of Cuba and Brazil.[45]

One prominent religious belief system that should be noted is
that of Ethiopianism. It began in the nineteenth century and developed
during the twentieth century. It was concerned with the redemption
of Blacks in the New World so that the power and prestige of the
ancient state of Ethiopia could be restored to them. Ethiopia was a
symbol of freedom because it had always avoided colonial rule and
remained independent. Generally the adherents of this philosophy
believe that freedom and salvation will be theirs when they return
to the mighty African nation of Ethiopia.[46] In Jamaica the "Ras
Tafari movement," begun in 1930, has organized around this ideology.
The basic belief is that all persons of African descent will be enabled
to return to their motherland of Africa and sometime in the future
the Black man will be avenged by compelling the White man to become
his servant.[47]

Our foregoing discussion reveals that religion served a number of
functions for Blacks and Whites during the slavery era and in its
immediate aftermath. Thus, it is not so important as to what constitutes a valid or even civilized religion but the uses to which it is
put. On balance, Black religion played a positive role in the Afro-
American's life by providing him with an outlet for the expression of
his deepest feelings and a refuge in a hostile White world. In a political

sense, it was most likely a negative force by its emphasis on compliance with oppressive institutions. At the same time it was also a weapon of struggle against slavery when properly used. Given the conditions of that era, it is questionable about how effective religion would have been if it had inspired all bondsmen to revolt. Being a minority in a strange land, it is possible that their everyday acts of covert resistance to slavery was all that was practical. And, a revolutionary religion would not have made that much of a difference.

SOCIOLOGICAL THEORIES OF RELIGION

Most sociological studies of religion among Whites have fallen into three categories: (1) religion and economic organization, (2) religion as an opiate, and (3) the functionalist approach. As a multiputpose institution, Black religion fits into each of those categories. It has a many faceted dimension which must be studied through the perspective of Black sociology. Until we develop a definitive theory of the role of Black religion, the following approaches can be used to explain how Black religion functions within given epochs and in particular settings.

Religion and Economic Organization

The classic theory on the relationship between religion and economics is presented in the work *The Protestant Ethic and the Spirit of Capitalism,* by Max Weber. According to Weber (1930), there were certain elements in Protestant religions—in contrast to Catholicism—which encouraged commerce. It was the Protestant view that the individual attained worldly success by his own efforts rather than the Catholic doctrine that his faith was predestined. By practicing the virtues of thrift and hard work, the Protestant could achieve salvation. These religious values also led to the accumulation of wealth necessary for the successful development of a capitalist economic system.[48]

The religious organizations of Black people also promoted, and sang the praises of, the capitalist ethic. By their own example Black churches encouraged the practice of capitalism. Dubois (1907) reported that "it was in order to establish their own churches that Negroes began to pool their meagre economic resources and buy buildings and the land on which they stood." He also believed that the Black church was the first institution to inculcate in Black males the economic rationality of the American culture.[49] Frazier (1964) found, too, that the Black church played an important role in economic cooperation and the accumulation of capital. One Black minister, Reverend Washington Brown, formed a group called "The Grand Fountain of True Reformers." Under its auspices a number of different businesses such as a newspaper, a bank, a real estate firm, and others were formed.[50]

Other more contemporary Black religious groups have promoted the idea of a Black capitalism. This business orientation has been particularly strong among Black religious organizations referred to as *cults*. One religious movement was the Universal Negro Improvement Association headed by Marcus Garvey. Although it was purported to be a nationalistic organization which believed in returning to a true Black religion and Black God, much of its activities consisted of starting businesses on a grand scale. Under its banner commercial ventures were started, such as grocery stores, laundries, restaurants, hotels, and the ill-fated Black Star Line of ships. Garvey (1926) was once quoted as saying, "Capitalism is necessary to the progress of the world, and those who unreasonably and wantonly oppose or fight against it are enemies to human advancement."[51]

One of the currently prominent religious economic organizations is the Nation of Islam (the Black Muslims). There is some question about their economic philosophy since their national newspaper, *Muhummad Speaks,* reports news most favorable to non-White socialist nations and condemns most vigorously economic exploitation of non-Whites by White capitalists. This group owns a number of businesses such as grocery stores, restaurants, barber shops, etc., which are run on the basis of providing a profit return. At the same time it operates schools and hospitals for its members. Ofari (1970) charges that their business operation differs little from that of White corporations. Rather than having the private profit from their commercial ventures benefit a single owner, it goes to a small group of private owners for their sole benefit.[52]

Whether or not that is true, the philosophy of the Nation of Islam does incorporate certain elements of the Protestant ethic. It has adopted a code of behavior similar to the Puritan ethic of capitalism, discipline, hard work, upright behavior, businesslike methods, and respect for authority. Its past leader, Elijah Muhammad, advised his followers: "Observe the operations of the White man. He is successful. He makes no excuses for his failure. He works hard—in a collective manner. You do the same."[53] Others have observed that when he talked about the all-Black state the Muslims want to create, he constantly referred to our banks, our businesses, our corporations. Rarely did he mention social agencies or cultural institutions.[54]

Within the mass-based Black churches, there is also the promotion of Black capitalism. Drake and Cayton (1945) found that most of the larger Black churches advertised Black-owned businesses on the theory that successful Black entrepreneurs were "advancing the race." It was common for Black ministers to encourage their congregation to patronize certain Black morticians, physicians, and retail stores. Church newspapers would advertise the services and products of some Black stores. There were even instances of ministers who appointed special agents or representatives within their church to plug specific stores or products.[55] Ofari (1970) has asserted that this collaboration between Black preacher and capitalist was an attempt to increase the power, prestige, and financial resources of the Black elite within Black America.[56]

Religion as an Opiate

Throughout history the religious institutions of a society have rarely been in the vanguard in the fight against racial or class oppression, nor have they been spearheads of reform. In fact, religion has been more often used as an instrument of social control. Marx and Engels (1955) labeled it "an opiate of the working class." According to them it had a "common interest with the ruling classes in keeping in subjection the great working mass of the nation" and that it early uncovered the possibilities religion provided for making the working class compliant to the will of the masters it had pleased God to place over them.[57]

As discussed earlier, the slaveholders also soon discovered that the bondsmen who were converted to Christianity or some part of its doctrine were more obedient slaves and less inclined to escape or participate in insurrections. Christianity was primarily used by slaveowners as a code of conduct which would prepare its adherents to orient their behavior toward acceptance and salvation in an afterlife. It was from the very beginning an opiate for the slaves to divert their attention and concern from the very oppressive institution of slavery. Its intent was to eradicate any desire to join some strong independent force that could deliver the slave from the harsh conditions forced upon him.

Fanon's (1963) theory of colonialism explains how the church operates in colonial societies. He writes: "The church in the colonies is the white people's church. She does not call the native to God's ways but to the ways of the white man, of the master, of the oppressor. And, as we know in this matter many are called but few chosen."[58] One investigation of what was being preached in Black churches was conducted in 1926 by Mays and Nicholson (1933). They found that out of 100 sermons delivered in urban Black churches, only 26 dealt with practical problems and the rest were concerned with other-world concerns or doctrinal and theological topics.[59]

A most eloquent and harsh indictment of the effect of Christianity on Afro-Americans was delivered by Malcolm X (1966). He declared:

> My brothers and sisters, our white slavemaster's Christian religion has taught us Black people here in the wilderness of North America that we will sprout wings when we die and fly up into the sky where God will have for us a special place called heaven. This is white man's Christian religion used to brainwash us Black people! We have accepted it . . . believed it . . . practiced it! And while we are doing all of that, for himself, this blue-eyed devil has twisted his Christianity, to keep his foot on our backs . . . to keep our eyes fixed on the pie in the sky and heaven in the hereafter— while he enjoys his heaven right here—on this earth—in this life.[60]

In general religion tends to have a conservatizing effect on individuals. Despite the apparent contradiction between Judeo-Christian values and racial prejudice, a number of studies have revealed a positive relationship between racial prejudice and religiosity.[61] It has the same conservative influence on American Blacks. A study by Gary Marx (1967) revealed that the less militant an Afro-American's attitude about civil rights the greater the probability that he was very religious. In other words, the more subjective importance Blacks gave to religion, the less likely they were to support militant activities. Using a scale to measure other-world versus secular orientation, he found even greater differences. Only 15 percent of those classified as other-world in outlook were militant compared with 39 percent who rated high on the "temporal" religious scale.[62]

Various authorities on the subject are in disagreement over whether Black religion is an opiate for Afro-Americans and, if so, when it became one. Some have claimed that it has always been a barrier to Black progress while others contend that the Black church has throughout its history been a positive institution for Black people. In the view of a prominent Black theologian, Black religion became dysfunctional in the 1920s when White Protestant evangelicalism replaced the Black folk religion and relegated it to verbal expression from the pulpit is such a way that action was stifled.[63]

The Functionalist Approach

Closely identified with an anthropological perspective, the functionalist approach is supported by the works of Durkheim (1947) and Radcliffe-Brown (1961).[64] The view from which functionalism starts is that religion is always a means to an end and must be understood in the context of the situation. It regards religion as a cultural tool by means of which man has been able to accommodate himself to his experiences in his total environment. It is the structure of human thought, feeling, and action to things which man believes to transcend everyday experiences with himself, his fellows, and the natural world. It constitutes what Durkheim calls the "sacred" and it is regarded as the very core of religion.[65]

Applying elements of the functionalist approach to Black religion, we can understand that religious worship brings about the sharing of beliefs and practices by a group with a common history and a shared destiny. The religious experiences in Black churches serve the purpose of giving strength, identity and a reason for being to its members. In some Black churches a sense of group cohesiveness is established through stimulating singing, the tempo of the music, and clapping of hands. Through such activity inhibitions are lost and the individual becomes one with the group, thus establishing a sense of group identity.[66]

The functions of religious ceremony and ritual are very symbolic in nature. In the case of Blacks the worship of God represents their social reality. Living in a hostile and alien world, they seek a figure who will look out for their interests. If they had equal participation in a society, they might look to their cultural institutions for this protection. Internal colonialism forces them to look to a powerful abstract figure to attain this necessary feeling of security. Due to their powerlessness, God is seen as potent, he is everything. Otherwise there is no hope of achieving relief from their oppressed condition.

As we have seen in the use of religion during slavery and the survival of Africanisms in New World religious forms, the Black form of religious worship has served the cohesive, vitalizing, and euphoric functions that the functionalists attribute to that institution. It provides a structured world view and a system of defense and attack in a basically hostile environment. With the use of Ethiopanism and African traditions of ritual and ceremony, Afro-Americans are made aware of their cultural heritage. The traditions of the past are reinforced and perpetuated, faith is renewed, values are conveyed and deeply imbedded in the consciousness of the participants.

While religious activity serves much the same purpose for White Americans, it has always occupied a more important place in the life of Afro-Americans. The church was the only institution that furnished an effective organization of this group and met many needs beyond that of the worship of God and instruction in religious ideology. That was only its manifest functions, but its latent functions consisted of meeting a further variety of Black needs.

LATENT FUNCTIONS OF THE BLACK CHURCH

Sociologists define the latent functions of institutions as those unintended and sometimes unrecognizable byproducts of its actions.[67] Much of our previous discussion has actually covered the important latent functions of religion and the church for Afro-Americans. In addition to them, there are other effects of collective religious worship on the Black social structure that should be briefly noted. We might classify them into the following categories:

Maintaining Family Solidarity

As in most societies, the Black church often stands as a conserver of morals, a strengthener of family life, and final authority on right

and wrong. By its power of expulsion from the church it could require that its members be in conformity with certain moral norms.
For example, after slavery some Black churches expelled women for
bearing children out-of-wedlock. It encouraged the establishment of the
monogamic family and urged Black males to become more diligent
providers for their wives and children. Among Southern Blacks the
church would provide temporary support for a home where the
father had deserted the family.[68] Scanzoni (1971) found in his study
of "stable" Black families that the majority of the respondents had
parents who attended church at least once a week. Consequently,
the link he saw between the Black family and religion was the trans-
mittal and reinforcement of values leading to optimum fulfillment of
dominant expectations regarding economic and conjugal behavior.[69]

Status Conferral

This is a rather unique function of the Black church. Giving Blacks
a sense of recognition and somebodiness is important in a society
where all Blacks are regarded as inferior vis-à-vis all Whites. Even
on an objective index of status, most Afro-Americans fall into the
bottom level. Hence, the janitor can elevate his self-esteem via his
role as a superintendent of the Sunday school. The domestic servant
can gain appreciation by serving as leader of the church choir and the
railroad porter could achieve a sense of importance and prestige in
his role as a senior deacon. Because the Black church has provided
a place where individuals could participate and be accepted and valued
by standards of their own community rather than that of the White
majority, it has preserved the self-respect of many Blacks who would
have been otherwise overwhelmed by their dehumanizing experiences.
One psychiatrist has cited the decline of the Black church as a primary
reason for the marked increase in the Black suicide rate.[70]

Leadership Development

Because the Black church was the most thoroughly owned and controlled public institution, it provided the most accessible means of
developing Black leadership abilities. The church furnished the opportunity for a display of talent and initiative. Blacks of limited means
and education could hold church positions that required no training,
for example, speakers, singers, and keepers of the minutes. Such church

roles provided for the learning of leadership abilities not available in the dominant society. As Frazier (1964) has pointed out, "The church was the main area of social life in which Blacks could aspire to become the leaders of men."[71] It was an arena in which the struggle for power and the thirst for power could be satisfied. One result of the Black church's unique position in leadership training has been the disproportionate number of Black ministers who have monopolized leadership positions in the Black community.

Center of Black Protest

Despite the conservative character of many Black churches, they have provided continued protest against all forms of racial oppression. Churches have been used for mass meetings, forums, and other types of programs geared to make Blacks aware of the major social issues confronting them. Black ministers have led and participated in economic boycotts against discriminating businesses, they have marched on picket lines, etc.

Expressive Functions

The Black church has provided one of the primary vehicles for the release of emotional tensions accumulated through the experiences faced in a racist society. Its structure and content are designed to reduce emotional states of tension. The singing of spirituals, style of preaching, and group interaction all help to promote a group solidarity and give the participants a sense of identity. The worship services, which allow frenzied singing, shouting, and praying, give individuals the opportunity to give vent to their emotions in a culturally acceptable fashion. This form of religious worship symbolizes the existence of a race—a group struggling alone and realizing strength, if only temporarily—through its attempt to blend and unite people who share the same experiences. It should be noted that this function meets the needs of Black women more than men. There are usually more women than men in Black churches and outwardly they react more emotionally than the males. While women will shout and scream in order to release their emotions, men often confine themselves to clapping their hands and saying amen.[72]

Social Intercourse and Amusements

In the past Southern Black churches served as the center of community life. Dubois (1899) claimed that the Black church was a center of social intercourse to a degree unknown in White churches, even in rural areas. A variety of recreational and amusement activities were available to church participants in the form of church-sponsored concerts, suppers, socials, plays, picnics, etc. Now many Black churches open their doors seven nights a week in order to provide this social life to the Black community. The Sunday services also serve as a time for exchange of gossip, courting, and friendly conversation.[73] Even in large urban areas Black churches are centers of social activity. Chicago's Black churches provided access to concerts, movies, and mass meetings for meetings of the Black community.[74]

Because of its central role in Black life, the church has served a number of latent functions. Not only did religious instruction provide the newly arrived African the opportunity to learn to read but churches—both Black and White—established the first schools for freedmen and emancipated slaves. The spirituals have served as the basis of other Black musical expressions such as jazz and rhythm and blues. Storefront churches have performed as transitional stations for rural Southern migrants to the urban North. Harrison (1966) observed that they served as revitalization movements: deliberate, conscious, organized efforts of migrants to create a more satisfying mode of existence by refurbishing rural religious behavior to an urban environment.[75]

THE ROLE OF THE BLACK MINISTER

No discussion of the sociology of Black religion would be complete without examining the role of the Black preacher. His place in Black history is best summed up by Dubois (1903):

> The preacher is the most unique personality developed by the Negro on American soil. A leader, politician, an orator, a boss, an intriguer, an idealist—all these he is, and ever, too, the center of a group of men, now twenty, now a thousand in number. The combination of a certain adroitness with deep-seated earnestness

of tact and consummate ability, gave him preeminence and helps maintain it.[76]

Undoubtedly, he has played an important leadership role in Black struggles. He was often the best trained leader in the Black community. When the Black church was the center of the community he exercised power over the daily lives of its inhabitants by his ability to expel members from his congregation and the moral censure of wayward and dissident individuals. In the larger community he could speak out in behalf of the Black masses because the Black church was the one public institution comparatively free of White control. This was particularly true in the North where the fear of White violent reprisals was not as great as in the South. He could speak to the issues facing Blacks since there were no higher church authorities to discipline him and no Whites to use economic reprisals. Because he was so free of White influence, Blacks expected him to do more than spend his time on pastoral duties.[77]

According to Work and Dubois (1903), the Black ministry developed through three distinct historical stages and was passing into a fourth stage as they wrote. The stages are described as follows: (1) The minister of slavery days and early freedom was largely ignorant but led the people in all areas including intellectual and political as well as religious. (2) The church-building, congregation-managing preacher was needed to build large church buildings and minister to large numbers. He did not need to meet high intellectual or moral standards if he could effectively cope with the financial and control function required. (3) The business-manager preacher was asked to raise and administer money in order to keep the church financially solvent. He was stronger intellectually and morally and possessed a certain expertise in business matters. (4) Called the "intellectual and moral minister," he was the man who was well skilled in the philosophy of theological matters and had strong moral standards.[78]

Who becomes a minister and how does he enter this occupation? One of the most common types of ministers is what Frazier (1964) called a "Jackleg preacher."[79] This was a semiliterate or uneducated person who gathered around him poor Blacks who were seeking a religious leader in the city. Often the Black male who becomes a preacher does so because it is the only occupation of prestige, and sometimes wealth, that does not require any training. All that is demanded is that one receive a "call" to preach the word of God. Entering the ministry, then, provides a way for an uneducated Black male to gain status within the Black community.[80] One result of this special attraction to the ministry is the large ratio of churches compared with the size of the Black population. Another indication of the appeal of the ministry was the 1930 U.S. Census finding that although Blacks comprised 9.7 percent of the total population at that time, they constituted about 16.8 percent of all clergymen. However, it is estimated that the proportion of Black ministers was actually much higher since Black ministers holding two jobs may not have reported the clergy occupation.[81]

Most Black ministers have no formal training. Moreover, as other occupational positions become available to them, the numbers in the ministry decrease. Since the thirties, there has been an absolute as well as a relative decline in the number of Black preachers. Few Black youth are presently attracted to this occupation because of the low salaries paid ministers and their feeling that the church has become irrelevant to Black people. In 1971 there were only 808 Black students enrolled in theological schools. Among that group, 32 were studying in Roman Catholic schools and 776 in Protestant or non-denominational schools.[82]

Although Black ministers reportedly receive rather low salaries, a very common charge against them is that the church is a racket for lining the pockets of the preacher. If there is any stereotype of the Black preacher, it is that he is a Cadillac-driving, woman-chasing person. Ofari (1970) contends that "it was no accident that the Black minister grew to be . . . one of the wealthiest . . . members of the Black community." Through their example, he claims, many other Black opportunistic hustlers have been inspired to set up their own church and rip off the Black community. Anyone who could secure a few chairs and a room could call himself "Reverend" because he had gotten the "call." Increasingly, the church became simply another business whose main concern was the wealth accumulated and not the number of people given leadership and help.[84]

Another image of the Black minister is sexual. Because of his high status in the Black community it was natural that many women would find sexual appeal in his prestigious status, command of oratory, wealth, and flamboyance. However, the normative role of a minister is distinctly nonsexual. When warning his members against succumbing to temptations of the flesh, he is expected to be their perfect example by his display of sexual abstinence. Hernton (1971) comments that the common songs, myths, jokes, and ditties about the sexual activity of the Black preacher are legend. However, it is also asserted that not only have Black women historically been sexually attracted to their preacher but that Black men, too, have identified with his unrestrained sexuality. This sexual image of the Black preacher is regarded by some as the last survival of the African sexual heritage in Black America. He represents a phallic symbol that was commonly worshiped in some African societies.[85]

It is in his role as protest leader that Black preachers have achieved their greatest prominence. While some of the outstanding Black leaders have been ministers, a number of studies reveal that although the largest proportion of the Black leadership class are ministers, the vast majority of them are mostly interested in their pastoral role. Only a small minority display any strong concern with the Black liberation struggle. Even those ministers who have been involved were reluctantly drawn into it by the demands of the community.[86] Although Black ministers have been credited with leading much of the civil rights movement, that movement was actually started and organized by secular groups such as college students, workers, and other organizations.

Johnstone (1969) has developed a typology of Black preachers according to their involvement in civil rights activity:[87]

1 *The militant* is a preacher who identifies himself as a member of inner-core planning and executing civil rights action groups. He is an aggressive, take-charge activist who not only speaks out on civil rights issues but also acts on the basis of his beliefs. Examples of this type of minister would be those who have participated in economic boycott programs, demonstrations, and marches.

2 *The moderate* is differentiated from the militant by his inclination to be the peacemaker, the gradualist, the middle-of-the-roader. While opposed to racial oppression, his form of protest is more subtle and accommodating. He believes in conciliatory techniques that will hopefully bring about improvement in the Black man's lot without alienating the White population.

3 *The traditionalist* is a minister who believes his role should be confined to meeting the spiritual needs of his congregation. Becoming actively involved in Black protest activities is low on his list of priorities. Even his concept of the condition of Blacks may be framed in religious terms, i.e., salvation will come in the afterlife. Some traditionalists are even unaware that there is a problem and want to be left alone to preach the gospel.

There are other latent role functions of the Black minister that make him of some value to the Black community. The church, for instance, often serves as a structural bridge between the family and successful entrance into certain occupational roles. It can furnish resources that supplement those of the family and the school. Scanzoni (1971) asked members of his stable Black family group if there was anyone who took an interest in them and helped them. After school teachers, the other person picked most frequently was their minister followed by the Sunday school teacher. These were the adults outside the family who were willing to give time and energy to supply needed encouragement, counsel, and direction to many Black youth.[88]

An important but ignored role of the Black preacher is the linkage he represents between eras and generations to Afro-Americans. Hamilton (1972) has noted that while Blacks have been subjected to the disruption and transformation of their social institutions in the transition from Africa to America, the one person they had to depend upon for bridging their transitional stages was the preacher. His was the only familiar role carried over from earlier periods. He linked up the past and the present and it was through his presence that a certain continuity and stability was achieved for a group besieged by instability and abrupt changes. While the Black church did not represent in pure form what had existed in Africa, the preacher was their medicine man, the healer, the bearer of their religious tradition.[89]

Illustrative of the diversified roles of Black preachers are the cases of three men. The first, Edward Wilmot Blyden, was a leading scholar of Black religious thought in the nineteenth century. His works on Black religion provided the ideological base for Ethiopianism. He is generally credited with providing the intellectual defense of African culture in response to European criticisms.[90] It was his view that Africans have a distinct place in history, a culture of value and a personality of their own. For a number of years he tried through his writings and other efforts to show Blacks the limitations of American society and European-oriented religion. Blyden was one of the leading exponents of the philosophy that Afro-Americans were an African people and should not only take pride in their cultural heritage but return to their land of origin to build an Africa for Africans.[91]

A leading religious figure of the twentieth century was Dr. Martin Luther King, Jr. He is generally thought of as the leader of the civil rights movement of the sixties. It is not commonly known that the development of the techniques of nonviolent direct action occurred years before he ever appeared on the scene. And, after he became a figure of prominence as head of the Southern Christian Leadership Conference, it was actually a Black student group (SNCC) that performed most the work involved in organizing direct action protests. Yet, King and his organization got most of the publicity and the public contributions because his style and tactics appealed more to the White population. He spoke in terms of Christianity, love, and nonviolence. Such language appealed to Whites since it conveyed the impression that he was a friend of the Whites and posed no real threat to them.[92] King was also more amenable to compromise with the White power elite and had close ties with colonial leaders and their emissaries. Such ties even compromised his nonviolent posture, as was evident in his signing a petition calling upon the U.S. Government to use the force necessary to give Israel free access through an Egyptian Canal or his endorsement of the government sending in troops to crush the Black rebellion in Detroit.[93]

Adam Clayton Powell was a minister who was actively involved in all aspects of the Black liberation struggle until his death in 1971. He was also the most powerful Black politician in this country. With a church of 11,000 people as his power base he was elected as a congressman from New York City in 1944. Years before his election to that post he had participated in economic boycotts, marches, and demonstrations. After serving in Congress for a number of years, he became Chairman of the House of Representatives Committee on Education and Labor. While having some weaknesses, he was one of the most radical and uncompromising Black ministers in America. He was one of the first prominent Black leaders to endorse the concept of "Black power" and was the founding chairman of the National Conference on Black Power.

As the Black church declines in influence so will the Black preacher's ability to assume leadership in all spheres of Black life. Just as many Blacks turn to alternative institutions to satisfy the needs once filled by the church, other persons from secular fields will supplement them in leadership positions. Many of these changes are coming about because of the need for rationalization of the Black struggle. The people require a movement based on an understanding of their history, an objective evaluation of their condition, and a correct analysis of the strategies and tactics needed. Pure religious inspiration, which was used in a variety of ways, may have had its place at one time. And, it can be said that overall it worked quite well.

NOTES

1 Louis Schneider, "Problems in the Sociology of Religion," in Robert E. Faris (ed.), *Handbook of Modern Sociology,* Rand McNally, Chicago, 1964, p. 776.

2 Melville J. Herskovits, *The Myth of the Negro Past,* Harper & Row, New York, 1941, p. 207.

3 W. E. B. DuBois, *The Souls of Black Folk,* McClurg, Chicago, 1903, chap. 10.
Fustel de Coulanges, *The Ancient City,* Lee and Shepard, Boston, 1899, p. 280.

5 Benjamin E. Mays and J. S. Nicholson, *The Negro's Church,* Institute of Social and Religious Research, New York, 1933, p. 201.

6 Hart M. Nelsen, et al. (eds.), *The Black Church in America,* Basic Books, New York, 1971, p. 8.

7 Harry V. Richardson, "The Negro in American Religious Life," in John P. David (ed.), *The American Negro Reference Book,* Prentice-Hall, Englewood Cliffs, N.J., 1966, p. 402.

8 Joseph R. Washington, Jr., *Black Religion,* Beacon, Boston, 1964, p. 31.

9 Reverend Wyatt T. Walker, quoted in William Brink and Louis Harris, *The Negro Revolution in America,* Simon and Schuster, New York, 1964, p. 103.

10 Charles S. Johnson, *Growing Up in the Black Belt,* American Council on Education, Washington, 1941, pp. 135–136.

11 Frederich Engels, "On the History of Early Christianity," in Karl Marx and Frederich Engels (eds.), *On Religion,* Foreign Language Publishing House, Moscow, 1955, p. 317.

12 Gayravd S. Wilmore, *Black Religion and Black Radicalism,* Double-day, Garden City, N.Y., 1973, pp. 19–20.
13 John S. Mbiti, *African Religions and Philosophy,* Praeger, New York, 1969, pp. 15, 16, 29–57.
14 John Hope Franklin, *From Slavery to Freedom,* Knopf, New York, 1967 edition, pp. 32–33.
15 Ibid.
16 Emile Durkheim, *The Elementary Forms of the Religious Life,* The Free Press, Glencoe, Ill., 1947, pp. 43–44.
17 E. Franklin Frazier, *The Negro Church in America,* Schocken, New York, 1964, pp. 10–11.
18 Kenneth Stampp, *The Peculiar Institution,* Knopf, New York, 1956, p. 158.
19 Franklin, op. cit., p. 201. However, much of the abolitionist movement also came from the White church groups.
20 Frazier, op. cit., pp. 16–19.
21 Liston Pope, "The Negro and Religion in America," *Review of Religious Research,* vol. 5, pp. 144, Spring 1964.
22 Vincent Harding, "Religion and Resistance Among Anti-Bellum Negroes 1800-1860," in August Meier and Elliot Rudwick (eds.), *The Making of Black America,* Atheneum, New York, 1969, p. 182.
23 Franklin, op. cit., p. 200.
24 Ibid., pp. 207–208.
25 Charles V. Hamilton, *The Black Preacher in America,* Morrow, New York, 1972, p. 44.
26 Frazier, op. cit., pp. 27–28.
27 Hamilton, op. cit., pp. 47–48.
28 Frazier, loc. cit.
29 Dubois, op. cit.
30 St. Clair Drake, *The Redemption of Africa and Black Religion,* Third World, Chicago, 1970, pp. 12–18.
31 Melville J. Herskovits, "On the Provenience of New World Negroes," *Social Forces,* vol. 12, pp. 247–262, December 1933.
32 Melville J. Herskovits, "Social History of the Negro," *Handbook of Social Psychology,"* Clark University, 1935, Worcester, Mass., pp. 256–257.
33 Dubois, *The Souls of Black Folk,* chap. 10.
34 Cf. George P. Jackson, *White and Negro Spirituals,* Augustin, New York, 1943.
35 Eileen Southern, "An Origin for the Negro Spiritual," *The Black Scholar,* vol. 3, pp. 8–9, Summer 1972.

36 Frazier, op. cit., pp. 13–14.
37 Southern, op. cit., p. 12.
38 Henry H. Mitchell, *Black Preaching,* Lippincott, Philadelphia, 1970, p. 72, 95.
39 Dubois, *The Souls of Black Folk,* chap. 10.
40 Herskovits, *The Myth of the Negro Past,* p. 106.
41 Erika E. Bourguignon, "Afro-American Religious Traditions and Transformations," in John Szwed (ed.), *Black America,* Basic Books, New York, 1970, pp. 190–202.
42 Remy Bastien, Vodoun and Politics in Haiti, in Richard Frucht (ed.), *Black Society in the New World,* Random House, New York, 1971, pp. 290–307.
43 Cyril R. James, *The Black Jacobins,* Random House, New York, 1963, pp. 86–87.
44 Melville J. Herskovits, "African Gods and Catholic Saints in New World Negro Belief," *American Anthropologist,* vol. 39, pp. 635–643, October–December 1937.
45 Bourguignon, op. cit., p. 194.
46 Drake, op. cit., pp. 50–53.
47 Vittorio Lanternari, *Religions of the Oppressed,* Random House, New York, 1963, pp. 159–163.
48 Max Weber, *The Protestant Ethic and the Spirit of Capitalism,* Allen and Unvin, London, 1930.
49 W. E. B. DuBois, *Economic Cooperation Among American Negroes,* Atlanta, Atlanta, 1907, p. 54.
50 Frazier, op. cit., p. 38.
51 Amy Jacques Garvey (ed.), *Philosophy and Opinions of Marcus Garvey, Volume 11,* Universal, New York, 1926, p. 76.
52 Earl Ofari, *The Myth of Black Capitalism,* Monthly Review, New York, 1970, pp. 49–65.
53 E. U. Essien-Udom, *Black Nationalism,* Dell, New York, 1962, p. 182.
54 Whitney Young, "The Role of the Middle-Class Negro," *Ebony,* vol. 17, p. 69, September 1963.
55 St. Clair Drake and Horace Cayton, *Black Metropolis,* Harcourt, Brace, New York, 1945, p. 429.
56 Ofari, op. cit., p. 51.
57 Karl Marx and Frederich Engels, *On Religion,* Foreign Languages Publishing House, Moscow, 1955, p. 303.
58 Frantz Fanon, *The Wretched of the Earth,* Grove, New York, 1963, p. 42.

59 Mays and Nicholson, op. cit., p. 245.
60 Malcolm X, *The Autobiography of Malcolm X*, Grove, New York, 1966, p. 200.
61 Cf. George Simpson and Milton Yinger, *Racial and Cultural Minorities*, Harper & Row, New York, 1972 edition, pp. 527–531.
62 Gary Marx, "Religion: Opiate or Inspiration of Civil Rights Militancy Among Negroes," *American Sociological Review*, vol. 32, pp. 64–72, February 1967.
63 Washington, op. cit., p. 37.
64 Durkheim, op. cit; A. R. Radcliffe-Brown, *Structure and Function in Primitive Society*, The Free Press, Glencoe, Ill., 1961.
65 Durkheim, op. cit., p. 47.
66 Hylan Lewis, *Blackways of Kent*, University of North Carolina, Chapel Hill, 1955, pp. 131–135.
67 Robert Merton, *Social Theory and Social Structure*, The Free Press, Glencoe, Ill., 1967, pp. 19–84.
68 E. Franklin Frazier, *The Negro Family in the United States*, University of Chicago, Chicago, 1948, p. 95.
69 John Scanzoni, *The Black Family in Modern Society*, Allyn & Bacon, Boston, 1971, pp. 51–52.
70 James P. Comer, quoted in *Ebony*, vol. 28, p. 160, September 1973.
71 Frazier, *The Negro Church in America*, p. 43.
72 Mary Elizabeth Mumford, "A Case Study of the Sanctified Church," in *Religion and Magic Among the Negroes of Washington, D.C.*, Howard University Department of Sociology and Anthropology, Washington, 1946, pp. 21–26.
73 W. E. B. DuBois, *The Philadelphia Negro*, University of Pennsylvania, Philadelphia, 1899, p. 202.
74 Drake and Cayton, op. cit., pp. 416–417.
75 Ira E. Harrison, The Storefront Church as a Revitalization Movement, *Review of Religion Research*, vol. 7, pp. 161–162, Spring 1966.
76 Du Bois, *The Souls of Black Folk*, pp. 190–191.
77 Drake and Cayton, op. cit., pp. 427–428.
78 Monroe Work and W. E. B. Dubois, "The Negro Ministry in the Middle West," in *The Negro Church* (W. E. B. Dubois, ed.), Atlanta University, Atlanta, 1903, pp. 83–85.
79 Frazier, *The Negro Church in America*, p. 53.
80 Gunnar Myrdal, *An American Dilemma*, Harper, New York, 1944, p. 875.

81 Fifteenth Census of the United States: 1930, *Population,* vol. IV, pp. 32–33.
82 Hamilton, op. cit., pp. 208–213.
83 Drake and Cayton, op. cit., pp. 419–429.
84 Ofari, op. cit., pp. 50–51.
85 Calvin Hernton, *Coming Together,* Random House, New York, 1971, pp. 17–19.
86 Washington, op. cit., 37–38.
87 Ronald L. Johnstone, "Negro Preachers Take Sides," *Review of Religious Research,* vol. 11, pp. 81–89, Fall 1969.
88 Scanzoni, op. cit., pp. 117–120.
89 Hamilton, op. cit., pp. 32–36.
90 Hollis Lynch, *Edward Wilmot Blyden: Pan-Negro Patriot 1832–1912,* Oxford, New York, 1970.
91 Andrew Billingsley, "Edward Blyden: Apostle of Blackness," *The Black Scholar,* vol. 2, pp. 3–12, December 1970.
92 August Meier, "On the Role of Martin Luther King," *New Politics,* vol. 4, pp. 52–59, Winter 1965.
93 Robert Staples, "Ghetto Rebellions and the Colonial Revolution," *The CORElator,* vol. 5, pp. 2–4, September 1967.
94 Hamilton, op. cit., pp. 111–112.

SUGGESTED READING LIST

Cleage, Albert B.: *Black Christian Nationalism,* Morrow, New York, 1972.
Cleage, Albert B.: *The Black Messiah,* Sheed and Ward, New York, 1968.
Cone, James H.: *Black Theology and Black Power,* New York, Seabury, 1969.
Cone, James H.: *A Black Theology of Liberation,* Lippincott, Philadelphia, 1970.
Drake, St. Clair: *The Redemption of Africa and Black Religion,* Third World, Chicago, 1970.
Frazier, E. Franklin: *The Negro Church in America,* Schocken, New York, 1964.

Johnston, Ruby Funchess: *The Religion of Negro Protestants,* Philosophical Library, New York, 1956.

Mays, Benjamin E. and J. W. Nicholson: *The Negro's Church,* Institute of Social and Religious Research, New York, 1933.

Mbiti, John S.: *African Religions and Philosophy,* Praeger, New York, 1969.

Mitchell, Henry H.: *Black Preaching,* Lippincott, Philadelphia, 1970.

Nelsen, Hart M. et al. (eds.): *The Black Church in America,* Basic Books, New York, 1971.

Washington, Joseph R., Jr.: *Black Religion,* Beacon, Boston, 1964.

Wilmore, Gayraud S.: *Black Religion and Black Radicalism,* Doubleday, Garden City, N.Y., 1973.

Social Class
in Black America

In certain quarters it has long been contended that America is a classless society. Contemporary public opinion is that we have become largely a middle-class society, the first of its kind in history. But, the inequality of income that exists makes it clear that if we are all equal, some are obviously more equal than others. One school of sociology, functionalism, explains the stratification of people as a universal condition that exists in all societies. Individuals occupy different levels of prestige, power, and wealth, they say, because every society must motivate its members to fill the various positions that are essential for the production of goods and services and the functioning of its institutions.[1]

Few concepts in sociology are so abstract and complex, and yet so fundamental, as social class. By definition it refers to a stratum of people of similar social position.[2] When it comes to describing the composition of each stratum and its lifestyles, the task is difficult for a number of reasons. Among them is the fact that social class is an analytical concept that is neither (1) universally accepted in the social sciences, (2) conceived in precisely the same way by all students of social stratification, nor (3) commonly designated by the same label.[3]

This difficulty is magnified when attempting to describe the Black class structure. In fact, there is considerable doubt in some circles as to the existence of a Black class structure, especially vis-à-vis the White population. While there may be differences in income levels among Blacks, race is itself a status grouping—with all Whites holding a superior status and all Blacks regarded as inferior. Historically the status level of the two racial groups was regarded as a caste rather than a class system. In a caste society, people are divided into higher and lower castes according to the behavior expected of them.[4]

A number of social scientists have accepted and explained the elements of a racial caste system in the United States. Myrdal (1944) regarded Blacks as a lower caste in America since they were subject to certain disabilities solely because of their Blackness and not because of poverty and lack of education. His distinction between caste and class was that the caste system is closed and rigid while the class system is, in a sense, always open and mobile.[5] Cox (1959) explained that the primary function of the caste system was to stereotype existing conditions and to repress the desire of the individual to advance his own interests at the expense of, or in opposition to, those in his community.[6]

There may be less agreement today on whether a formal caste system exists in the United States. Recent events indicate that some Black mobility is allowed in this social structure. Moreover, there have always been differences in America's caste system and that of classical caste societies. The caste structure here had to be enforced by laws and the threat of force while it was maintained by tradition and sanctioned by religion in classical caste societies. In the United States the subordination of Blacks was opposed to the teachings of Christianity and the political ideology of the country.[7]

Before examining the significance and dynamics of class for Blacks, it will be useful to view class as seen through the three conceptual models used in earlier chapters.

THEORIES OF SOCIAL STRATIFICATION

Marxian Concept

This theory of stratification has been one of the leading sources of inspiration for sociological analysis in the area of social differentiation.

Basically, Marx (1932) saw all societies as divided into two groups: the oppressed and the oppressor. In modern industrialized countries these two groups are defined as the proletariat (the working class) and the bourgeoisie (owners of the means of production) with the petty bourgeoisie as a marginal group of small businessmen, farmers, professionals, etc. Other elements that define class membership such as self-concept, values, lifestyles, etc., are secondary to the Marxian point of view. One's class standing stems from his relationship to the means of production. You either own the factories, businesses, and banks or your labor is sold to those who do. If you do not see yourself as a member of the working classes (assuming you are an employee), that is simply what Marx labeled "false class consciousness."[8] Real class consciousness results when the workers take up loyalties to their own class and ignore the ruling class's definition of reality.

Domestic Colonialism

This model is similar to the Marxian concept in that it acknowledges the division of social systems into two types of classes: the exploited and the exploiter. However, it diverges from Marxist theory in its view that those two classes are based primarily on racial membership. The colonizer, who is White, will be the ruling class and most members of the colonized will be Black. A further differentiation in the colonial society is the selection of certain members of the colonized to serve as elites with certain privileges and functions under the colonial process. It is the allowance of limited mobility in colonial societies that creates a bourgeois elite out of the subordinate racial group, and this group has considerably different privileges and functions than the traditional bourgeoisie.[9]

In traditional stratified societies, the bourgeoisie played the role of accumulating and investing capital, developing industry and commerce to a higher level, and providing the society with a minimum share of prosperity. Under colonialism, the native middle class is created by the colonial ruling class to play the role of middleman in the exploitation of the natives. It shares the values of the colonial power structure and rejects the culture and lifestyles of its own people. At the same time its function is to act as an intermediary between the natives and the settler in order to serve as examples of "mobility" in colonial society and to ward off nationalist aspirations— or at least to channel those aspirations into controllable forms.[10]

Not all of the colonized elite serve their masters in the way desired. Among this group one also finds the colonized leaders in their liberation struggles. Hence, although some act as intermediaries between the natives and the settlers, others have become leaders, activists, and theorists in the movements for national liberation. Some of the more prominent members of the native elite who have employed their skills in the decolonization movement are Kwame Nkrumah, Sekou Toure, Stokeley Carmichael, etc.

While the native bourgeoisie is entitled to certain privileges and goals denied members of the working masses, they are still subject to restrictions placed generally on the entire group. Hence, upperclass Blacks are still treated the same as other Blacks in certain areas. There are many places they cannot live, places they are not accepted, and things they cannot do simply because they are Black. This is why, as Blauner (1972) explains, one cannot reduce race relations to class relations. Racism denies an individual's participation in society in markedly different ways than does class dominance and exploitation. In a racist, colonized society members of the racially subordinate group are dehumanized, their dignity violated, and personalities degraded in a much more all-encompassing way than class exploitation.[11]

Pan-Africanism

Since this model is based on the continuity of African cultural strands and a commonality of status resulting from racist oppression, it of necessity minimizes the significance of social class for people of African descent. The concept of Blacks as an African people means they share the African values of brotherhood, communalism, and cooperation. Robert Hill (1973) gives vent to this feeling when he states, "There is no difference in values between middle and lower-income Blacks. The class issue is phony." Since division of Blacks into socioeconomic groupings tends to highlight differences among Blacks rather than similarities, Hill declares that it is a divisive technique of the White ruling class.[12]

All three conceptual models contain some vital elements of the class issue for Blacks. Whether there is a Black stratification system or not, the question of class has considerable import for the Black population and should be examined. In this chapter we will find out that one cannot make absolute statements about Black social

class based on any one conceptual model. Obviously, there are differences in income, education, and occupations among Blacks and
these must inevitably affect their life chances and lifestyles. At the
same time we will discover that there are enough variations within
the same stratum of Blacks to discount many theories of Black value
differences. The most appropriate place to start is with a transcultural
view of Black status dynamics.

DEVELOPMENT OF THE BLACK CLASS STRUCTURE

Regardless of the functionalist position that social classes are universal,
there was little stratification of people in precolonial Africa. In that
society land was held in common, goods were shared, and everybody
was a worker. The individual always had a certain measure of security
because he could depend on the wealth of the community in which
he was a member. African society was organized along what Marx
labeled "primitive communism lines." The individual contributed what
he could and received what he needed. The elderly, ill, widows,
and orphans were all cared for under African communalism. Landlords and capitalists were virtually unknown in most African societies
until the arrival of the European. The idea of class or caste did not
exist in African society.[13]

In transition from Africa to the New World, Afro-Americans remained a homogenous status grouping. During the era of slavery, all
bondsmen were Black, deprived, and powerless while Whiteness was
correlated with freedom, power, and privilege. Even under slavery,
however, social differentiation began to appear. The slaveholders
started to create a ranking of slaves by assigning them specialized
tasks for the sake of economic efficiency and by isolating domestics
and artisans from the field hands as a control technique.[14] Forsythe
(1973) explains that general social, economic, and political changes
of that era brought about a class society within the ranks of the slave
population. The emerging capitalism of that epoch could not develop
to its fullest without the assistance of class division among Blacks. He
states that the rigidity of a society based on racial caste was too inflexible to be adaptive to the needs of economic exploitation. Slavery
had experienced many problems with physically coerced labor and
needed the cooperation of its workers. Thus, the divide-and-rule
tactics.[15]

There is some question about the effectiveness of the divide-and-conquer strategy. Although house slaves enjoyed certain advantages by living in the slavemaster's household, Stampp (1956) reports that slaves showed remarkable loyalty toward one another. It was the exception and not the rule for a slave to betray a fellow slave. To betray Black people to White people was a serious offense in their eyes and such a person became an object of social ostracism. A spirit of cooperation was more common among the bondsmen. When a newly purchased slave was sent to the slave quarters, he was immediately initiated into the secrets of the group. For example, he was told what he had to do to avoid the lash.[16] According to Murray (1970), there were Judases as well as snobs among the house slaves but as a general rule they brought infinitely more tactical information from the big house to the slave quarters than any information they ever took back.[17]

After slavery the spirit of African communalism and cooperation survived in the form of Black fraternal orders and benefit associations. A number of these organizations sprung up to aid widows and orphans of deceased members, furnish opportunities for social intercourse, provide insurance against sickness and death, etc.[18] This cooperative effort by former slaves prompted one newspaper editor to write in 1898:

> Compared with modern civilized groups, the organization of action among American Negroes is extremely simple . . . and yet there are among them 23,000 churches, with unusually wide activities and spending annually at least $10,000,000. There are thousands of secret societies with their insurance and social features, large numbers of beneficial societies. . . . There is the slowly expanding seed of cooperative business efforts. . . . Finally there are the slowly evolving organs by which the group seeks to stop and minimize the anti-social deeds and accidents of its members. This is a picture of all human striving—unusually simple—but strikingly human and worth further study and attention.[19]

The social differentiation of the Black population continued to evolve in the postslavery era. At the end of slavery approximately one-tenth of the Black population were free persons already. Among this group, the upper class consisted of families that held considerable property and could claim aristocratic White ancestry or descent from a free ancestor. Unskilled free Blacks with a small income composed the lower class and a large group of artisans with moderate incomes and a stable family life made up the middle class. In many instances, this group was hostile to the newly freed slaves. Many of them derived their income from providing services only to Whites—and denying them to Blacks. Thus, some Black barbers cut only White men's hair and some Black caterers catered only for Whites.[20]

This group was fairly small in numbers and remained so for years. Until recently most Blacks were concentrated in the South and that region had only a small number of professional and clerical workers.[21] In such a situation it seems more appropriate to call these workers colonial elites since they were all still subordinate to Whites of every social class. It was mainly in the North that a more complex form of stratification among Blacks emerged. To understand the nature of this social differentiation of the Afro-American population, we must examine the relationship between class and race (see Table 7-1).

CLASS AND RACE

Although numerous theories exist on the meaning of social class, the most prominent is that of W. Lloyd Warner and Paul Lunt (1942) who defined class as: "Two or more orders of people who are believed to be and are accordingly ranked by the members of the community in socially superior and inferior positions."[22] As a prerequisite to belonging to a particular social class, one must gain acceptance as an equal by those who belong in the class. One must not only be accepted by other members of that class but must participate in such informal activities as visiting, dancing, receptions, teas, and larger informal affairs.[23]

Using the criteria of acceptance and participation automatically places almost all Blacks at the bottom. However, class standing is also based upon the following four criteria: income, education, occupation, and family background.[24] Employing these criteria we can make some kind of comparison and try to fit Blacks into the typology of Warner et al.

Table 7-1 A Comparison of Black and White Class Indexes

	Whites	Blacks
Income	Most important determinant of status. Inherited wealth gives one greater esteem. Inequality of incomes allows greater privilege and status to those who have large amounts of money.	Significant in influencing life chances and lifestyles. It is not a prerequisite for either acceptance or participation in most social circles. Differences in income are not great within the Black group.
Education	Seems to be most significant only in obtaining high-paying professional positions. Those with highest levels of education do not receive highest income. Even in lower class unionized workers earn more than white-collar employees.	Close correlation between status and educational level. Highly educated persons have most esteem because of value placed on education. The largest number of Blacks in high-paying jobs are also the most educated, e.g., doctors, lawyers.
Occupation	Occupations have a prestige of their own, apart from the income and educational factors associated with them. It is probably the best indicator of class values and lifestyles. Although certain jobs may pay high salaries, they can be low in prestige, e.g., plumbers, electricians. Others may be high in prestige but low in income, e.g., college professors.	An important factor in status. It is very closely associated with one's education and income. Occupational diversity was very low until recent years with teachers and doctors being the most numerous and prestigious status grouping. Education was usually the only route to social mobility and entry into those positions.
Family Background	Higher status is derived from coming from an old, established family of means. It mainly serves to divide members of the upper class from newly arrived persons with newly obtained wealth. Individuals in the old upper class receive a higher status because their longer tenure in that group has allowed them to acquire the culture and formal manners of the upper class.	Of little importance to most Blacks, who share a similar background of slave ancestry. The massive amount of race-mixing makes tracing descent a very hard task. Among Blacks who were free before emancipation family ancestry has greater significance. This factor has little effect on determining status in the wider community since no Blacks are of aristocratic stock.

The Black class structure, in the typology of Warner et al., is pyramidal, with a large lower class, a small middle class, and a negligible upper class. The White class pattern is diamond-shaped with small lower and upper classes and a large middle class.

Table 7-2   Median Income of Black Families as a Percent of White Median Family Income, 1964–1971

Year	%
1964	54
1965	54
1966	58
1967	59
1968	60
1969	61
1970	61
1971	60

Source: U.S. Bureau of the Census, The Social and Economic Status of the Black Population in the United States, 1971, p. 29.

To understand exactly how Blacks fit into the general class pattern we need to examine the three most reliable indexes of class standing: education, employment, and income. In a comparison of the median income of Blacks with Whites, one notes a slow but steady narrowing of the income gap between the two races. Between 1964 and 1970 the differential narrowed from Blacks' earning 54 percent of the income of Whites to 61 percent. However, after 1970 the gap began to widen again as Blacks slipped back to earning only 60 percent of White income in 1971. The average difference in Black and White incomes in 1971 was over $4,000.[25]

The differential in income is even greater because these figures do not weigh the fact that many more Black families (two-thirds) derive their family income from multiple earners than White households (one-half). The income gap between Black and White families with the husband as sole breadwinner did not significantly close in the last decade. In fact when both the Black husband's and working wife's annual income were added, the total amounted to only $23 more than that earned by a White male head of household whose wife was not employed.[26]

Education and occupation make little difference in the income gap between Blacks and Whites. Educationally, for example, the proportion of Blacks graduating from high school and college increased slightly but it made little impact on the income gap.[27] Indeed, the relative income gap between Blacks and Whites increases with education. When Siegel (1965) computed the estimated lifetime income of Blacks as a percentage of White estimated lifetime income at three educational levels, he found the Black elementary school graduate would earn 64 percent of his White peer's lifetime income, but the Black college graduate's lifetime earnings would be only 50 percent of his White counterpart's lifetime income.[28] Hence, highly educated Blacks suffer the brunt of income discrimination more intensely than those with less education. A probable reason for this disparity is that high-status jobs more likely require certain social skills and friendship and family ties than lower-paying positions. In a society in which they are social outcasts, higher-educated Blacks do not possess the social skills or kinship networks to gain entry to many positions reserved for Whites.

Much of this racial difference in income, moreover, is due to sheer economic exploitation on the basis of race. Differences in Black and White incomes occur even within the same occupation. The 1970 census reveals that Blacks still earn less than Whites for comparable work. Although White professional and managerial workers earned $13,726 in 1972, Blacks in the same occupational category only received $9,467. Among craftsmen, foremen, and kindred workers, the White income was $10,553, the Black salary was $8,488.[29] Furthermore, at the current rate of progress, Whites will continue to monopolize white-collar jobs while Blacks are disproportionately located in low-paying manual occupations. Purcell and Cavanagh (1972) estimate that it will take 70.2 years before the percentage of Blacks in sales jobs reach parity with Whites and 86.7 years before the professionals catch up.[30]

Over the past forty years, the rate of unemployment among Blacks has been steadily twice that of Whites. In 1973 Black unemployment was at its highest level since 1961. Overall, 10 percent of Blacks were officially unemployed in 1973 compared with 5 percent for Whites. The proportion of Blacks living in poverty (income of under $4,275 for a family of four) has increased while White poverty has declined sharply.[31] In 1972 over a third of the Black population was poverty stricken compared with 9 percent for Whites. All these figures indicate a trend toward concentrating more Blacks in the low-income stratum while making almost all White Americans middle class.

If income and educational levels are used to compute class standing, approximately 28 percent of Black families would fall in the middle class (those families earning over $10,000 annually), the majority of them in the lower middle class. Another 70 percent would be in the lower-class category with the remainder (2 percent) slightly above the middle class. Over 50 percent of Blacks, twenty-five to twenty-nine years old, have completed high school in 1971. About 20 percent of young Blacks are currently enrolled in college. At the same time a considerably larger number of Blacks do not finish high school and the college completion rates of Whites under 35 years of age is four times that of Blacks.[32]

THE BLACK CLASS STRUCTURE

In 1973 a pair of authors created a mild furor when they published an article which claimed that the economic picture for Afro-Americans is clearly improving and that 52 percent of Black Americans can properly be classified today as middle class. According to Wattenberg and Scammon (1973), a substantial number of Black families outside the South under age thirty-five have achieved income parity with Whites similarly situated. In those families where the wife also is employed, income equality has been achieved and even surpassed. Furthermore, they accused White liberals and Black leaders of a conspiracy to hide the fact that the liberal legislative policies of the sixties have succeeded in elevating the relative economic status of Black people.[33]

As we have already demonstrated, a tiny number of Blacks have achieved something resembling income equality with Whites but 90 percent of all Black families still lag behind.[34] In terms of the real Black class structure, Munford (1972) gives us one of the most accurate typologies.[35] They are:

1 *Service Stratum.* This category is composed of less than 10 percent of the Black population. It consists of two different groups: the professionals and entrepreneurs. They are labeled a service group because their primary function is to provide or sell services. The professionals have traditionally been comprised of teachers, doctors, lawyers, ministers, entertainers, athletes, etc. Although their range of income is fairly large, they constitute the nearest thing to an upper class in Black America. Most of them will have similar lifestyles, associate with one another and marry within this group. There will be some differences in their numbers and lifestyles depending on the region of the country in which they live and the size of the area in which they reside.[36]

The business sector of this group counts among its members those Blacks engaged in service enterprises such as banking, insurance, publishing, and entertainment. Not only are they small in numbers but their influence in the business world is minimal. They represent less than 3 percent of the nation's total businesses and their combined assets are less than one-half of 1 percent of the assets of the Bank of America. When counted together the $195 million in 1972 total sales of all the Black enterprises did not match the $203 million in sales achieved by one White corporation ranked five-hundredth by *Fortune* magazine.[37]

2 *Middle-Income Families.* These are families characterized by regular employment in a community besieged by joblessness. They will be found in jobs in the post office and other governmental positions that provide job security if not high wages. In the private sector, they will hold recently obtained positions as clerks, banktellers, secretaries, telephone and telegraph workers, etc. It is worth noting here the large proportion of Blacks employed in jobs in government agencies. In 1969 the percentage of Blacks employed in the public sector was 26.0 compared with 28.1 for Whites.[38] Since this sector accounts for the largest source of white-collar jobs for Blacks, the small difference between Blacks and Whites is quite significant. Blacks have gravitated toward the public sector since they face less discrimination there because of their voting strength, and the use of civil service tests

reduces the opportunity for Whites to use kinship and friendship ties to gain jobs at the expense of Blacks.[39]

While some members of this class have come under attack for being devoted to petty bourgeois social values and moral prescriptions borrowed from White, Protestant, lower-middle-class Anglo-Saxons,[40] St. Clair Drake's (1967) description rather accurately fits the majority of them. According to him: "What sociologists call the Negro Middle class is merely a collection of people who have similar life styles and aspirations, whose basic goals are living well, being respectable and not being crude. Middle-class Negroes, by-and-large, are not concerned about mobility into the Negro upper class or integration with Whites. They want their rights and good jobs as well as enough money to get those goods and services which make life comfortable."[41]

3 *The Proletariat.* Among its members are those Blacks employed in factories and skilled crafts. Most of them are employed in heavy industry, for example, automobile factories, electronics and aircraft industries, etc. Although they will often make more money than the two higher classes, they are subject to seasonal employment and periodic layoffs in the fragile American economy. They are even more vulnerable than White workers because they are commonly the last hired and first fired in these jobs. The same is true of those few Blacks allowed entry into craft unions. Any downturn in housing construction, for instance, will automatically eliminate most of the Black work force since they were permitted into these unions only in recent times. The proletariat is estimated as comprising 45 to 68 percent of the Black population, depending on the definitions used to assign workers to this group.

4 *Lumpenproletariat* (or under class). These are Blacks who are chronically unemployed and who shift from one section of the community to another. They are high school dropouts, transients, the unskilled, and emigrants from the South. A large proportion are young Afro-Americans who suffer high unemployment rates, have prison records, and possess few skills that are marketable in the industrial world.

This group has always been seen as the dregs of society. Even Marx (1909) saw them as a marginal, fringe group operating outside the moral boundaries of capitalist society.[42] In colonial society, however, this group is seen as the main revolutionary force because it has nothing to lose. The members of this stratum exist in a chaotic and unorganized environment and are characterized by disorganization, violence, gambling, drinking, use of narcotics, and marital and family instability.[43] In Marxian terms they exist because they constitute an industrial reserve army in the event of economic expansion. Thus, capitalism maintains this class element at the lowest level of subsistence to be used when its industries require additional workers. At the same time they provide competition to the proletariat by seeking their jobs and hence depressing wages in certain industries. Since they are not maintained at levels sufficient to support families, they are inclined toward sexual permissiveness and marital breakup because they cannot carry the responsibility of supporting families.[44]

5 *Rural Peasants.* A largely neglected group, the rural peasants exist in significant numbers in the South where they work as sharecroppers, small farmers, and domestic servants. Though smaller in number than the other classes, they comprise a significant class of Blacks because they are subjected to a superexploitation and supply many of the members of the lumpenproletariat in the cities. Over fifty years ago the majority of Blacks were located in this class. The mechanization of agriculture and better opportunities in the city led most of them to migrate to urban areas where they became a part of the landless proletariat.[45]

In societies that meet the classical definition of a colonial order, this class is regarded as the most revolutionary segment of the working classes.[46] In industrial America, however, the lumpenproletariat must carry out this historical role. Due to their isolation from the social, economic, and political events taking place the rural peasants do not have the level of political consciousness or potential to make an effective challenge to the prevailing colonial order. The mechanization of agriculture makes them a dispensable class in a technological society. Those who work as servants simply do not have the power or resources to paralyze an industrial society by withdrawal of their services or taking control of the essential means of production.

CLASS SIMILARITIES AND VARIATIONS

Lifestyle differences by class are usually a function of three factors: (1) values that are expressed in a preference for one lifestyle or another, (2) economic means that limit or maximize the ability of individuals to indulge in certain activities or possess desired goals, and (3) awareness of alternative forms of behaving and more effective techniques of doing something. Listed here are some Black lifestyles with variations highlighted by virtue of their greater interest to the social scientist.

Aspiration Values

Regardless of their status level, most Blacks have high levels of educational aspiration. Sometimes their aspirations are so high as to be unrealistic. A recent study found that Blacks generally possessed high aspirations for the type of educational level they hoped to reach but relatively low occupational goals.[47] These high educational goals are demonstrated in the number of Blacks attending college who come from low-income families. Over 75 percent of the Blacks enrolled in college are from families in which the head had no college education.[48]

Consumption Patterns

Available studies indicate some class differences in consumer behavior. Blacks consume more liquor than Whites and Scotch whisky is their favorite alcoholic beverage, especially among the middle class, because it is considered a status drink.[49] The lower-class group makes fewer purchases of magazines and professional journals than the middle-income group. Blacks in general spend a larger proportion of their income on clothing and cars than Whites.[50]

Marriage and Family Patterns

The lack of research on middle-class Black families does not provide much data for this comparison. Dating and premarital sexual behavior begin earlier for lower-income Black females, but the differences in Black sexual behavior are not that great. Upwardly mobile Black women engage in a more conservative form of sexual behavior because a premarital pregnancy can mean dropping out of school and ruining one's chances of gaining entrance into the middle class. If the middle-class Black female becomes pregnant before marriage there is a greater likelihood of her obtaining an abortion than her lower-income sister. Middle-class marriages are less frequently dissolved by divorce or separation and there are fewer women who head households.[51]

A significant class difference is the number of children born to middle-income and lower-income Black families. Lower-class Black women have one of the largest birth rates while Black middle-class women have the lowest. Again, this differential reflects pragmatic choices rather than differences in values. Children are strongly regarded as a positive value by middle-class Black families but many perceive a very direct link between large families and low incomes. Black women also need to stay in the labor force in order to maintain their middle-class status. Moreover, higher education makes Black middle-class women more aware of, and effective in using, birth control.[52]

Political Behavior

This is the area of greatest similarity among Blacks. They register and vote in about the same number. Middle-class Blacks participate more in civic and political organizations. One study shows that Blacks of all social classes are closer to one another in their political orientation than they are to Whites of comparable incomes and education.[53] Only a small proportion of Blacks are registered, or vote for, Republicans. A class difference does exist in that lower-class Blacks more often vote a straight Democratic ticket while middle-class Blacks occasionally split their tickets. Lower-income Blacks are more commonly registered Democrats while middle-class Blacks tend to register as Independents.[54]

Hamilton (1973) claims that this class collaboration in politics occurs because the Black middle class consists of salaried employees in government employment, and their job interests determine the sort of position they will take on certain public policy issues. The interests of the middle class, he declares, are politically compatible with those of the lower class because the Black middle class is based in the public sector rather than the private, profit-oriented sector of the economy as is the White middle-class.[55] Hence, the critical variable in political behavior is race, which is particularly relevant since so many White politicians campaign for votes on the basis of subtle racist slogans such as law and order or antibusing.

Recreation and Entertainment

Since the elimination of racial barriers to public facilities, there are probably greater class differences in this area. A number of middle-class Blacks have the same recreational outlets as their White counterparts: bridge, social clubs, golf, water sports, skiing, fishing, and hunting.[56] Because of less income the lower class has a more limited

social life and spends its leisure time visiting friends, going to bars
and movies, watching television, etc. In Washington, D.C. the non-
professional working-class Blacks go to cabarets and go-gos while the
professionals prefer cocktail parties and nightclubs.[57] There are some
class differences in musical tastes with middle-class Blacks preferring
jazz and classical music over rhythm and blues and gospel. Middle-
income Blacks also attend the legitimate theater, lectures, and museums
more often than lower-income groups.[58]

Religion

Blacks have a very similar religious origin. Almost all of them were
originally Baptists or Methodists. However, when they change religious affiliation it is usually to a higher-status religion. Kronus (1971)
found that middle-income Blacks were more likely to have changed
their religious affiliation and usually to a higher-status denomination.
Middle-class Blacks had a much higher frequency of Catholic affiliation (high status) and a much lower frequency of Baptist affiliation
(low status).[59]

Even when both groups are in the same religion, they are organized along different lines. In the lower classes there are more
storefront churches with preachers, some semiliterate, who conduct
a very emotional sermon which exhorts the members to "be in the
world but not of it."[60] The middle-class church is more sedate, with
a college-trained minister, who gives a sober message to the congregation. Its service is more subdued compared with the very expressive
and emotion-laden atmosphere of the lower-class church.

Residence and Associations

Among Blacks owning one's own home is a commonly shared value.
Hence, the type and location of their homes are very important.
Having decent furniture is a strong value.[61] Also, the Black community is physically separated by class. Middle-class Blacks rarely
live in the same neighborhoods as the lower class and usually do not
want to. In recent years there has been a trend toward moving to
the suburbs. During the sixties the Black percentage increase in the
suburbs was slightly larger than the White—29 compared with 27.5—
although the numerical increase was smaller, 820,000 to 15.3 million.[62]

Most of this growth took place in areas adjacent to the Black ghetto or in locations where there was already a concentration of Blacks. Only about 12 percent of Blacks who moved to the suburbs actually found themselves in racially integrated environments. Moreover, they pay much higher prices than Whites for comparable housing in suburban settings.[63]

Moving to the suburbs was not an attempt to get away from other Blacks. When Bethel (1972) asked her subjects what factors influenced their movement to the suburbs, they gave the following reasons: availability of housing, price of housing, proximity to work, safety, amenities, better housing, better schools, lack of congestion, and other public services. The key reason here is probably safety, as middle-class Black families fled the central city to escape the spiraling crime rate in that environment. As suburbanites they continued to orient their lives around the city itself and retained their friends still in the city and most of their social and business activities as well.[64]

When we look at friendship cliques, we find that more middle-class Blacks have interracial contacts outside work than their lower-class counterparts. Kronus (1971) discovered, however, that only 15 percent of his middle-class Black sample had any meaningful contact with Whites outside the sphere of work.[65] Ethnic preference studies show that Blacks preferred to associate primarily with Blacks of their own social class.[66] It was not so much the economic means of individuals with which they were concerned but class traits such as being well-mannered, highly rated, interested in the future, and always on the job. The class traits they disliked were: being loud, rowdy, or disrespectful and getting one into trouble. In particular they wanted to avoid drug addicts, criminals, alcoholics, and those persons who draw trouble at any place and time.[67]

Self-Conception

Self-conception refers to the individual's subjective definition of his class location. In this regard self-reporting may not be that reliable a measure of class identification. Ione Vargas (1973) has observed that Black professionals have been so castigated for being middle class that many of them state that they are not middle class. On the other hand, she says, some Blacks living in poverty are so in fear of being called culturally deprived and disadvantaged they quickly label themselves middle class.[68]

For a number of reasons, Blacks have a higher level of class consciousness than other groups in the United States. Even those who would objectively fall into the middle class act in strong defense of the working class and call for a society free of class exploitation. When Leggett (1964) studied class consciousness among White and Black workers, he found considerable variations within the two groups. Blacks were twice as likely to express high class consciousness as Whites. He concluded that Black workers, because of both their racially reinforced class consciousness and their greater vulnerability to unemployment, can be expected to be in the vanguard of any class conflict.[69]

Skin Color

Color was traditionally a badge of status among Blacks for several reasons. Lighter skin color carried higher status because of its proximity to the skin pigmentation of the dominant racial group. Many Blacks in the middle class were fairskinned since they were the illegitimate children of a mixed racial union. The White parent (usually the father) would see that they received certain educational advantages not as available to Blacks of a darker hue. Even mulatto women of the lower class had easier access to the middle class because of their skin color. For the longest time light skin pigmentation was regarded as an important requirement for marriage in the middle class. A man who had achieved success in his occupation and had a good income would marry a fairskinned woman in order to consolidate his social status.[70]

These middle-class Blacks had internalized the values of the dominant racial group. Pettigrew (1966) and his colleagues found that not only were middle-class Black males married to an unusually high number of mulatto women but they were also more inclined to hold favorable attitudes toward Whites and to be politically conservative.[71] In the recent past whole Black societies were divided along skin color lines. Some universities admitted only fairskinned females, clubs and churches consisted exclusively of fairskinned Blacks, and some employment opportunities were made available solely to this group.[72] Most of this status division by skin color is now a relic of the past.

Work Orientation

This trait illustrates that Blacks have a greater commonality of interests than differences. Cutting across class lines, one finds a strong belief in hard work and education. One study found that even poor Black youth who have grown up in welfare families have a more positive attitude toward the desirability and necessity of work than children of the White middle class.[73] Another researcher discovered that a slightly larger number of Black workers expressed a desire to take a job as a car washer rather than go on welfare, even if the pay for the two sources of income was the same.[74] At the same time Blacks are twice as likely as Whites to be very dissatisfied with their work.[75]

Two examples of variations within the lower class are cited by McQueen (1971) and Edwards (1968). McQueen identified two types of Black families: very poor and those just above the poverty level. Between these two groups he found significant differences in planning and thriftiness, providing security and protection for the future, quest for respectability, self-reliance, and mobility aspirations. The group just above poverty scored higher on all these dimensions and was characterized by a strong Protestant ethic orientation.[76]

Edwards (1968) studied a group of 28 Black families, half of whom were Christians, and half belonging to the Black Muslims. Although all these families lived in the same ghetto the Muslim families were typically middle class in their behavior. The Muslim father worked hard, sometimes at two jobs, attended church faithfully, and was the ultimate authority in his family. Muslim wives left all wage earning and decision making to their husbands. The children were expected to be well-behaved and to work hard at school. Drinking or smoking was not allowed in their homes, nor was profane language spoken at any time. Marital quarrels were avoided or at least did not involve physical violence. In general, the Christian couples had opposite patterns.[77]

These two cases illustrate the wide variations *within* classes as well as *between* classes. The division of Blacks into different class strata on the basis of a minor difference in income obscures the dependent relationship they all have to the colonial ruling class, a relationship that controls all facets of their lives and permeates their institutional structures. Moving from an annual income of $5,000 to $10,000 does not change their access to political power or to the economic resources of the colonial power structure. Changing their sexual habits or cultural tastes will do nothing to alter the basic relationship they have to a White-dominated society, nor will it reallocate the unequal distribution of wealth or life chances.

FUNCTIONS OF CLASS DIVISIONS

In the foregoing discussion we have demonstrated that the issue of class is secondary to a group whose standing and treatment are determined by their racial membership and who essentially constitute one class—the oppressed. However, in a colonial society, the assignment of different class levels to the Black population serves some very useful functions, hence the class perspective is likely to be pushed. Class divisions create and maintain Black factionalism along class lines and foster disunity in a group that is systematically exploited by the colonial ruling class. Individuals who subjectively set themselves apart from other Blacks because of a belief that they have antagonistic class interests weaken the Black community's ability to forge a group unity to combat the exploitation to which all Blacks are subjected.

Class division is an age-old technique of ruling classes to create distinctions within the oppressed groups in order to weaken their ability to resist colonial rule. Chrisman (1970) notes that this cultural strategy of the Anglo-American state is one of the main reasons it maintains its dominance. The two principles of this strategy are: (1) always maintain divisions between classes and races and (2) always offer assimilation of classes and races. The technique of playing off race interests against class interests has the effect of preventing different races from uniting in a struggle along class lines. And, it retards a struggle along racial lines because of class conflict within the Black community, which turns the Black bourgeoisie, the proletariat, and the lumpenproletariat against one another.[78]

Indications are that this strategy has had mixed success. The radicalization of Black college students has brought about one of the closest collaborations between the Black bourgeoisie and the lumpenproletariat ever witnessed.[79] At the same time the cooptation of Black elites through token concessions such as Black capitalism programs, antipoverty posts, and financial payoffs is at its highest level ever. An obvious break in Black unity occurred in 1972 when a number of prominent and well-respected Black leaders endorsed a presidential candidate whose administration was labeled by the NAACP as being anti-Black.

Some years ago Dubois (1952) predicted that as discrimination based on race subsided, class would become more important in determining Black attitudes toward labor, wealth, and work.[80] As in classical colonized societies, the decolonization process allows native elites to rule directly the same system as previously existed under colonial rule. In sociological terms this means a shift from a racist caste system to a class system. The substance of exploitation remains the same but the oppressor is a member of the same racial group. Although Black elites may someday control the institutions of the Black community, the chances are that they will still identify with and serve the interests of the colonial ruling class.[81]

These colonial elites constitute a small minority of the Black population and should not be confused with most Blacks regarded as middle class. Proctor (1971) puts it quite well in his statement that "the gap that is alleged to exist between the Black masses and the bourgeoisie is largely a myth and a lazy description of a complicated phenomenon." Most of the Black middle class, he notes, are first-generation arrivals from city slums and only a bachelor's degree away from squalor and welfare. Very few Black families are deeply entrenched in the middle class and in many cases the wife's employment is the only thing that keeps them out of poverty.[82]

Because some Blacks are poor does not mean they fail to share the same values and aspirations as other, more advantaged Blacks. Hylan Lewis (1967) points out that the behavior of the majority of poor Black families is a pragmatic adjustment to the external and internal stresses and deprivations they are subject to in the quest for essentially common values. He believes it would be more productive to conceive of different types of Black families as responding in different ways to the facts of their position and to relative isolation rather than to the requirements of a lower-class culture.[83] In other words the poor, too, aspire to have an education, live in comfortable and decent housing, and be safe from crime and other problems of poverty. But in a colonized society, only limited mobility is permitted for colonials and the rest must make the best of what they have.

THE FUTURE OF BLACK SOCIAL CLASSES

In predicting the future development of Black class stratification it is necessary to look at two parallel trends. One is the continued movement of some Blacks into the middle class and the division of this group into two different substrata: those who align themselves with the Black masses and identify with their struggle for liberation and the neocolonial elites who will accept the values of the ruling class and serve its interests by serving as intermediaries between the oppressor and the oppressed. The other trend is the enlargement of the lumpenproletariat, which perpetuates a pyramdial class structure and which may encourage class antagonisms in the Black community. Somewhere in the middle will be the bulk of Black working people who may identify with the struggle of either group—one for neocolonial control in the form of Black dominance in community businesses and politics—the other group working to destroy the structure of class and racial exploitation. Unlike the past, this group may take an important leadership role in the future.

The most inevitable trend in Black class patterns is the growth of the lumpenproletariat. In a society undergoing its greatest growth in skills, the largely unskilled Black underclass may become an army of the permanently employed. The ascendancy of automation and cybernation, where machines do the work of men, reduces the need for labor in all sectors but the fringe areas. Yet the movement of Black peasants from the rural South will continue to bring in large numbers of unskilled people to whom the only jobs available will be as cooks, servants, or waitresses for affluent Whites.[84]

Even in these menial jobs Blacks can face serious competition from unskilled Whites who may become surplus labor as a result of automation and cybernation. History shows that Whites are content to leave low-status jobs to Blacks in relative periods of economic prosperity but invoke their racial privilege to enter those Black employment areas when in strong need of work.[85] Already, the unemployment rate for Black youth is as high as 65 percent in certain inner city areas. Some Blacks are permanently dropping out of the work force because of their inability to find jobs. For example, between 1960 and 1972, the Black male labor force participation rate—those working and those unemployed but still applying for work—has declined from 83 to 73 percent.[86]

Perhaps the most significant change has taken place in the radicalized Black middle class. As one observer wrote, "A new militant Black middle-class is developing in the United States. It is very different from the old Black bourgeoisie—it is a class that views its destiny as being tied directly to the destiny of the poor."[87] This is evidenced in the positions of Black professional organizations that differ radically from their White counterparts. Black medical associations have endorsed a national health care system, Black teachers have called for community control of schools, and Black psychologists have opposed the use of IQ tests for school placement.[88]

An equally significant change has occurred in the lifestyle of the Black bourgeoisie. Ladner (1973) mentions the example of a Black doctor who values art and classical music but also participates in cabarets, enjoys gospel music, and the annual New Year's Day ritual of eating chitterlings.[89] Among Los Angeles's Black elite, Blacks are increasingly being judged on how they relate to or identify with the problems of the ghetto. In the social world of the Black bourgeoisie, there is more of an emphasis on fund raising, a greater obligation to contribute financially to Black causes. One socialite comments that "if you aren't contributing financially to the cause you haven't arrived socially." The wife of a Black millionaire remarked, "I feel a personal commitment with my brother in the ghetto."[90]

While the Black bourgeoisie may be committed to Black causes, this does not mean they want to live in the ghetto. The neighborhoods of the underclass remain a repository of all the problems, crime, violence, drugs, which internal colonialism has created and maintained. It has become a no-man's land where no one wants to go for any legitimate purpose, and it has been abandoned to whatever uses the dispossessed may want to put it.[91] The Black middle class exists in a very fragile world and guards its hard-fought gains jealously and thus erects a defense against the erosion of its achievements. Moreover, since it exists on the fringe of the middle class it does not have the resources to solve the problems of the Black underclass.

There are suggestions about what efforts the Black middle class can make to expedite Black liberation. Lerone Bennett (1973) lists the following: (1) define and maintain a communitywide policy leading to Black control of the resources and culture of the Black community, (2) seize control of the structures that define and control Black people, and (3) assume responsibility for the financial support of Black institutions and movements.[98] Others have demanded that the Black bourgeoisie must commit suicide as a class. This act of class suicide means that they must be willing to set aside personal gain and join in the priorities of the Black poor, the unemployed, and the workers.[94]

A few limited attempts have been made to cut across class lines in the Black community. In Tanzania, for example, the concept of Ujamaa (i.e., familyhood) is being put into practice. Within the Ujamaa village individuals live and work as extended family units. They are jointly organized as cooperative farms by the government and citizens groups.[95] In the United States a new value system has been proposed by Leroi Jones (1969) for Afro-Americans. He has defined this new value system as based on seven principles, among them unity, collective work and responsibility, self-determination, cooperative economics, purpose, creativity, and faith.[96]

The question must be asked whether Blacks can develop an equalitarian subsystem in a society so overwhelmingly structured on class inequality. Most likely the answer is negative. A more probable development is the emergence of a class of Black petty bourgeoisie who will undertake the exploitation of the Black masses that is now done directly by the White colonial power structure. Hence, we shall witness larger numbers of Blacks being elected to public office, programs created to develop a Black capitalist class, and Black functionaries replacing Whites in the role of colonial mediating positions such as teachers, social workers, policemen, etc.[97]

One of the solutions left for us to address is the possible unity of working class Whites and Blacks. At this point in time it is difficult to foresee this event taking place. It would require the White worker to give up his racial privileges for a united class struggle and there is no indication that he is willing to make that sacrifice. Because Blacks are increasingly becoming the lumpenproletariat, Whites are rapidly being assimilated into the middle class. They have experienced a much larger entry into white-collar jobs than the total increase in the total work force. As we have already noted, the number of Whites in poverty is declining sharply while Blacks increased their numbers in this category. Given these factors and alternatives, we will continue to live in a class- and race-divided society until the contradictions of monopoly capitalism make themselves felt.

NOTES

1 Kingsley Davis and Wilbert E. Moore, "Some Principles of Stratification," *American Sociological Review,* vol. 10, pp. 242–249, April 1945.
2 Paul B. Horton and Chester L. Hunt, *Sociology,* McGraw-Hill, New York, 1964, p. 261.
3 Harold Hodges, *Social Stratification,* Schenkman, Cambridge, Mass., 1964, pp. 12–13.
4 John Dollard, *Caste and Class in a Southern Town,* Yale, New Haven, Conn., 1937, p. 62.
5 Gunnar Myrdal, *An American Dilemma,* Harpers, New York, 1944, p. 669.
6 Oliver Cox, *Caste, Class and Race,* Monthly Review, New York, 1959, pp. 299–302.
7 Gerald Berreman, "Caste in India and the United States," *American Journal of Sociology,* vol. 66, pp. 120–127, September 1960.
8 Karl Marx and Frederich Engels, *The German Ideology,* International, New York, 1930, pp. 48–49.
9 Frantz Fanon, *The Wretched of the Earth,* Crone, New York, 1963, pp. 35–39. The term bourgeoisie, or middle class, refers to having a slightly higher position than the masses and the internalization of the dominant group's cultural values.
10 Ibid.
11 Robert Blauner, *Racial Oppression in America,* Harper & Row, New York, 1972, pp. 145–146.
12 Robert Hill, Research Director of the National Urban League, quoted in *Ebony,* pp. 125–126, August 1973.
13 Julius Nyerere, "African Socialism: Ujamaa in Practice," *The Black Scholar,* pp. 2–7, February 1971.
14 Kenneth M. Stampp. *The Peculiar Institution,* Vintage, New York, 1956, Chap. Eight.
15 Dennis Forsythe, Race, Color and Class in the British West Indies, unpublished manuscript, 1973.
16 Stampp, loc. cit.
17 Albert Murray, *The Omni-Americans,* Outerbridge and Dienstfrey, New York, 1970, p. 89.
18 John Hope Franklin, *From Slavery to Freedom,* Knopf, New York, 1967 edition, pp. 406–409.
19 Ibid., p. 409.
20 E. Franklin Frazier, *The Negro in the United States,* Macmillan, New York, 1949, p. 275.

21 Hylan Lewis, "Innovations and Trends in the Contemporary Southern Negro Community, *Journal of Social Issues,* vol. 10, pp. 19–27, November 1954.

22 W. Lloyd Warner and Paul Lunt, *The Social Life of a Modern Community,* Yale, New Haven, Conn., 1942, p. 82.

23 W. Lloyd Warner, Marchia Meeker, and Kenneth Eells, *Social Class in America,* Science Research Associates, Chicago, 1949, p. 00.

24 Milton M. Gordon, *Social Class in American Sociology,* McGraw-Hill, New York, 1963.

25 U.S. Bureau of the Census, *The Social and Economic Status of the Black Population, 1971,* 1971, p. 29.

26 U.S. Bureau of the Census, *Current Population Reports: Social and Economic Characteristics of the Black Population in Metropolitan and Non-Metropolitan Areas: 1970 and 1960,* no. 37, 1971, table 8, p. 23.

27 U.S. Bureau of the Census, *Social and Economic Status of the Black Population . . .* , loc. cit.

28 Paul Siegel, "On the Cost of Being Negro," *Sociological Inquiry,* vol. 35, pp. 41–57, Winter 1965.

29 U.S. Bureau of the Census, *The Social and Economic Status of the Black Population, 1973,* 1974, Ser. P-23, no. 48, p. 59.

30 Theodore Purcell and Gerald Cavanagh, *Blacks in the Industrial World,* The Free Press, New York, 1972, p. 43.

31 "Blacks Income Is Still Lagging," *The San Francisco Chronicle,* A6, July 23, 1973.

32 U.S. Bureau of the Census, *Social and Economic Status of the Black Population 1971,* pp. 79–88. Until 1973 there had been a steady increase in the percentage of Blacks attending college. The American Council on Education reports a decrease in the proportion of Blacks entering the nation's colleges and universities in 1973. Cf. *The San Francisco Chronicle,* p. 6, February 4, 1974.

33 Ben J. Wattenberg and Richard Scammon, "Black Progress and Liberal Rhetoric," *Commentary,* pp. 35–44, April 1973.

34 Cf. Herrington J. Bryce, "Putting Black Economic Progress in Perspective," vol. 28, *Ebony,* pp. 59–62, August 1973.

35 C. J. Munford, "Social Structure and Black Revolution," *The Black Scholar,* vol. 4, pp. 11–23, November–December 1972. I use only the types of social classes defined by Munford. Their characteristics are a combination of the ideas and research of other social scientists including Munford. These types represent the internal Black class structure.

36 See E. Franklin Frazier, *The Black Bourgeoisie,* Collier, New York, 1962, for an analysis of Black middle-class life in the forties and fifties. For a recent examination read Sidney Kronus, *The Black Middle Class,* Merrill, Columbus, Ohio, 1971.

37 U.S. Bureau of the Census, *Social and Economic Status of the Black Population, 1971,* pp. 74–75.

38 Raymond S. Franklin and Solomon Resnik, *The Political Economy of Racism,* Holt, Rinehart and Winston, New York, 1973, p. 75.

39 The significance of the small percentage difference between Blacks and Whites in the public sector is the large gap in white-collar positions by race in private industry. A study sponsored by the Department of Labor found that in 1970 there were only 5,000 Black professionals in companies with 100 or more employees. Cf. "A Study of Black Job Advancement," *The San Francisco Chronicle,* p. 1, September 11, 1973.

40 Munford, op. cit., p. 13.

41 St. Clair Drake, "The Social and Economic Status of the Negro in the United States," in Talcott Parsons and Kenneth B. Clark (eds.), *The Negro American,* Beacon, Boston, 1967, p. 14.

42 Karl Marx, *Das Kapital,* Kerr, Chicago, 1909.

43 Fanon, op. cit., p. 48.

44 Elliot Liebow, *Tally's Corner,* Little, Brown, Boston, 1966, pp. 29–71.

45 Frazier, *The Negro in the United States,* op. cit., pp. 196, 692.

46 Eric Wolf, *Peasant Wars of the Twentieth Century,* Harper & Row, New York, 1969.

47 Bob Hayes, "Roadblocks of the Black School Child," *The San Francisco Examiner,* p. 29, January 29, 1974.

48 Robert Hill, Emerson-Hall, New York, *The Strengths of Black Families,* 1972, p. 30.

49 James E. Stafford, Keith Cox, and James Higginbotham, "Some Consumption Pattern Differences Between Urban Whites and Negroes," *Social Science Quarterly,* vol. 49, pp. 619–630, December 1968.

50 Kronus, op. cit., pp. 47–48.

51 For a summary of these differences see Robert Staples, *The Black Woman in America: Sex, Marriage and the Family,* Nelson-Hall, Chicago, 1973, chaps. 2, 4, 5.

52 Ibid., chap. 5.

53 Dennis Ippalito, William S. Donaldson, and Lewis Bowman, "Political Orientations Among Negroes and Whites," *Social Science Quarterly,* vol. 49, pp. 548–556, December 1968.

54 Kronus, op. cit., pp. 48–51.

55 Charles V. Hamilton, quoted in "Class Patterns in Black Politics,"
    Ebony, p. 38, August 1973.
56 C. Eric Lincoln, "The Negro's Middle Class Dream," *The New
    York Times Magazine*, p. 35, October 25, 1964.
57 Lu Barbara Bowman, "Clubs, Not Bars Attract Black Singles," *The
    Washington Post*, pp. A1, A10, October 18, 1972.
58 Kronus, op. cit., p. 48.
59 Ibid., pp. 45–46.
60 St. Clair Drake and Horace Cayton, *Black Metropolis*, Harcourt,
    Brace, New York, 1945, pp. 611–657.
61 Abram Kardiner and Lionel Ovesey, *The Mark of Oppression*,
    Norton, New York, 1951, p. 62.
62 U.S. Bureau of the Census, *Social and Economic Status of the
    Black Population, 1971*, p. 23.
63 "Where the Blacks Are," *Newsweek*, p. 53, February 22, 1971.
64 Pauline Bethel, "The Movement of Blacks to the Suburbs in the
    Washington-Virginia-Maryland Metropolitan Area," unpublished
    master's thesis, Howard University, 1972.
65 Kronus, op. cit., p. 29.
66 Alvin Gains and Max Meenes, "Ethnic and Class Preferences Among
    College Negroes," *Journal of Negro Education*, vol. 29, pp. 128–
    133, Spring 1960.
67 Sophia McDowell, "Patterns of Preference by Negro Youth for White
    and Negro Associates," *Phylon*, vol. 32. pp. 290–301, Fall 1971.
68 Ione Vargas, "The Black Middle-Class Defined," *Ebony*, p. 46,
    August 1973.
69 John Leggett, "Economic Insecurity and Working Class Conscious-
    ness," *American Sociological Review*, vol. 29, pp. 226–244, April
    1964.
70 Frazier, *The Black Bourgeoisie*, pp. 198–199.
71 Thomas Pettigrew, et al., "Color Gradation and Attitudes Among
    Middle-Income Negroes," *American Sociological Review*, vol. 31,
    pp. 365–374, June 1966.
72 W. Lloyd Warner, Buford H. Junker, and Walter A. Adams, *Color
    and Human Nature*, American Council on Education, Washington,
    1941, pp. 292–296.
73 Leonard Goodwin, *Do the Poor Want to Work?*, Washington,
    Brookings, 1972.
74 Curt Tausky and William J. Wilson, "Work Attachment Among
    Black Men," *Phylon*, vol. 32, pp. 23–30, Spring 1971.
75 Bryce, op. cit., p. 61.
76 Albert McQueen, "Incipient Social Mobility Among Poor Black

Families," a paper presented at the National Conference on Family Relations, Estes Park, Colo. August 1971.

77 Harry Edwards, "Black Muslim and Negro Christian Family Relationships," *Journal of Marriage and The Family*, vol. 30, pp. 604–611, November 1968.

78 Robert Chrisman, "The Formation of a Revolutionary Black Culture," *The Black Scholar*, vol. 1, pp. 2–9, June 1970.

79 Harry Edwards, *Black Students*, The Free Press, New York, 1970.

80 W. E. B. Dubois, *Battle for Peace*, Masses and Mainstream, New York, 1952, pp. 76–77.

81 Cf. Earl Ofari, *The Myth of Black Capitalism*, Monthly Review, New York, 1970, pp. 87–100.

82 Samuel Proctor, "Survival Techniques and the Black Middle-Class," in Rhoda Goldstein (ed.), *Black Life and Culture in the United States*, Crowell, New York, 1971, p. 286.

83 Hylan Lewis, "Culture, Class and Family Life Among Low-Income Urban Negroes," in Arthur Ross and Herbert Hill (eds.), *Employment, Race and Poverty*, Harcourt, Brace and World, New York, 1967, p. 171.

84 Eldridge Cleaver, "On Lumpen Ideology," *The Black Scholar*, vol. 3, pp. 2–10, November–December 1972.

85 Drake and Cayton, op. cit., p. 235.

86 Bryce, op. cit., p. 61.

87 Charles L. Sanders, "Black Assertion Among Black Professionals," *Journal of the National Medical Association*, vol. 63, p. 460, November 1971.

88 Ibid., pp. 460–465.

89 Joyce Ladner, "The Black Middle Class Defined," *Ebony*, p. 44, August 1973.

90 Sharon Fay Koch, "Changing Attitudes of L.A.'s Black Elite," *Los Angeles Times*, p. A1, April 16, 1972.

91 Lee Rainwater, "Post 1984 America," in Helen Lopata (ed.), *Marriages and Families*, Nostrand, New York, 1973, pp. 389–390.

92 Proctor, op. cit., p. 281.

93 Lerone Bennett, Jr., "Black Bourgeoisie Revisited," *Ebony*, p. 55, August 1973.

94 Earl Ofari, "The Dilemma of the Black Middle Class," *Ebony*, vol. 28, p. 143, August, 1973.

95 Joyce Ladner, "Tanzanian Women and Nation Building," *The Black Scholar*, vol. 3, pp. 22–29, December 1971.

96 Leroi Jones, "A Black Value System," *The Black Scholar*, vol. 1, pp. 54–60, November 1969.

97 Eldridge Cleaver, "The Crisis of the Black Bourgeoisie," *The Black Scholar*, vol. 4, pp. 2–11, January 1973.

SUGGESTED READING LIST

Cox, Oliver: *Caste, Class and Race,* Monthly Review, New York, 1959.

Ebony, "The Black Middle Class," vol. 28, August 1973.

Frazier, E. Franklin, *The Black Bourgeoisie,* Collier, New York, 1962.

Hare, Nathan: *The Black Anglo-Saxons,* Marzani and Munsell, New York, 1965.

Kronus, Sidney: *The Black Middle Class,* Merrill, Columbus, Ohio, 1971.

Leggett, John: "Economic Insecurity and the Working Class Consciousness," *American Sociological Review,* vol. 29, pp. 226–234, April 1964.

Munford, C. J.: "Social Structure and Black Revolution," *The Black Scholar,* vol. 4, pp. 11–23, November–December, 1972.

Muraskin, William Alan: *Middle Class Blacks in a White Society,* University of California, Berkeley, 1975.

Nyerere, Julius: "African Socialism: Ujamaa in Practice," *The Black Scholar,* vol. 1, pp. 2–7, February 1971.

Ofari, Earl: *The Myth of Black Capitalism,* Monthly Review, New York, 1970.

Parsons, Talcott and Kenneth B. Clark (eds.): *The Negro American,* Beacon, Boston, 1967.

Thomas, Tony (ed.): *Black Liberation and Socialism,* Pathfinder, New York, 1974.

U.S. Bureau of the Census: *The Social and Economic Status of the Black Population, 1971,* 1971.

Wattenberg, Ben J. and Richard Scammon: "Black Progress and Liberal Rhetoric," *Commentary,* pp. 35–44, April 1973.

Willie, Charles V.: "The Black Family and Social Class," *American Journal of Orthopsychiatry,* vol. 44, pp. 50–60, January 1974.

Black Crime and Delinquency

CRIME IN AMERICA

Criminal behavior is considered one of America's most serious social problems. At one time it ranked first among the public's concerns. Today it is still a preoccupation of many citizens who fear walking the streets at night, live behind doors with multiple locks, carry weapons on their person, or keep watchdogs and firearms in their homes for protection. Some of America's cities look like armed camps with guards wherever anything of value is located. The impact of this fear of crime is reflected in the daily lives of many Americans, who refuse to talk to strangers, have their phone numbers unlisted, refrain from dining out, and stay away from certain forms of transportation such as buses and subways.

The fear of crime and increasing use of precautions persist despite official statements that crime affects only a small number of people and that changes in the judicial system and larger and more efficient police forces have brought about a decline in criminal acts. But, it has been known for years that official statistics reflect only the minimal level of criminal activity. The FBI is the central source for all criminal statistics and it depends on police reports from major cities. Most crime statistics are grossly misleading inasmuch as rural areas are often not represented and the crime that is reported may differ radically because of variations in police-reporting procedures.

Moreover, the majority of crimes are not reported to the police since people feel that they would not do anything about the incident, would not catch the offenders, or would not want to be bothered. This finding comes from an independent survey of 10,000 households conducted by the National Opinion Research Center. On the basis of its findings the real crime rate is actually triple the rate officially recorded. In only half the cases was the crime reported to the police; 25 percent of the time that the police were called nobody responded, and only 75 percent of the complaints made were regarded by the police as violations of the law.[1] Another index of the real incidence of crime is the Gallup Poll finding that one person in every three living in densely populated center city areas has been mugged, robbed, or suffered property loss in 1972. One person in five in suburban areas had been the victim of one or more of the five types of crime asked about in the survey.[2]

Up to this point we have been discussing the prevalence of crime without any specific definition of it. Webster defines crime as "an act committed in violation of a law prohibiting it, or omitted in violation of a law ordering it."[3] If we accept this definition literally, it brands practically all American adults as criminals. However, the public fear mentioned above relates to crimes like robbery, burglary, and assaults. These are crimes involving theft or violence against the person, and these crimes are the ones that law enforcement agencies usually enforce the laws against. Yet the greatest amount of violence and largest amount of money illegally taken is not through the robberies of homes and small stores. Neither is the greatest amount of violence against the person usually in the form of an assault, rape, or murder. It is the way in which crime is defined that determines how people perceive the problem of crime, who is arrested for criminal conduct, and the remedies used to reduce crime.

Before examining the relationship between colonialism and crime, we need to look at the various types of crime that exist in American society. Among the four most prominent categories are:

Ordinary Crimes

These are acts that are committed by the majority of American citizens. Some of them will be minor offenses that constitute no threat to "law and order," for example, traffic violations, some forms of sexual conduct, use of language offensive to others, etc. Many states have a number of laws that are unenforced and unenforceable, and it is estimated that the average person breaks at least one law every day. Another category of crimes falls in a middle range, which could be labeled serious crimes but are committed by large numbers of the population. Among the more common crimes of this nature are cheating on income taxes, falsifying job or loan applications, employee theft, etc.

Even some of the more serious crimes may be put into this category simply because they involve the majority of the population. According to one study of a middle-class, affluent White sample, at least 90 percent had committed 1 of the 49 crimes listed, with the average number being 18 apiece. Moreover, among those crimes listed were larceny (89 percent), tax evasion (57 percent), car theft (26 percent), and robbery (11 percent). There are other studies that show that the average American citizen violates the law and that many of these violations are quite serious. However, few of these crimes were reported and the criminal avoided arrest and prosecution.[4]

Political Crimes

These are acts committed by a public official who seeks power for himself, his party, or certain interest groups by violating the constitutional and ethical norms of the political order and interpreting the law in an exclusive and politically divisive way. The political criminal seeks to maintain or acquire power by excluding classes and races and ethnic, religious, or political groups by denying or obstructing their participation in the political and economic order.[5] This definition covers a multitude of sins, most of which are illegal and rarely punished. The Watergate scandal has heightened public awareness of these types of crimes.

Among the political crimes of commission are acceptance of campaign contributions for future government favors or taking a bribe to grant government contracts. Some of the more marginal cases are politicians or government employees who have a financial interest in companies bidding on government contracts that they pass judgment on. In the case of businesses regulated by government agencies, price increases allowed often coincide with sizable donations to the campaign coffers of the administration in power. Another common practice in government is for those public officials in office to maintain a partnership in a law firm that represents a number of clients seeking government contracts or special interest legislation.

In maintaining their power the political criminals will violate the rights of other groups and political parties. While this is most obvious in the case of the Watergate scandal, when the Republican administration used illegal means to prevent the Democratic party presidential candidate from winning the 1972 presidential election, that same administration was even more vociferous against dissident minority parties. In the wake of the Watergate scandal, the federal government admitted to electronic surveillance (wiretapping) of the Socialist Worker's party. It further acknowledged the existence of a memorandum from the Director of the Federal Bureau of Investigation directing his agents to begin an attack against groups and individuals "who spout revolution and unlawfully challenge society to obtain their demands. In the main those groups consisted of people opposed to War, Poverty and Racism."[6]

The list of political crimes can be expanded to cover more serious offenses such as the illegal conduct of a war that killed and wounded millions of people, both military and civilian, when the government was guilty of failing to enforce certain laws that exist to protect the poor and racial minorities. The present government is notorious for failing to enforce laws that prohibit racial discrimination in jobs, housing, and education. On the local level public officials are lax in enforcing housing codes and requiring slumlords to maintain their property in decent condition. Dishonest merchants, particularly in the ghetto, often charge excessive or fraudulent prices for inferior merchandise. As Nagel (1968) has commented: "The poor, too, want law and order."[7]

Corporate Crimes

This category refers to illegal acts committed by manufacturers, businessmen, and the upper class. Although the public perceives crime in terms of the thousand-dollar bank robbery or physical assault on an individual, the largest amount of money stolen and violence reaped are functions of corporate crime. This type of criminal activity is often referred to as white-collar crime, which was first publicized by Edwin Sutherland (1949), the noted criminologist. He observed that the prison population in 1923 was overwhelmingly from the working class and that only about 2 percent could be considered middle class or higher. He then set out to explore whether the frequency of white-collar crime matched the distribution of the classes in prison.[8]

In his exploration Sutherland uncovered a high prevalence of lawlessness in the business world. Among those illegal practices were restraint of trade and misrepresentation in advertising, financial fraud, violation of trust, etc. Over 980 decisions had been rendered against 70 corporations with the number of violations ranging from 1 to 50.[9] Lundberg (1969), in a more recent study, reported that from 1945 to 1965 the Federal Trade Commission issued almost 4,000 cease-and-desist orders for illegal violations by businesses for a number of crimes. Almost 60 percent of the top corporations in the United States have been convicted at least four times for violating government acts and rulings.[10]

Although corporate crimes are just as illegal as ordinary crimes, they are handled quite differently. Ordinary crimes are often discouraged by fines, imprisonment, and even execution. Corporate crimes usually escape penal sanctions and may receive only orders to cease and desist, sometimes a fine, or the loss of a license. Most ordinary crimes reported wind up in the criminal court while corporate crimes are dealt with by civil courts, inspectors, administrative boards, or commissions.

Corporate crimes are dealt with quite lightly although the amount of money involved and the hazards to the public are much greater. A government study has noted that the price fixing by 29 electrical equipment companies alone probably cost utilities and therefore the public more money than is reported as stolen by burglars in a year.[11] Another study has estimated that in one year as much as $7 billion changed hands in kickbacks, payoffs, and bribes.[12] Whereas the crimes of robbery, burglary, and larceny appear quite often in police statistics, the number of reported offenses for these crimes account for less than one-sixth the estimated total dollar loss for all property crimes.[13]

The deaths and injuries caused by illegal acts cannot be accounted for by the numbers of assaults, rapes, and homicides each year. By far the largest causes of death are automobile accidents and unsafe consumer products. Cars with defective parts cause thousands of deaths each year, and over 30 million Americans are injured and 30 thousand killed each year because of unsafe consumer products other than automobiles.[14]

Among the other types of crimes we might put into this category are the illegal acts of organized crime and individual white-collar crime. Organized crime refers "to economic enterprises organized for the purposes of conducting illegal activities or operating legitimate ventures by illegal methods."[15] Some of the activities of this group are gambling, prostitution, and drugs. They fall into the category of corporate crime because many of their activities are hidden by legitimate businesses controlled by a few individuals or families and they operate in collusion with other legitimate businesses and public officials.[16]

The individual white-collar criminal includes such types as the embezzler who steals from his employer or the wealthy upper-class male who avoids paying thousands or even millions of dollars in taxes through evasion or deceit. Although millions of Americans may empathize with the individual who cheats on his income tax, a former commissioner of the Internal Revenue Service asserts: "It is indeed strange that the theft of a used car worth $500.00 rates a three year prison sentence whereas the theft of $50,000.00 of tax rates only a small fine and no prison time. Yes, theft; what else is tax evasion?"[17]

Crimes of the Underclass

These are the crimes for which people are most often arrested, prosecuted, and convicted. They derive from economic conditions that force people to steal for survival. It is the crimes of the underclass that ipso facto determine what the crime problem is in the United States. In a society where wealth is unequally distributed, and the poor are locked in a life-and-death struggle for survival, crime is but one of a number of limited responses to their deprived situation.

The majority of crimes brought to the attention of the courts are committed for money.

Although the burden of poverty rests equally on all members of the underclass, it is colonized Blacks who bear most heavily the oppressive aspects of the American criminal justice system. Due to the inequity of colonial rule, Blacks are more likely to be arrested, brutalized by the police, disenfranchised in the courtroom, and punished most severely.

COLONIALISM AND CRIME

In a colonial setting the subject group is set apart geographically from the dominant group, which exposes it to a different set of cultural standards that have no legitimacy in the colonizer's society. The native has a status which is always unequal to that of the White settler. Because his own cultural values have no legitimacy in the settler's world, he must always conform to the standards that are alien to him and which he has no resources to meet.[18] This vicious cycle determines the form of Black crime in the United States, and the political and economic inequalities inherent in a colonial setting inevitably influence the Afro-American's chances for equal justice under the law.

Achieving justice for Blacks under the legal system is difficult because the laws reflect the racial inequality in this country. The legalization of the colonial order is best represented in the Constitution. While the Constitution is regarded as the bulwark of human equality and freedom, it denied the right to vote to Afro-Americans and made the political franchise an exclusive right of White property owners. In this same Constitution are three provisions that legally established the subjugated colonized status of Blacks. One clause allowed White slaveholders to count their slaves as three-fifths of a person when determining how many representatives a state might send to Congress. A second clause prohibited the Congress from passing any laws restricting the slave trade until 1808. The third one provided that runaway slaves had to be returned by any other state in which they might have sought refuge.[19]

Crimes of the colonizer are deeply rooted in the history of this country. It was founded on violence against the native Indians who had their land taken away and were subjected to a systematic pattern of genocide and the subversion of their culture. The first crime of the settlers against Afro-Americans was their abduction from the continent of Africa to the shores of North America where they were forced into involuntary servitude. Hence, the history of the dominant racial group is founded in the crimes of abduction, genocide, and slavery.[20] Yet instead of prison sentences the colonizers have been rewarded with the spoils of their illegal acts and their crimes were legitimated in the society's history books and in the country's cultural values.

It is in the power to define what constitutes a crime that is the essence of colonial relationships. How crime is defined reflects the relationship of the colonized to the colonizer. The dominant racial group defines those acts of crime that fit its needs and purposes and classifies a criminal as an individual who commits certain kinds of illegal acts while other such acts are exempted from prosecution and can avoid public condemnation because they are not perceived as being criminal or a threat to society.

As a result of the colonizer's power to define what crimes are to be punished, we find prominent gaps in the seriousness of a crime and the punishment meted out for it. For instance, a Black youth alleged to have stolen $10 from a grocery store may be sent to prison for ten years while business executives may be involved in a million-dollar stock fraud that will result in a suspended sentence and perhaps a fine. Such differentials in disposal of criminal cases have little to do with the issue of crime but are a mere reflection of one's standing in the colonial hierarchy. Marcuse (1970) understood this quite well when he wrote, "The language of the prevailing law and order . . . not only defines and condemns the enemy, it also creates him; and this creation is not the enemy as he really is but as he must be in order to perform his function for the establishment."[21]

The phrase "all men are equal before the law" may be occasionally true in the application of the law before those accused of a crime. However, as Balbus (1973) points out, it is equally correct that legal equality in the face of the existence of economic inequality is repressive.[22] Even Max Weber (1971) noted that the men of property were served much better by formal legal equality than the poor.[23] Assuming the existence of an equitable enforcement of the law, this serves to buttress and legitimate the present colonial order. It gives permanence to laws passed by the ruling class for their own advantage. Its purpose is to ensure respect for those laws useful only to members of the racially dominant group and their leaders, which is injurious to the mass of colonized Blacks and maintained only by the fear of punishment.

Whatever the purpose of law, it is quite clear that Blacks did not participate in writing the laws to which they are subjected. A common view of the law is expressed by Julius Lester (1968): "The American Black man has never known law and order except as an instrument of oppression. The law has been written by white men, for the protection of white men and their property, to be enforced by white men against Blacks in particular and poor folk in general."[24] Probably the most recent example of this use of the law was in the sixties when many Black Southerners were arrested for seeking service at White lunch counters while White Southerners could easily request service at Black lunch counters if they desired without penalty.

In a very real sense Blacks are not protected by American law because they have no power to enforce those laws. They have no law of their own and no defense against the laws of the colonizer. It is the external imposition of the law that undermines any belief Blacks might have in the legitimacy of the legal system. One group of politically conscious Blacks charged: "In court you ask us to submit to a code of laws . . . your laws, not our laws (Black and poor people) but your laws—your laws because we were never asked if we consented to having them as our laws, nor are these laws relevant to our ghetto reality. They are your laws, and we find them racist and oppressive."[25]

Even when economic need is absent, the colonial system creates a proclivity toward crime by Blacks because of their feelings of alienation from the dominant society. The alienated man feels he is not part of his society, that he is powerless to determine his life chances, and that the values of the dominant culture are not his own. When Afro-Americans are denied participation in the total society, excluded from both its duties and privileges, they do not develop the feeling of responsibility that is necessary for social stability. In the ghetto Blacks are regularly cheated by dishonest merchants who rob them of needed funds by service charges for cashing welfare checks, excessive interests, hidden interests, poor merchandise, and inflated prices.[26] Since most of these merchants are White, many Blacks define all Whites as the "enemy" against whom anything goes.

Most societies depend on the individual's internal controls to prevent crime waves. In turn the individual refrains from criminal behavior because he believes that the system under which he lives is a just one. However, Blacks have much less faith in the political system than Whites. A number of studies have documented the lack of Black faith in the government, and some recent investigations reveal that less than a majority of Afro-Americans believe elected officials can be trusted.[27] Lipset (1963) defines legitimacy as "the capacity of the system to engender and maintain the belief that the existing political institutions are the most appropriate ones for the society." Groups regard a political system as legitimate or illegitimate, he suggests, according to the way in which its values fit with theirs.[28] In a society where large numbers of the populace, and their political leaders, believe that people are poor because they deserve to be, there can be little Black agreement with those values.

However, Blacks and Whites do share cultural goals that are established for all members of the society. These are certain common success goals for everybody but the means for attaining them are distributed unequally throughout the population. In the case of Blacks they are the most disadvantaged group because of their colonized status. Merton (1957) notes that when the dominant culture restricts access to socially accepted ways of attaining these goals for deprived minorities, they will display deviant behavior on a large scale.[29]

It is generally believed by criminologists that high crime rates are a function of poverty. Where studies exist they show that it is the poor Black who is most likely to be arrested, convicted, and sent to jail for the violation of a law.[30] The McLennans (1970) note that Blacks living under conditions similar to Whites have similar crime rates.[31] When Epps (1967) compared the delinquency rates of high school juniors in Seattle, he found that within the same social class there was no significant differences in Black or White delinquency rates.[32]

While the effect of class is important in reducing differentials in Black and White crime rates, colonialism structures the class pattern in such a way that most Blacks wind up in the lower stratum of the class structure. There are three times as many Blacks living in poverty as Whites and the gap is growing wider each year. On the average Blacks earn only 60 percent of the annual income of Whites.[33] Moreover, many of the White poor will not be counted in crime statistics because of their demographic character. Much of White poverty is concentrated in certain groups that have low crime rates: the aged, those in rural areas, and among female heads of households.[34]

Colonialism operates in such a way as to perpetrate economic inequalities in a society based on race. The poor Black person is often arrested for no reason other than his colonized status, e.g., being observed in a White neighborhood after dark. Once individuals get arrest or prison records, they are regarded with suspicion forever by potential employers. Rarely will they ever obtain positions of trust, thereby being relegated to low-paying and menial jobs. This is the same condition that leads people into crime in the first place. The criminal justice system is inherently biased against the poor and Blacks (increasingly the same person). In the words of Anatole France (1919): "So long as society is founded on injustice the function of the laws will be to defend and sustain injustice. And the more unjust they are the more responsible they will seem."[35]

RACE AND CRIME

In the minds of the White citizenry, race and crime are closely associated. This is why politicians who formerly campaigned on a pro-segregationist position have switched to a hardline stance on law and order. It is assumed that the criminals they will crack down on will be Black thieves and rapists, not white-collar criminals. The same people who vote for the law-and-order political candidate are more likely to believe that poverty is deserved because of laziness and incompetence, that Blacks are moving too fast to gain their rights, etc.[36] A clear indication that law and order really mean Black subjugation is the fact that the groups most in need of police protection, Blacks, rarely vote for a law-and-order candidate.

This association between race and crime is not a recent phenomenon. One writer wrote: "Students are of the opinion that with the possible exception of the Aztec, the earth has never known a bloodier race than the African Negro."[38] Much of this stereotyping by the dominant racial group is necessary in order to explain why the racially subordinate group is forced to live in segregated, substandard conditions and must be held under tight control. In the nineteenth century some criminologists asserted that certain racial groups possessed inherent criminal tendencies.[39] More recently a leading physician and close friend of former President Nixon proposed that the government begin the mass testing of six- to eight-year-old children to determine if they have criminal behavior tendencies. For those so inclined, he suggested "treatment camps" for the young hardcore criminal.[40]

The theory of inherent criminal traits among racial groups is weakened by the cross-cultural evidence. In East Africa 71 percent of the 41 tribal groups studied had lower homicide rates than the Whites of either South Carolina or Texas in 1949–1951. Generally, there is much less crime in African societies than in the United States.[41] Moreover, the White fear of Black criminality is rather strange since the available data reveal that when certain criminal acts are interracial, the victim is more often Black than White.[42] Perhaps much of the White fear of Black crime is motivated by the same concern the slavemaster had over his slaves' attacking him. It is the fear that in a colonized society the natives will attempt to break their chains and escape from the reservation.

A similar analogy is found in the writings of Fanon (1963) on colonialism in Algeria. The French settlers noted that criminality in Algeria was a problem and the authorities unanimously agreed that the Algerian was a born criminal. This theory was taught in the universities for over twenty years. In response to these theories, Fanon contends that "the Algerian's criminality is not the consequence of the organization of his nervous system but the direct product of the colonial situation." In the context of oppression the colonized man cannot internalize the moral values of the oppressor, but must concern himself with survival. For him, to steal means to keep on existing.[43]

The iron hand of colonial rule, however, confines most Black crime to its own community. Although settlers have more money to steal and hostility is felt more frequently toward Whites, the victims of Black theft and violence are primarily other Blacks. A colonized status effectively prevents Blacks from gaining access to White neighbor-hoods where they are likely to arouse suspicion and be stopped by the police. Furthermore, most Afro-Americans are acutely conscious that the penalties for crimes against Whites are much higher than when the victim is Black. Certain types of crime are excluded for Blacks because of their racially subordinate position. Embezzlement, extor-tion, fraud, forgery, and counterfeiting all require a position of trust or equal status with the victim that Blacks seldom have.

Most Black crimes are categorized as minor offenses, e.g., drunk-eness, disorderly conduct, vagrancy, gambling, etc. The majority of serious property crimes like burglary, larceny (theft over $50), and auto thefts are committed by Whites. More Blacks than Whites are arrested for serious crimes of violence such as murder, rape, and aggravated assault. The majority of these Black crimes will have Black victims.[44] Fanon (1963) suggests that this violence stems from the violence with which the supremacy of White values is affirmed, that the settler introduces violence into the native's life. Once the native internalizes these values, they will initially be expressed in aggressive-ness against his own people. The settler or policeman can assault the native with impunity but he attacks his fellow Black at the slightest hostile or aggressive glance cast upon him. Ultimately, this behavior leads to armed resistance to colonialism.[45]

One sees the analogy between African colonialism and its North American form in two examples. In Elkin's (1959) study of slavery he suggests that the slaves internalized the values of the slaveholders. One of those values would be the slaveowner's use of violence against the slaves in order to intimidate them.[46] Pettigrew (1962) makes the important point that most Blacks come from the South, which has a tradition of violence. Although most Black violence is concentrated in the North, large numbers are emigrants from the South. He believes that it is the legacy of White Southern values that causes much Black violence against the person.[47]

THE ROLE OF THE POLICE

It is in the form of police attitudes and practices that we see the oper-ational effects of colonialism. Fanon (1963) spoke of the policeman as the "official instituted go-between, the spokesman of the settler and his rule of oppression."[48] In the United States James Baldwin's (1963) assessment was that "they represent the force of the white world and that world's profit and ease, to keep the Black man corraled up here in this place."[49] Others have described the White policeman's role in Black ghettos as an army of occupation protecting the interests of outside exploiters and maintaining the domination over the ghetto by the central metropolitan power structure.[50]

Whether the policeman carries out this function or not, it is quite clear that White policemen are disliked and feared by a large number of ghetto Blacks. Almost every survey taken reveals that a larger number of Blacks than Whites hold unfavorable attitudes toward the police.[51] This is true even of the Black middle class since police behavior is determined more by the external appearance of skin color than class standing. Members of the Black middle class are commonly accosted by the police, ordered to pull their cars to the curb, and addressed as boy or nigger.[52] Such incidents once led Louis Lomax (1962) to comment: "I don't know a single Negro who doesn't get a flutter in his stomach when approached by a white policeman."[53]

Blacks have two major complaints against the police: (1) they are concerned with protecting White businesses in the ghetto more than the life and property of the residents and (2) they are often disrespectful and abusive.[54] Police brutality has been a common charge lodged against White police officers. In the two-and-a-half-year period from January 1958 to June 1960, the United States Department of Justice received 1,328 complaints charging police brutality. Almost half of the complaints came from Blacks.[55] Since these cases always involve the police investigating the police, none of those cases led to the prosecution, and certainly not the conviction, of any police officer. Given such insensitivity to their charges by those who control the police force, it is little wonder that the police have become the focal point of sniping attacks and Black hostility and noncooperation.[56]

White policemen can act in this arbitrary fashion with Blacks because they know that this colonized group has no recourse to any agency of power or control over the police. Furthermore, the call for support of your local police is often a vote-getter since many Whites see the police as necessary to hold back a tide of Black insurgency.[57]

Another reason for the White policemen's abusive behavior with Blacks is that they represent the most authoritarian and racist section of the White population. Of the policemen interviewed by the President's Crime Commission Task Force on Police, 72 percent of them expressed clear anti-Black prejudice.[58] Other studies consistently show that White policemen hold racist attitudes, have little sympathy for the condition of Black ghetto inhabitants, and believe Blacks need more restraint than Whites. According to one veteran observer and former policeman, "The department recruits a sizable number of people with racist attitudes, socializes them into a system with a strong racist element and takes the officer who cannot advance and puts him in the ghetto where he has day-to-day contact with the Black citizens."[59]

Many White officers covet assignments in the Black community because it is financially lucrative. They find it easier to collect extortion money from petty ghetto criminals and are less likely to be detected, investigated, or convicted since Blacks believe it to be futile to report corrupt police officers. They also have a greater opportunity to receive outstanding merit citations based on the number of arrests they make of crimes that they solve. These awards allow them to achieve more rapid promotion, greater authority, and higher salaries.

Considering the characteristics of policemen assigned to the Black community, it is of little surprise to find that for the years 1920–1932, out of 479 Blacks killed by White persons in the South, 54 percent were slain by White police officers.[60] More recently, outside the South, we find that 75 percent of the civilians killed by Chicago police in 1971 were Black.[61] The state of California reports that Blacks, who make up 7 percent of its population, represented 48 percent of those killed by policemen in 1971.[62] A more indirect form of police violence against the subject group is revealed in the finding that the majority of Black males who committed suicide in New Orleans were enmeshed in troubles with the police. Most of these suicide victims had a fear of the police and saw them as the symbol of White authority in the Black community.[63]

The colonial order acknowledges its dependence on the White policeman by its resistance to Black demands for community control of the police and/or more Black police officers. In no American city does the proportion of Black police officers match their proportion in the general population. The highest ratio of Black policemen to the Black population is in Philadelphia where Blacks make up 20 percent of the police force and 29 percent of the population. New Orleans has the lowest with Blacks comprising 45 percent of the total population and 5 percent of the police force.[64] In that same city the predominantly White Patrolmen's Association of New Orleans has objected to the police chief's announced goal of hiring one hundred more Black police officers.[65] White officers in other cities have resisted any attempts to exclude White policemen from Black communities.

In the trend toward indirect colonial control (neocolonialism) Blacks are being hired in record numbers to police the Black community. The cofounder of the Afro-American Patrolmen's League in Chicago states that Black policemen are hired to control the Black community. This benefits the settler group because it realizes that control is more absolute if done by a member of the community, who knows its inner workings. It also provides the illusion of hope to the community that it has some means of redress simply because the colonizer's agent is Black. But the Black policeman cannot give justice to his people because he must protect and maintain the same institutions and systems as the White policeman.[66]

To avoid this conflict the Black policeman must alienate himself from his community. His new loyalty must be to White culture and White standards. Now that he joins the colonizer's system he must reject the lifestyle of the native. Fanon (1963) reminds us that under a colonial regime the ideas put forward by the colonizer also influence the natives, especially those selected to play the role of native elites.[67] Hence one finds that the Black policeman is often charged with the same practice of police brutality as his White counterpart. One study demonstrated that 18 percent of the Black police officers were openly prejudiced against other Blacks.[68]

However, not all Black policemen accommodate themselves to protecting White colonial rule. In many cities they have formed separate police officers associations and called for more justice and less law and order in Black communities. The New York City Afro-American Police League endorsed the proposal for a civilian review board while the predominantly White police association opposed it and spent a great deal of money to have it rejected.[69] Several factors contribute to the Black policeman's different attitude toward law enforcement besides loyalty to his group. They enter police work for economic reasons rather than a desire to uphold all of the society's laws and maintain the order of the status quo.[70] Because they are Black, most White police officers do not accept them, and in some cases Black police officers have actually been beaten or jailed by their White colleagues.

Much of the Black crime rate can be explained by White police attitudes toward Blacks. Since the society gives policemen the power to arbitrarily arrest citizens, Blacks are very prone to being picked up for standing on a corner or wearing dark glasses at midnight. Such cases are common, as illustrated in this conversation between a judge and a defendant:

Judge: What did you do? How did you wind up in jail here?
Defendant: I don't know, I was just standing there.[71]

Failure to move on or to give a good account of one's presence to a policeman is an offense under many laws. Since many Black people spend their time in the streets there is a greater likelihood they will be picked up for minor offenses or no offense other than being Black and looking suspicious. It is estimated that about 90 percent of all Black males can expect to go to jail or prison sometime in their life.[72]

THE JUDICIAL SYSTEM

Colonialism permeates the entire criminal justice system. The political regime is the main executioner and controls the dispensation of justice from police apprehension to prison, and all these institutions serve the function of maintaining colonial rule. The political state would be unable to set into motion its racist machinery were it not sanctioned and supported by the judicial system. Not only has the judicial branch failed to prosecute or convict those police officers accused of brutality toward Blacks but it acts in concert with them to imprison large numbers of a group whose only crime is being Black and poor.

Afro-Americans are disadvantaged in receiving a fair trial because of a number of barriers. Being poor they are often unable to afford a lawyer to defend them. In federal larceny cases, 52 percent of the Blacks did not have their own lawyers, as compared with 25 percent of the Whites.[73] If they are provided a public defender or court-appointed attorney, his only service will be to negotiate the multiple counts against the defender into one lesser charge to which the defendant agrees to plead guilty.

Since colonial administrations seldom allow natives to attain professional skills and become members of the bourgeosie, there are very few Black lawyers to represent Black defenders before the court. Black lawyers make up about 1 percent of all lawyers while comprising 12 percent of the total population.[74] Actually, more Blacks finish law school but have difficulty passing the bar exams. Southern states often have the highest rate of Black failure on bar exams and lawsuits have been filed against state bar associations alleging a systematic exclusion of Blacks from the practice of law.

Even when Black lawyers are available, Black defendants sometimes choose White attorneys to defend them. The odds are so stacked against the Black defendant that he chooses a White lawyer with the hope that having one can neutralize the impact of White racism on the final outcome of his case. Colonialism creates this kind of dependency in the native to rely upon members of the dominant group so that he might receive the ordinary rights of White citizens. For Blacks justice is a privilege, not a right.

Most Blacks accused of a crime will be arrested by a White policeman, tried by a White judge and jury, and sentenced to a prison with a White warden and White prison guards. The majority of Blacks who come before a court will face a trial by a judge instead of a jury.[75] This may derive from the Black belief that upper-class Whites (who are judges) will be more lenient than a jury composed of working-class Whites. A large majority of judges are political appointees and owe their position to the colonial administration. For obvious reasons, there are few Black judges. Of the nation's 21,000 judges, only 250 are Black and most of them are in the federal court system. Few Blacks serve on local and state courts and there are almost none in the South.[76]

One of the judge's most important functions is that of setting bail for the accused defendant. The requirement that a defendant post a cash bond to ensure his appearance in court is one of the most glaring inequities in the criminal justice system. It is quite obvious that the wealthy have no difficulty in posting bail and returning home to await their court appearance. But, the poor Black defendant is often unable to raise the thousands of dollars in bail required for offenses. With the overcrowded court calendars some defendants have actually spent years in jail because of their inability to post bail. Others have lost their jobs while they languished in jail without even having been convicted of a crime.

A trial by jury does not appreciably help the Black defendant's chances for a fair trial. There is a great likelihood that the Black defendant's jury will be predominantly White. Blacks are systematically excluded from juries by a number of measures. Prosecutors try to weed them out in selecting the final panel for fear they will be too soft on the Black defendant. Sometimes they are excluded by more subtle and indirect means such as requirements of voter registration, property ownership, literacy, and psychological tests.[77]

Few Blacks will receive a neutral hearing before a jury of "normal" White Americans. One study of jury decision making tested an index that ranked the characteristics which created the most sympathy among jurors. The highest amount of sympathy went to defendants under the age of twenty-one and Blacks were the group jurors felt least sympathetic toward.[78] As Fanon (1967) reminds us, in a racist society the normal person is therefore racist.[79]

Another disadvantage faced by the Black defendant is the illegitimacy of his cultural values. There are several examples of words and phrases used by Blacks that have a totally different meaning in the White community. These cultural differences are particularly crucial in certain types of crimes such as assault and battery and public obscenity. But White society insists that the Black community is lacking in values and that differences in cultural symbols, i.e., language, are not recognized in a court of law. There are other linguistic barriers in the courtroom that affect the Black defendant. Often, he may not comprehend the legal jargon of the attorneys and give answers based on his mistaken interpretation of the language used in the courtroom.[80]

Given the fact that various officials and judicial processes reflect and are responsive to values and interests of the racially dominant group, it is predictable that the Black defendant will be shortchanged in the decision of the court and the length of his prison sentence. Most of the available data demonstrate that Blacks are less likely to be put on probation or given suspended sentences than Whites. In general the sentences they receive for the same crime are higher than those for Whites. Southern courts were the most discriminatory. Blacks received an average of 16.8 years compared with 12.1 years for Whites in seven Southern states.[81]

There are three standards of justice for criminal cases involving Blacks: one for Black acts against Whites, a second for Black crimes against Blacks, and another for White crimes against Blacks. In general the crimes of Whites against Blacks receive light or no penalties while Black offenses against other Blacks are lightly punished. However, the illegal acts that Blacks commit against Whites often receive very serious punishment, especially in cases involving violence or rape. For example, in those seven Southern states mentioned above Black-White crimes result in average sentences of 28.0 while Black-Black crimes averages 21.2 years and White-Black crimes only 20.7 years.[82]

It is in the sentences meted out for capital offenses that we see blatant proof of unequal treatment in the courts. For colonized Blacks in the United States capital punishment is only a transfer of the function of lynch mobs to the state authority. Under the auspices of the political state, Blacks have been executed for less serious crimes and crimes less often receiving the death penalty, especially rape, than Whites. They were of a younger age than Whites at the time of execution and were more often executed without appeals, regardless of their offense or age at execution. Over 53 percent of the 3,827 men and 32 women executed since 1930 were Black. In 1972 the proportion of Blacks on death row was 52 percent. It is in the South where discrimination in capital punishment is most evident. Practically all executions for rape took place in the South. In that region 90 percent of those executed for rape were Black. Most of their rape victims were White while no White male has ever received the death penalty for raping a Black woman.[83]

Again the colonial pattern emerges. The two things the settler fears most are the robbery of his possessions and the rape of his women. The reason for this is that, besides extraordinary wealth, he also has access to most of the women in the population. What native women he cannot lure away with his wealth he physically conquers. Hence, out of fear that the native will retaliate, he punishes with unrelenting fury the crime of sexual violation of upper-caste women.

About 85 percent of the Black rape offenders executed had White victims although the overwhelming majority (95 percent) of the Black male's rape victims were Black women.[84] Myrdal (1944) explains this phenomenon in his observation that "what whites ask for is a general order according to which all Negroes are placed under all white people and excluded from not only the white man's society but also from the ordinary symbols of respect. No Negro shall ever aspire to them and no white shall be allowed to offer them."[85] And it is this fear of the native invading his domain and destroying his property which motivates the settler to punish severely any native who attempts to become familiar or intimate with the symbol of White privilege—the White female.

VICTIMLESS CRIMES

These are illegal acts in which no victim is directly involved. More importantly these are crimes that often are arbitrarily defined by the police and they usually are the sole witness. The existence of these laws is increasingly being called into question. Many people believe that individuals should be able to control their own lives and destinies without interference from the society as long as physical or material damage to others is not involved.

While victimless crimes represent much less threat to the society they actually account for about 80 percent of all arrests for Blacks and Whites.[86] The significance of the high arrest rates is that Blacks are more prone to engage in these activities, face a greater likelihood of being arrested for them, and are more subjected to the capricous whims of policemen who are given a great deal of latitude in arrests for this form of criminal behavior. Among the victimless crimes we shall examine are alcoholism, drug addiction, gambling, prostitution, and a miscellaneous grab bag of vaguely defined crimes.

Alcoholism

Formally known as the crime of public intoxication, alcoholism accounted for 280,706 Black arrests and about 20 percent of all arrests of Blacks in 1972. It ranks as their number one offense.[87] Because of the oppressive conditions under which they live Blacks consume more alcoholic beverages to cope with the stress in their lives and escape from reality. No law ever stopped a man from drinking and alcoholism is not going to be solved by putting people in jail because it is a medical problem, not a crime.

Enforcement of the law on alcoholism fits well into the typical pattern of colonialism. The colonial order creates the conditions that lead Blacks into heavy drinking. They control the disposition of licenses to engage in liquor sales. Since this is a profitable enterprise leading to significant economic gains, few Blacks are allowed to participate in the alcoholic beverage industry. Hence Whites create the conditions that motivate Black indulgence in alcohol consumption from which they benefit financially. Upper-class Whites can do their drinking in bars, clubs, and restaurants, because of their greater wealth, where they are less exposed to arrest for intoxication.[88] Poor Blacks, who live in substandard homes, are more likely to remain in the streets and the constant surveillance of the ghetto by police forces makes them more vulnerable to detection and arrest.

Drug Addiction

Drug abuse is another medical problem that is defined as a crime. In some cases it is questionable whether it should even be considered a medical problem since most doctors do not consider marijuana, the most common offense, harmful. Over 84,000 Blacks were arrested for narcotics violations in 1972 and they accounted for some 22 percent of all drug arrests.[89] A number of studies have found a strong relationship between heroin addiction and minority group status.[90] In some parts of the inner city, addicts represent as much as 10 percent of its total population.[91] The use of heroin by poor Blacks can only be seen as an effort to cope with the stresses related to survival.

A heavy drug addict population provides the police with a rationale to patrol the Black community to "protect" its inhabitants from their criminal behavior. At the same time they are managing to control and intimidate its residents by their presence. It is well known that Blacks are not in control of the manufacturing, importation, and sale of drugs. The point of origin of heroin is often from Turkey to France, where it is processed and smuggled into this country from Latin America and Canadian ports. But the public clamor for new controls to get the addict off the street leads to repressive laws that increase the penalties for pushers. The effect of these laws is to punish the poor ghetto addict (who must sell to support his habit) while dealing leniently with the manufacturer who is not directly involved in drug sales or the middle-class drug user who can afford to purchase his drugs.

Gambling

Gambling is defined as the nonsanctioned playing of games of chance for money or some other stake.[92] Making it a crime represents a pure moral judgment on the part of lawmakers and reflects a retention of puritanical standards. The rule is honored more in its breach than observance. Probably no law is more inconsistent or violated more often than this one. In one state gambling is legal and some other states have legalized lotteries. Even churches are known to run bingo games for their members. Yet, 70 percent of all persons arrested for gambling are Black. It is quite implausible that some 12 percent of the population accounts for 70 percent of the illegal gambling in the United States.[93] One must assume that these arrest statistics reflect the tendency of policemen to concentrate on arresting Blacks for this crime because they can do so with impunity.

Prostitution

Defined as selling the services of oneself for purposes of sexual intercourse,[94] prostitution also represents a moral judgement based on the puritanical principle that all sexual activity must be confined to marriage. Moreover, it is inconsistent. The state of Nevada permits prostitution in several of its counties and many foreign nations have legalized prostitution, although it is confined to segregated areas. Again, we find an unequal application of the law. The percentage of Black women arrested for this crime in 1972 was 61 percent.[95] There are double standards operating here.

In most prostitution arrests only the woman is charged although the male is equally guilty of violating the law. One reason the Black prostitute's male partner is unbothered is that he is often a middle- or upper-class White male. Many of the Black women who go into prostitution do so because of racist oppression and poverty. Some Black women are forced to carry out this function because they are just poor women out of a job and cannot survive any other way.[96]

The second double standard exists between the predominantly Black street walker and the predominantly White call girl. The street walker is more easily observed and subject to arrest than the call girl who entertains clients in her home or apartment. Due to the Black prostitute's colonized status she cannot become a call girl since the clients of call girls are usually wealthy White males who desire the call girl to be a part of their social life. Most call girls are found in the better cocktail lounges and restaurants where the presence of a Black woman would be suspect.[98]

A number of police and judicial practices victimize the Black prostitute. It should be noted that open prostitution is permitted in Black communities but is rarely found in White ones. The police maintain a much less rigorous standard of law enforcement in Black ghettos, where they tolerate illegal activities they would not tolerate elsewhere. In court Black prostitutes are also discriminated against. In Oklahoma City the police were filing state charges, which called for a possible $500 fine and a prison sentence, against Black prostitutes, but were filing municipal charges, which called for a $200 fine, against White prostitutes. In another locale, Washington, D.C., eight policemen were suspended for conspiring to illegally entrap Black prostitutes.[98]

Miscellaneous

These violations represent a variety of crimes that are vaguely defined and represent nothing more than a police officer's belief that he has sufficient evidence and information to legally take an individual into custody. Among these crimes are disorderly conduct, suspicious conduct, and vagrancy. Most of these charges are lodged against the poor and Blacks. The definitions of some of the crimes almost automatically exclude any but the poor. Vagrancy, for instance, refers to shiftless or idle wandering without money or work.[99] Others are subject to varying definitions although they commonly involve lack of respect or obedience to the forces of authority (usually the policeman himself). Considering the image of the police among Blacks it is no surprise that they are frequently arrested for this crime.

Policemen use these charges as an instrument of control over Blacks. Often Afro-Americans are picked up on charges of suspicious conduct for being in a White neighborhood. In the South the charges of vagrancy and breach of the peace were commonly used against civil rights workers who were protesting racial discrimination.[100] Very few of the people arrested on these charges are actually found guilty in a court of law. As one author points out, the vagrancy and public intoxication laws serve the aesthetic function of removing the failures of the American dream from public sight.[101]

PRISON AS A FORM OF SOCIAL CONTROL

As we have seen, a cross section of individuals are guilty of some violation of the law. But they are not all represented in the nation's prison population. George Jackson (1971) puts it well when he states, "There are no wealthy men on death row and so very few in the general prison population that we can discount them altogether."[102] *The Christian Science Monitor* reports that most prisons are cesspools for the poor, their walls and pickets holding men and women without money or influence, who had committed their crimes in the first place for that reason, and who went to court with a poor legal defense or no defense at all.[103]

It is not only the poor but Blacks and other racial minorities who fill America's jails. There are actually more Blacks in prison than in college and the number is rapidly increasing. In 1970, 43 percent of the prison population was non-White. The sentences they receive and racial differences in them are also increasing. White felons received an average of 48 months compared with 58.4 months for their Black counterparts in 1969. One year later the White felon's average sentence decreased to 45.9 percent with the average sentence for non-White felons increasing to 59.2 months.[104]

Blacks and Latins make up as many as 85 percent of the inmates in some prisons in large urban states. One study pointed out the class characteristics of the nation's prisoners. In investigating the background of convicted felons in Washington, D.C. during the years 1964–65, it was found that 90 percent had incomes of less than $5,000. Of that group, 78 percent were Black. Only 5.8 percent of the prison population engaged in high-status occupations such as professional, technical work, manager, proprietor, and similar groupings compared with 20.6 percent of the general nonprison population.[105]

It is this kind of disparity that has led many Black prisoners to define themselves as political prisoners. Traditionally, that term has been applied to persons jailed for overtly political acts which may or may not have been criminal offenses. Gradually that concept has been expanded to include oppressed racial minorities who are largely the victims of an oppressive politico-economic order.

One inmate at Attica explained it this way. The decisions to underfund Black schools, not to enforce housing codes, to deprive him of a decent job or welfare were political ones that affected his life. The end result of these political decisions had caused him and his family to be poor, uneducated, poorly housed and fed, and with few alternatives for survival. This, he believed, led directly to his committing crimes.[106] According to Chrisman (1971), "The Black prisoner's crime may or may not have been a political action against the state but the state's action against him is always political."[107]

Bettina Aptheker (1971) defines four groupings of prisoners who go to prison as a result of their political views and activities or who are victims of class, racial, and national oppression:[108]

1 Those who are imprisoned as a result of their political leadership and beliefs and become victims of politically inspired frameups. Examples of these types of political prisoners are Bobby Seale, Huey Newton, and Angela Davis.

2 Groups of people who have committed various acts of civil disobedience, or who refused to join the Armed Forces. Technically they have violated a law but their violations were obviously political acts.

3 People who lack a political perspective but are victims of class, racial, and national oppression. They represent the thousands of poor and minority people who are railroaded to prison by way of inadequate legal defense and political power.

4 Prisoners who were guilty of certain crimes but develop a political consciousness in prison. When they begin to express their political views they become victims of politically inspired actions against them by the prison administration and the parole boards. Examples of this type are the Soledad Brothers, Ruchell Magee, and the Folsom Strikers.

The official function of prisons is to rehabilitate those convicted of a crime against society. Huey Newton (1971) responds to this purpose with: "The prison cannot gain a victory over the political prisoner because he has nothing to be rehabilitated from or to. He

refuses to accept the legitimacy of the system and refuses to participate."[109] A more accurate purpose of prison is to maintain physical
and psychological control over those who refuse to abide by the laws
of colonial rule. Prison sentences are used to preserve the status relations in a colonial society. They serve as a brutal reminder to the
other natives who would dare disturb the existing order of colonial
relations. In essense, the prison is an instrument of racial and class
domination.

One could not possibly take seriously the society's claim that
prisons are designed to rehabilitate if one could observe their inner
workings. In prisons where the majority of the inmates are Blacks,
Chicanos, and Puerto Ricans, most of the guards will be White,
racist, and former policemen or soldiers. These prisoners will be subjected to the most dehumanizing conditions, including beatings by prison
guards, urine in their food, tortures and murders by prison authorities,
being placed naked in solitary confinement without sanitary facilities,
etc.[110] A common practice in prisons is the use of prisoners for medical
research. An Atlanta prison was using prisoners to test a malaria
serum. The prisoners were actually given malaria but treated before
it could kill them. However, at least three prisoners suffered ruptured
spleens from the disease and a few contacted hepatitis.[111] With such
horror stories in great abundance, a number of authorities have called
for the abolition of the nation's prison system.

JUVENILE DELINQUENCY

The same colonial processes that create and maintain Black adult
criminal patterns operate equally on the patterns of Black juvenile
delinquency. A significant difference is that until a few years ago
juveniles could be sent to prison in many states without even the
barest requirements of due process being observed. Until 1967 juveniles
were not provided with the right to have a lawyer, given the opportunity to face their accuser or cross-examine him, or require the
prosecutor to prove the charges against them beyond a reasonable
doubt. Any juvenile can be arrested by a police officer and taken into
custody if he has reasonable cause to believe that the juvenile has
engaged in criminal acts or is in danger of leading an idle, dissolute,
lewd, or immoral life.

A pattern of economic deprivation is usually the precipitating force for Black delinquency. As mentioned earlier, Black teenagers have the highest rate of unemployment in the United States, approaching 65 percent in some large cities.[112] Black males who find jobs are less likely to be delinquent than the ones who do not. But they cannot pick and choose; they must take the jobs they can get—usually hard and dirty work, at low pay—and regard themselves as fortunate if they find work at all.

Black delinquency rates are also functions of law enforcement patterns. Studies show that Black youth are accosted more often by police officers merely because their Blackness marks them as potential troublemakers.[113] One clear indication of this discriminatory treatment is the proportion of Blacks among innocent juveniles arrested by the police; in a group of 76 juveniles arrested, 10 were found to be innocent and 7 of the 10 were Black although less than one-third of the youths arrested were Afro-Americans.[114]

Lower-class Black youth living in high delinquency areas have a much higher risk of being discovered and adjudicated as delinquents. Through self-reporting studies of White middle-class youth it has been revealed that they have a much higher delinquency ratio than appears in official statistics of delinquency.[155] The police officer who observes a middle-class White youth committing an illegal act will send him home to his parents while the Black youth is more often detained for the same crime. Often after detaining the minority youth, the police officer will arrest and charge him, with little or no evidence, to avoid loss of face.[116] Goldman (1969) found that while only 33.6 percent of the offenses committed by White juveniles were referred to the court, 64.8 percent of the Black arrests were disposed of by court referral.[117]

Many White policemen treat Black youth differently because they dislike their rebellious behavior toward them. One White policeman complained that "they say the damnedest things to you and they seem to have no respect for you as an adult."[118] This may be true but most Black adolescents have a rational basis for their attitude toward the police. Greenberg's (1969) study established that in elementary school Black students expressed the same positive attitudes toward the police as their White peers. In high school they showed significantly more negative attitudes toward the police than White students.[119] Probably the experiences of Black youth between the two levels of school produce these negative attitudes. Harassing Black youth in White neighborhoods, breaking up groups of youth congregated on corners or in cars without provocation, the wanton shooting of Black youth for petty crimes, and arbitrarily searching them for weapons are acts calculated to produce negative attitudes.[120]

Ghetto youth learn early that the law symbolizes systematic and unpunished police brutality, judicial bias, governmental indifference, and racial hypocrisy. The police represent the store and pawnshop owners, the landlords, and other vested interests. At a young age ghetto children develop cynical attitudes toward politics and the legitimacy of the system as it relates to them.[121] The police are the most visible symbols of an illegal order and as Fanon (1967) suggests, "Under colonialism the oppressed reject all visible representations of colonial oppression."[122]

SUMMARY

In this chapter the colonial model has been used to explain the relationship between race and crime. While the fit between theory and empirical data is not perfect, it does illustrate the link between Black oppression and the disproportionate amount of crime found in its environs. The operational effects of colonialism are expressed in the high arrest rates, lengthy prison sentences, and political victimization of Blacks in prison, and the path that leads to jail is deeply rooted in the imposed pattern of Black subordination.

Using the colonial model does point the way to reducing some of the inequities of American criminal justice. Among one of the remedies suggested by this model is community control of the police, which would diminish the Black belief that the police in Black neighborhoods constitute an army of occupation. An autonomous police force composed of members of the native group would eliminate the illegitimate use of violence against the Black populace. Policemen would be controlled by the native community and required to live in their precinct. In this way Blacks would have greater assurances that the police are there to respond to their interests and values rather than to the needs of the White majority.

The judicial process needs to be reorganized along similar lines. Oppressed racial minorities should be allowed to have a trial by a jury of their peers. This means a jury whose experiences and values are similar to the defendants. Where this is not feasible we might consider proportional representation of Blacks on juries, the legal staff, and the bench. While these suggestions will not radically affect the socioeconomic conditions that generate crime, they will at least reduce the impact of racism on the administration of justice to the Black population.

Until such time as these changes take place, Black crime will continue to exist at or beyond its present level. A major concern of the Black community is the Black-on-Black crime in its environment. Some indigenous groups have organized to fight this type of crime in order to make their communities safe places to live. The colonial order has little concern for the safety of its natives and cannot be depended upon to solve their internal problems. Therefore, Blacks must assume the responsibility for policing their own communities and simultaneously fight against the victimization of Blacks by the criminal justice machinery of the colonial power structure.

NOTES

1 Phillip Ennis, *Criminal Victimization in the United States: A Report of a National Survey,* The National Opinion Research Center, University of Chicago, May 1967, chap. 5.
2 *The Washington Post,* p. A21, January 14, 1973.
3 *Webster's New World Dictionary,* World, New York, 1972, p. 335.
4 James Wallerstein and Clement Wyle, "Our Law-Abiding Law-breakers," *Probation,* vol. 25, pp. 107–112, April 1947.
5 Joseph Mouledoux, "Political Crime and the Negro Revolution," in Sethard Fisher (ed.), *Power and the Black Community,* Random House, New York, 1970, p. 269.
6 *San Francisco Chronicle,* p. 10, January 11, 1974.
7 Stuart Nagel, "The Poor, Too, Want Law and Order," *The Chicago Daily Law Bulletin,* April 26, 1968.
8 Edwin H. Sutherland, *White Collar Crime,* Dryden, New York, 1949, pp. 3–13.
9 Ibid., pp. 20–24.
10 Ferdinand Lundberg, *The Rich and the Super Rich,* Ballantine, New York, 1969, p. 137.
11 The President's Commission on Law Enforcement, *The Challenge of Crime in a Free Society,* U.S. Government Printing Office, Washington, 1967, pp. 47–48.

12 Ramsey Clark, *Crime in America*, Simon and Shuster, New York, 1970, p. 73.
13 The President's Commission on Law Enforcement, op. cit., p. 31.
14 Report of the Consumer Product Safety Commission, quoted in *Newsweek*, p. 91, October 15, 1973.
15 Ina Corinne Brown, *Understanding Race Relations*, Prentice-Hall, Englewood Cliffs, N.J., 1973, p. 134.
16 Donald Cressey, *Theft of the Nation*, Harper & Row, New York, 1969, pp. 99–107.
17 Johnnie M. Walters, in a speech to the Michigan State Bar Association, quoted in *The San Francisco Chronicle*, p. 32, October 11, 1973.
18 Robert Blauner, *Racial Oppression in America*, Harper & Row, New York, 1972, p. 140–146.
19 John Hope Franklin, *From Slavery to Freedom*, Knopf, New York, 1967 edition, pp. 141–144.
20 Arnold Birenbaum and Edward Sagarin (eds.), *Social Problems: Private Troubles and Public Issues*, Scribner, New York, 1972, pp. 291–300.
21 Herbert Marcuse, *Essay on Liberation*, Beacon, Boston, 1970, p. 74.
22 Issac Balbus, *The Dialectics of Legal Repression*, Russell Sage, New York, 1973, p. 5.
23 Max Weber, quoted in George Lukacs, *History and Class Consciousness*, Boston, M.I.T., Cambridge, Mass., 1971, p. 96.
24 Julius Lester, *Look Out Whitey: Black Powers Gonna Get Your Mama*, Dial, New York, 1968, p. 23.
25 "To Judge Murtagh: From the Panther 21" in Phillip Foner (ed.), *The Black Panthers Speak*, Lippincott, Philadelphia, 1970, p. 204.
26 David Caplovitz, *The Poor Pay More*, The Front Press, New York, 1963, p. 137.
27 David O. Sears, "Black Attitudes Toward the Political System in the Aftermath of the Watts Insurrection," *Midwest Journal of Political Science*, vol. 13, pp. 515–544, November 1969.
28 Seymour Lipset, *Political Man*, Doubleday, New York, 1963, p. 65.
29 Robert K. Merton, *Social Theory and Social Structure*, The Free Press, Glencoe, Ill., 1957, p. 180.
30 The President's Commission on Law Enforcement, op. cit., p. 45.
31 B. McLennan and R. McLennan, "Public Policy and the Control of Crime in Crime," in B. McLennan (ed.), *Urban Society*, Dunellen, New York, 1970, pp. 125–147.

32 Edgar Epps, "Socioeconomic Status, Race, Level of Aspiration and Juvenile Delinquency: A Limited Empirical Test of Merton's Conception of Deviancy," *Phylon*, vol. 28, pp. 16–27, Spring 1967.

33 U.S. Bureau of the Census, *Current Population Reports: The Social and Economic Status of the Black Population in the United States*, 1971, p. 29.

34 Michael Harrington, *The Other America*, Macmillan, New York, 1963, pp. 9–24.

35 Anatole France, speech at Tours, France, August 1919.

36 Jerome Skolnick (ed.), *The Politics of Protest*, Ballantine, New York, 1969, p. 289.

37 Carleton Putnam, *Race and Reason: A Yankee View*, Public Affairs, Washington, 1961, p. 44.

38 P. F. Secord, "Facial Features and Inference Processes in Interpersonal Perception," in R. Taguiri and L. Petrillo (eds.), *Person Perception and Interpersonal Behavior*, Stanford, Stanford, Calif., 1958, p. 303.

39 Marvin Wolfgang and Bernard Cohen, *Crime and Race: Conceptions and Misconceptions*, Institute of Human Relations, New York, 1970, pp. 5–13.

40 Angela Davis (ed.), *If They Come in the Morning*, Signet, New York, 1971, p. 55.

41 Paul Bohannon (ed.), *African Homicide and Suicide*, Princeton, Princeton, N.J., 1960, pp. 236–239.

42 Wolfgang and Cohen, op. cit., pp. 43–44.

43 Frantz Fanon, *The Wretched of the Earth*, Grove, New York, 1963, pp. 248–249.

44 "Crime in the United States 1972," *Uniform Crime Reports*, 1972, table 36, p. 131.

45 Fanon, op. cit., pp. 42–43.

46 Stanley Elkins, *Slavery*, University of Chicago, 1959, pp. 115–133.

47 Thomas Pettigrew and Rosalind Spier, "The Ecological Structure of Negro Homocide," *American Journal of Sociology*, vol. 67, pp. 621–629, May 1962.

48 Fanon, op. cit., p. 31.

49 James Baldwin, *Notes of a Native Son*, Dell, New York, 1963, p. 62.

50 Blauner, op. cit., pp. 89–90.

51 Leonard Savitz, "Black Crime," in Kent Miller and Ralph Dreger (eds.), *Comparative Studies of Blacks and Whites in the United States*, Seminar, New York, 1973, pp. 484–487.

52 Phillip Ennis, "Crime, Victims and the Police," in James Short, Jr. (ed.), *Modern Criminals*, Aldine, Chicago, 1970, pp. 87–103.

53 Louis Lomax, *The Negro Revolt,* New American Library, New York, 1962, p. 59.

54 *Report of the National Advisory Commission on Civil Disorders,* Bantam, New York, 1968, p. 302.

55 U.S. Civil Rights Commission, *Justice,* U.S. Government Printing Office, Washington, 1961, Book 5, p. 26.

56 Terry Ann Knopf, "Sniping: A New Pattern of Violence," in Peter Rossi (ed.), *Ghetto Revolts,* Transaction, New Brunswick, N.J., Books, 1973, pp. 153–174.

57 Skolnick, op. cit., chap. 7.

58 "Study Calls Police Bias Widespread," *The Washington Post,* p. A1, June 29, 1967.

59 Arthur Niederhoffer, *Behind the Shield: The Police in Urban Society,* Doubleday, New York, 1969, p. 178–198.

60 Gunnar Myrdal, *An American Dilemma,* Harper, New York, 1944, p. 542.

61 Testimony before Congressman Meltcalfe's hearing on Police Brutality, Chicago, August 30, 1972.

62 Report by Evell Younger, Attorney General of the State of California, cited in the *Los Angeles Sentinel,* p. A2, August 10, 1972.

63 William Swanson and Warren Breed, "Black Suicide in New Orleans," in Ari Kiev (ed.), *Transcultural Studies in Suicide,* forthcoming.

64 *Report of the National Advisory Commission . . . ,* op. cit., p. 321.

65 "White Police Object to Goal of 100 More Blacks," *Jet,* p. 13, November 29, 1973.

66 Edward Palmer, "Black Police in America," *The Black Scholar,* vol. 4, pp. 20–22, October 1973.

67 Fanon, op. cit., p. 250.

68 Donald Black and Albert Reiss, Jr., "Patterns of Behavior in Police and Citizen Transactions," *Studies in Crime and Law Enforcement in Metropolitan Areas,* Government Printing Office, Washington, 1967, p. 136

69 *The New York Times,* p. 29, May 9, 1966.

70 Savitz, op. cit., p. 497.

71 The President's Commission on Law Enforcement, op. cit., p. 145.

72 Ibid., pp. 216–228.

73 Stuart Nagel, "The Tipped Scales of American Justice," *Transaction,* vol. 3, pp. 3–9, May–June 1966.

74 Survey conducted by the American Judicature Society, cited in *Jet,* p. 32, August 30, 1973.

75 Nagel, loc. cit.

76 *Jet*, p. 32, August 30, 1973.
77 Wolfgang and Cohen, op. cit., pp. 79–80.
78 Harry Kalven and Hans Teusel, *The American Jury*, Little Brown, Boston, 1966, p. 211.
79 Fanon, "Racism and Culture," in *Toward the African Revolution*, Monthly Review, New York, 1967, p. 40.
80 Daniel H. Sivett, "Cross-Cultural Communication in the Courtroom: Applied Linguistics in a Murder Trial," a paper presented at the Conference on Racism and the Law, San Francisco, December, 1967.
81 Savitz, op. cit. p. 500.
82 Savitz, loc. cit.
83 William J. Bowers, "Racial Discrimination in Capital Punishment: Characteristics of the Condemned," unpublished manuscript, June 1972.
84 Ibid.
85 Myrdal, op. cit., p. 65.
86 *Uniform Crime Reports*, loc. cit.
87 Ibid.
88 Doug Joseph, "Alcoholic Beverages: Another Facet of White Exploitation of the Black Community," unpublished paper, Arizona State University, 1972.
89 *Uniform Crime Reports*, loc. cit.
90 Savitz, op. cit., p. 474.
91 "1 in 10 Addicted in Parts of the Inner City," *The Washington Post*, p. C1, April 4, 1972.
92 *Webster's New World Dictionary*, op. cit., p. 573.
93 *Uniform Crime Reports*, loc. cit.
94 *Webster's New World Dictionary*, op. cit., pp. 1, 141.
95 *Uniform Crime Reports*, loc. cit.
96 Robert Staples, *The Black Woman in America: Sex, Marriage and the Family*, Nelson-Hall, Chicago, 1973, pp. 73–94.
97 Ibid.
98 Ibid.
99 *Webster's New World Dictionary*, op. cit., p. 1566.
100 William Ryan, *Blaming the Victim*, Vintage, New York, 1971, p. 208.
101 J. Skelly Wright, "The Courts Have Failed the Poor," *The New York Times Magazine*, pp. 26–27, March 9, 1969.
102 George Jackson, "Towards the United Front," in Davis (ed.), op. cit., p. 157.
103 *The Christian Science Monitor*, December 13, 1971.

104 "National Prisoner Statistics—State Prisoners: Admissions and Re-
     leases, 1970," Bureau of Prisons, Washington, 1971, p. 1.
105 The President's Commission on Law Enforcement, op. cit., p. 45.
106 Bill Keene, "Who Is a Political Prisoner?" *The Hilltop,* p. 8,
     April 6, 1973.
107 Robert Chrisman, "Black Prisoners—White Law," *The Black Schol-
     ar,* p. 45, April–May 1971.
108 Bettina Aptheker, "The Social Functions of the Prisons in the
     United States," in Davis (ed.), op. cit., pp. 58–59.
109 Huey Newton, "Prison, Where Is Thy Victory?" in Davis (ed.),
     op. cit., p. 63.
110 Jessica Mitford, *Kind and Usual Punishment: The Prison Business,*
     Knopf, New York, 1973, pp. 259–266.
111 "Guinea Pig Experiments Are Conducted in Prisons," *Jet,* p. 20,
     August 24, 1972.
112 U.S. Bureau of the Census, *The Social and Economic Status . . . ,*
     p. 45.
113 Irving Piliavin and Scott Briar, "Police Encounters with Juveniles,"
     American Journal of Sociology, vol. 70, pp. 206–214, September
     1964.
114 Ibid.
115 James Short and F. Ivan Nye, "Reported Behavior as a Criterion
     of Deviant Behavior," *Social Problems,* vol. 5, pp. 207–213,
     Winter 1957–58.
116 The President's Commission on Law Enforcement, op. cit., p.
     146.
117 Nathan Goldman, "The Differential Selections of Juvenile Of-
     fenders for Court Appearances," in William Chambers (ed.),
     Crime and the Legal Process, McGraw-Hill, New York, 1969,
     p. 264–294.
118 Piliavin and Briar, op. cit., p. 212.
119 Edward Greenberg, "Black Children and the Political System: A
     Study of Socialization to Support," a paper delivered at the
     American Political Science Association Meeting, New York,
     September 1969.
120 Blauner, op. cit., p. 98.
121 Schley Lyons, "The Political Socialization of Ghetto Children,
     Efficacy and Cynicism," *The Journal of Politics,* vol. 32, pp.
     288–304, May 1970.
122 Frantz Fanon, *A Dying Colonialism,* Grove, New York, 1967,
     pp. 121–124.

SUGGESTED READING LIST

Balbus, Issac: *The Dialectics of Legal Repression,* Russel Sage, New York, 1973.

Bayley, David H. and Harold Mendelsohn: *Minorities and the Police: Confrontation in America,* The Free Press, New York, 1969.

Bell, Derrick A.: *Race, Racism and American Law,* Little, Brown, Boston, 1973.

Berry, Mary: *Black Resistance, White Law: A History of Constitutional Racism in America,* Appleton-Century-Crofts, New York, 1971.

Blackburn, Sara (ed.): *White Justice: Black Experience Today in America's Courtrooms,* Harper & Row, New York, 1971.

Bohannon, Paul (ed.): *African Homocide and Suicide,* Princeton, Princeton, N.J., 1960.

Bowers, William J.: *Executions in America,* Lexington, Lexington, Mass., 1974.

Chrisman, Robert: Black Prisoners–White Law, *The Black Scholar,* vol. 1, p. 45, April–May 1971.

Davis, Angela (ed.): *If They Come in the Morning,* Signet, New York, 1971.

Feagin, Joe R. and Harlan Hahn: *Ghetto Revolts: The Politics of Violence in American Cities,* Macmillan, New York, 1973.

Ianni, A. Francis: *Black Mafia,* Simon and Schuster, New York, 1974.

Knight, Etheridge: *Black Voices from Prison,* Pathfinder, New York, 1970.

Mitford, Jessica: *Kind and Usual Punishment: The Prison Business,* Knopf, New York, 1973.

Niederhoffer, Arthur: *Behind the Shield: The Police in Urban Society,* Doubleday, New York, 1969.

Pinkney, Alphonso: *The American Way of Violence,* Random House, New York, 1972.

Reasons, Charles E. and Jack L. Kuykendall: *Race, Crime and Justice,* Goodyear, Pacific Palisades, Calif., 1972.

Savitz, Leonard: "Black Crime," in Kent Miller and Ralph Dreger (eds.), *Comparative Studies of Blacks and Whites in the United States,* Seminar, New York, 1973.

Wolfgang, Marvin and Bernard Cohen: *Crime and Race: Conceptions and Misconceptions,* Institute of Human Relations, New York, 1970.

Chapter 9

Majority Groups

In most traditional sociology texts there is usually a section or chapter on minority groups and the problems they encounter in a society where the majority culture excludes them from equal participation in certain areas. While the treatment of this subject by liberal sociologists is generally sympathetic to racial minorities and favorable toward a greater minority share in the society's values, the practice of minority exclusion is usually viewed as the minority group's problem. Euphemistic terms such as "prejudice" and "discrimination" are used instead of "racism" and "oppression." Such majority group attitudes and practices are commonly attributed to past events, e.g., slavery, psychological factors, and the universal tendency toward ethnocentrism in all human beings.

The purpose of this chapter is to describe the nature of majority groups, how their racial attitudes are formed and maintained, their gains from minority group subordination and how their dominance is maintained, and some of the disadvantages of minority group exclusion. Before explaining majority group behavior, we should understand that the concepts of majority and minority groups are applicable only to pluralistic societies that have diverse racial and ethnic groups, not racially homogeneous countries. Hence the United States, being one of the most ethnically heterogeneous countries in the world, is particularly pluralistic whereas Sweden is not.

When we speak of the nature of majority groups, it should be explained that it is a qualitative not a quantitative concept. Numerical superiority does not necessarily mean a group has the political, economic, or social power in a given society. For example, Blacks in Rhodesia are a numerical majority but a political and economic minority. The 250,000 Whites who rule that country are the qualitative majority despite the five million Blacks who inhabit it. A similar situation exists in certain parts of the United States, such as Washington, D.C., where Blacks comprise the statistical majority, but are still subject to White oppression. Hence the majority is the group with more power on the basis of which it can exclude powerless groups from equal competition and privileges on the grounds of ethnic, racial, religious, cultural, or sex differences.[1]

In reality majority-minority relations are power relationships because they deal with the distribution of power in a society. At the same time the majority of American Whites do not rule this nation either. Therefore, it is necessary to distinguish majority groups from the ruling class of American society. We refer to majority groups as the members of the dominant racial group whose interests are represented in the political, economic, and social institutions of the society and whose status is superior to that of the racially subordinate group. The ruling class is that elite fraction of the dominant group who actually control the wealth, resources, and institutions. In this chapter we are specifically concerned with the collective dominance of Whites qua Whites over Blacks. This is not the only form of dominance, nor ultimately the most important, since class and sex oppression also exist in the American social structure.

In American society there are degrees of oppression, but race is the most salient and pervasive foundation on which it is based. All other aspects of class and sex oppression are subordinate to it at this point. It was this fact that once led W. E. B. Dubois (1961) to remark over sixty years ago that the problem of the twentieth century would be the color line.[2] People in this nation have a multiple set of identities but their primary self-identification is race. They think of themselves as "White" or "Black" because it determines their lifestyles and life chances in a racist society. Being Black or White affects every element of individual existence including access to jobs, education, housing, food, and even life or death.

The basic reason for the institutionalized dominance of one racial group over another is usually considered to be racism. Yet historical and objective analysis reveals that racial dominance usually precedes the idea of racial superiority. This, at least, is reflected in Memmi's (1968) definition of racism as "the generalized and final assigning of values to real or imaginary differences, to the accusor's benefit and at his victim's expense, in order to justify the former's own privileges or aggression." It is his belief that racism is a functional rationalization and symbol for oppression. As an example, he cites the fact that racist attitudes are always directed at the vanquished, not the powerful. It is usually the colonized who are the victims of racism, not the colonizer. The reason for this, according to Memmi, is to justify the ghettoization and colonial exploitation of subject peoples by the racist.[3]

It is our intent to describe exactly how and why majority groups use racism as a tool to subjugate people of color. This is in contrast to the traditional sociological approach to race relations as a minority problem because Blacks possess certain characteristics, e.g., skin color or cultural values, that have elicited the White pattern of racial exclusion and discrimination. Although much of majority group dominance is built into major social institutions, which are the primary mechanism of racial subordination, that subject has been dealt with elsewhere (see Chapter 4) as has the role of the ruling class in creating and perpetuating racism.

Defining majority groups as the collective group of Whites who benefit from minority subordination does not mean that they are a monolithic group. Many Whites do not actively participate in the oppression of minorities, nor do they favor such practices. They do not ask for racial privileges based on the subjugation of powerless racial groups, nor do they have to. Their racial privileges are built into the institutions and customs of American society and rebound to them automatically by virtue of the almost total exclusion of certain racial groups from equal competition in reaching the society's goals.

All members of the dominant majority have not always possessed preferential status in the United States. This country's history is replete with the oppression of many White groups who were subject to discrimination of some kind. Even today certain sectors of the White population are divided into warring camps, for example, White youth and women. Many White radicals are just as opposed to oppressive elements in American society as Blacks. However, even disloyal members of the opposition can claim their privileges as a member of the dominant racial majority any time they wish. Political ideologies are not as immutable as skin color as the history of Black involvement in White-dominated radical movements well illustrates.

Still, it must be recognized that the benefits of racism accrue primarily to members of the ruling group. In a society structured in such a way that the positive values are not available to people on the basis of need or allocated on the basis of their contribution to its total wealth, the rulers find it relatively easy to secure White collaboration in the distribution of economic opportunities along racial lines. We have to understand the reasons and methods by which racial majorities hold on to their power so that we can simultaneously understand how their tendency toward racial dominance can be converted into building a society free of class and sexual exploitation.

MECHANISMS OF MAJORITY GROUP DOMINANCE

Assimilation

Chrisman (1970) charges that an important strategy of the Anglo-American state to retain its control is through the offer of assimilation to Blacks.[4] According to Gordon (1964), assimilation occurs on two different levels—the behavioral and the structural. Behavioral assimilation refers to the minority person who takes on the cultural patterns and values of the dominant culture. Structural assimilation is the process of integrating into the social world of the majority group, including its cliques, clubs, and neighborhoods.[5] Most assimilation by Blacks has been of the behavioral type although there is a significant increase in the structural level of assimilation.

Because of their physical isolation from Whites, few Blacks have had the opportunity to acquire Anglo-Saxon cultural values in any systematic way. Those who did were a small minority until recent years. Cultural assimilation serves to maintain majority group dominance because the assimilated individual often becomes committed to the preservation of Anglo-Saxon values and institutions rather than to the liberation of his group. Since it is only a minority of Blacks who become culturally assimilated, they are given opportunities denied to the masses and their achievements are cited as examples of equal opportunity in America for those who follow the rules. The Black majority who remain oppressed are considered failures because of the inability or unwillingness to adopt the society's values and customs.

Structural assimilation has been an even rarer practice. Since it frequently involves intermarriage, White Americans have been strongly opposed to it. In fact the barriers to interracial marriage have been a primary method of majority group dominance. As King (1973) has observed, "Marriage between members of the ruling class and those whom they oppress inevitably undermines the rationale for the basis of oppression."[6] The social taboos on interracial marriage prevent challenge to the superior group in a number of ways. A low incidence of racial intermarriage makes Black accumulation of wealth improbable, prohibits Blacks from obtaining jobs through social contacts and kin connections, and prevents them from obtaining a familiarity with the social world of Whites, which is necessary for obtaining certain jobs that require such knowledge.[7]

Even when limited interracial marriages were permitted, they reflected the status of Blacks as a colonized group. Until recent years most of them involved Black men of a high socioeconomic status with White women of a lower status.[8] This type of marriage was called *hypogamy* and was such a common union that sociologists devised theories to explain it. A most common theory was that the Black male partner was exchanging his economic resources for the privilege of being married to a member of the racially superior group. Or, in other words, he was trading his socioeconomic status for her caste status.[9]

While many interracial marriages are formed for the same reasons as intraracial marriages, they carry strong political implications in a racist, colonized society. Since the dominant racial group assigns positive values to beauty and personality traits possessed primarily by the White female, she becomes a more desirable marriage partner to some Black males. This reflects the cultural dominance found in many colonized societies. According to one observer:

> Some men or some women in effect, by choosing partners of another race, marry persons of a class or a culture inferior to their own whom they would not have chosen as spouses in their own race and whose chief asset seems to be the assurance that the partner will achieve denaturalization and deracialization. Among certain people of color, the fact that they are marrying someone of the white race seems to have overridden every other consideration. In this fact they find access to complete equality with that illustrious race, the master of the world, the ruler of the peoples of color. . . .[10]

Many people prefer to think of the present increase in interracial marriages as a sign of racial progress. To a certain extent it is since the growing tolerance of such marriages illustrates that White America is diverging slightly from its rigid caste structure and permitting individuals free choice in their selection of marriage partners.[11] At the same time the characteristics of many interracial marriages are fostering majority group dominance. Among those characteristics are that (1) most of the marriages involve Black males and White females and (2) a disproportionate number of the Black male partners are of a high socioeconomic status.[12]

One of the problems created by the one-sided character of Black-White marriages is the disunity it creates in the Black community. Nathan Hare (1971) felt compelled to write an editorial stating that "all over this land the Black college movement is being torn apart by the infiltration of the white female who, because of centuries on a queenly pedestal, is able to take away from the small supply of Black male students."[13] The fact that these are the most successful Black males creates additional problems. One of them is the limited supply of Black males in this category available as marriage partners to middle-class Black women.[14] Another problem is the impact it has on the Black group's economic progress. Instead of interracial marriage being a vehicle for Black accumulation of White wealth, the reverse is the case. Young White women who violate their group's racial norms by marrying a Black male seldom have any economic resources of their own. By marrying higher-status Black males they stand to gain what little wealth he has, particularly since Black males have the shortest life expectancy rate and White women have the longest.[15]

None of these problems need exist in a less racist society but they are salient in a race-divided country such as the United States. A genuine breakdown of the racial caste system would equally involve Black men and Black women in intermarriage. But the marriage of Black women and White men would not serve the interests of majority group control as well. Even those very successful Black women in the entertainment world that intermarried were subject to economic exploitation by their White husbands.[16] Moreover, in Black-White unions where the White partner is female, the children of such marriages are legally Black but culturally White. As in most families it is the mother who transmits the culture to the child.[17]

Cooptation

Cooptation is a process similar to that of assimilation. Davidson (1970) considers it a procedure whereby the ruling class nonviolently brings into its fold, and thus controls, an entire minority group or individual members of that group who have challenged the dominance of the majority culture.[18] Usually the coopted Blacks are the more competent members who have demonstrated leadership qualities. This process is distinguished from assimilation in that it is a more deliberate strategy of the ruling elites and is not as pervasive as structural assimilation since it may involve only working within the dominant institutions and accepting their values.

The procedure of cooptation can be accomplished through a variety of ways. Education of native youth is a most common technique used in most colonial societies. In schools controlled by the colonizer, the colonized youth are programmed for accepting the superiority of White values and the inferiority of their own group's norms.[19] A basic difference, for instance, between French and British colonialism in Africa was the French use of cooptation to maintain its colonial rule. France pursued a strategy of gradually bringing its African elites into the French way of life. As they took on French cultural trappings, their status was progressively elevated until they attained full French citizenship. It was these same Black Frenchmen who were then sent back to their native countries to assume leadership posts.[20]

In the United States the process of cooptation has been refined to a great art. Beginning with the middle sixties, almost every Black leader that was not killed or imprisoned had joined some respectable part of the system. The heads of government agencies, university departments, and charitable organizations are a virtual roster of civil rights activists and revolutionary militants from the sixties. In part this resulted from the fact that many Black leaders were fighting only to join the dominant group's system. They were not struggling against the exploitative values of this society but only against their exclusion. A similar realization led Harold Cruse (1967) to conclude, "What really worries the establishment is not so much the cacophony of protest, but the problem of how to absorb the movement without too much stress and strain."[21]

Although the colonizer uses his educational system, money, and prestigious positions to coopt the talented members of the racially subordinate group, this tactic has met with limited success. Many of the coopted Blacks are able to operate within the system only so long as they can justify their role and functioning to themselves. Since the American system has been proceeding in the direction of neocolonialism, it has been easier for some Blacks to accept the limited opportunity available to them with the rationalization that they were helping to further Black progress. Expressions of overt racism are rare in American leadership circles today and Blacks rarely must directly confront their role as a pawn in racial oppression. What has happened, however, is that some Blacks who were coopted have begun to realize that their achievements within the colonial structure were at the expense of their own group. As a result, they moved radically toward a rejection of White culture and developed a nationalist ideology. Such cases were quite common under the Nixon administration. As Memmi (1967) states it: "The day has come when it is the colonized who must refuse the colonizer."[22]

Conventions and Etiquette

In a stable system of racial stratification, the preservation of majority group control is often a matter of conformity with local customs. The Southern part of the United States particularly had its concept of the Negro's "place" and a whole structure of behavior reinforced it. Persistent usage of certain terms tended to inculcate in both racial groups that their different statuses were the natural order of things. It was common, and natural, for Whites to address all Blacks by their first names and for Blacks to refer to Whites by courtesy titles such as Mr. or Mrs. Such a differential use of titles reflected the inequality of the racial groups in that setting.[23]

A number of other Southern customs maintained the social distance between the two racial groups. Taboos on shaking hands, Blacks entering White homes through the back door, Whites always having to initiate the conversation or physical touch, Black deference to Whites, etc., were all symbolic rituals which served to remind both racial groups of their "place" in Southern society.[24] Some of these customs were embodied in laws requiring racial segregation in certain public facilities. Moreover, community sanctions against the violation of informal customs could be quite severe. Even members of the racially dominant group were not free to go beyond certain limits in their behavior with Blacks. Undergirding the system of racial customs was the potential threat of violence, loss of employment, or ostracism.

In the North there was no such elaborate code of racial etiquette. Unlike the South, White Northerners had little contact with Blacks except that required for supervising them in their jobs. In general, Northern Whites avoided social situations such as eating, mating, and friendship with Blacks. This custom itself perpetuates minority group subordination by confining these people to jobs that do not involve social contacts with Whites. Rather than competency and qualifications, other standards that work against racial minorities are used.[25]

Historically, it was a custom in both the South and North that Blacks should not be put into jobs which required them to supervise Whites. There was also a concern about hiring Black males for jobs where they might have any social contact with White women. Special efforts were made to avoid situations in which Black men and White women could get together on a friendly basis, where erotic attraction might overcome taboos that did not exist in law. At the same time Black women were frequently placed in such situations with White men. And, in fact, White males took many liberties with them that would have been severely punished had Black men done the same with White women.[26]

Dependency

There are several types of dependency. In classical colonial societies it is assumed that the colonizer creates a dependency relationship in which the colonized identify with the power, privilege, and status of the ruling order. This psychological reaction of the native supposedly stems from the giving of gifts or services by a European to a native. The colonized henceforth begins to depend on the settler for these items and this creates in him a dependency complex which will further colonial rule.[27] Much of the basis of this theory rests on the stereotyping of the oppressed group as childlike in nature. A similar theory for Afro-Americans was developed by Stanley Elkins (1968). He asserted that slavery placed Blacks in a completely dependent role. All their rewards came from absolute obedience—not initiative and enterprise—a fact that strongly decreased the need for Black achievement.[28]

Little credence should be given these theories because dependency would create passive acceptance of one's condition. There is ample evidence that Blacks have resisted their oppression since arriving on these shores.[29] The dependency we consider relevant is more political and economic in character. In attempting to build institutions or attain economic success, Blacks find themselves in need of White assistance in some form or another. A major reason for this type of dependency is that the legacy of racism has deprived Blacks of the skills, contacts, and power to do many things without help from Whites.[30]

Two instances where Blacks held obstensible control but had to depend on Whites occurred in Newark, New Jersey and Gary, Indiana. In Newark a housing development was being built by a Black nationalist organization headed by Amiri Bayaka. Although a terribly high unemployment rate existed among the local Blacks, many Whites were employed in the construction project because they were the only ones who had the required skills. In Gary, Indiana where Blacks had elected one of their own as Mayor in the face of massive White resistance, there were hopes among them for political patronage in the form of high city positions. The Mayor also appeared to be committed to putting as many Blacks as possible in those jobs. However, most of the educated Blacks in the city were school teachers and social workers. Having had no access to other positions before, they were unprepared to fill them. Thus, the city had to rely either on Whites to fill key posts or unqualified Blacks who operated inefficiently.[31]

Any discussion of Black separatism must keep the above factors in mind. Moreover, it is difficult to escape White involvement in Black affairs because its control over the entire society is so pervasive. One aspect of White involvement—Black social movements—is virtually over except for the more conservative organizations. In previous years White activists generally had greater access to resources, were freer to act, closer to the centers of power, and frequently had crucially needed organizing experience. As a result, many Whites had leadership roles and made decisions in movements primarily affecting Blacks.[32] Not all White involvement in Black affairs is negative but it does serve to reinforce myths of Black inferiority and reliance upon Whites to accomplish anything of value.

On the individual level successful Blacks often find it necessary to rely on Whites to attain their goals and preserve them. It is common to find Black atheletes and entertainers represented by White agents. Until recently most Blacks in boxing had White managers. Black television stars use mostly White guests on variety shows in order to avoid the appearance of an all-Black program. White lawyers frequently manage the business affairs of wealthy Blacks. While this could be considered examples of interracial cooperation, it is seldom reciprocated by successful Whites. In some cases Whites possess the know-how to get certain things done better than comparable Blacks. Sometimes it is due to the belief of even Blacks that Whites are just naturally more capable. The net result is continued Black dependency on Whites.

Ethnocentrism

This concept was once defined by William Graham Sumner (1906) as "that view of things in which one's own group is the center of everything and all others are scaled and rated with reference to it."[33] While ethnocentric tendencies may exist in most societies, its prevalence in a nation where one racial group has all the power and others have none leads to cultural dominance by the dominant group. Whites use Anglo-Saxon cultural values as a yardstick to measure the worth of other groups. In general other cultural groups are ranked positive or negative according to the degree that they approximate the cultural characteristics of the White majority. However, it is not the only criterion for determining a racial minority's participation in the society at large. For example, Asian Americans have often excelled Whites in terms of certain Anglo-Saxon values but they are still excluded from the mainstream on the basis of skin color.[34]

Insistence on minority group conformity to majority group culture has different effects depending on the minority group and its individual member's class position. For the most part middle-class minority members have taken on Anglo-Saxon traits or are at least capable of adopting them when necessary, but certain minorities such as Puerto Ricans and Chicanos have low degrees of cultural assimilation. Lower-class members of other groups tend to retain the values of their own culture.[35] It is their failure to adopt values in conformity to Anglo-Saxon traditions that often becomes an ex-post facto rationale for their exclusion from majority group institutions.

Anglo-conformity is a term used by Gordon (1964) to describe the White culture's prescription that English institutions, language, and cultural patterns remain dominant and standard in American life. He insists that upholders of Anglo-conformity are not necessarily racists. Some are and others simply believe that since English culture represents the foundation of American society, newly entering immigrants should conform to its values.[36] Such a presumption ignores the fact that Blacks, at least, never had an opportunity to adjust to Anglo-Saxon culture and on a group level stood to benefit little by its adoption. Requirements that they categorically accept Anglo-Saxon cultural forms do not take into account the reality of Black life in America.

Hence, those who exclude Blacks from the mainstream for other reasons use their different cultural traditions as a smoke screen. Blacks are barred from predominantly White schools because of the looser morals they allegedly possess when the exclusion actually permits White schools to use the differences spent on Black and White schools to increase White advantages over Blacks in competition for jobs, income, etc. Many of the other Anglo-Saxon traits required have little to do with one's ability to perform a job competently. Whether a group believes in sex before marriage, the monogamous family, etc., is irrelevant to most job requirements. Although these values are imposed on all members of the society, the effect is considerably different for racial minorities who have not internalized those values and may find them in conflict with the mores of their own group.

The ultimate effect of ethnocentrism is to provide a justification for the exploitation of racial minorities on the basis of their maladjustment to Anglo-Saxon culture. Groups that insist on retaining their cultural heritage are labeled a threat to the American way of life. By using this kind of patriotic appeal, the White majority is unified in its resistance to lowering the barriers to minority group inclusion in the larger society. Ethnocentrism serves as a protection against change since the dominant racial group has certain privileges under the current arrangement. It has a better grasp of the internal workings of Anglo-Saxon culture which works to its advantage in a number of ways. Defense of the majority group's cultural system serves to preserve the colonial order and its cultural dominance.

Ideologies

Ideologies are a set of beliefs used to justify the present social order. One of the ideologies used to maintain White rule is what Schuman (1969) calls "the doctrine of free will," the belief by Whites that individuals are responsible for their own actions.[37] A logical inference from this belief is that the source of Black deprivation can be found in a lack of motivation to achieve success in a society which offers equal opportunity to all its citizens. This rationale for low status among Blacks differs from traditional racial ideologies because it attempts to explain the Black condition in nonbiological terms.

It is now more fashionable to believe that the inferior economic and educational status of Blacks is due simply to their failure to have high aspirations and work hard to achieve their goals. This belief is particularly strong among White ethnics who assert that hard work and education will lead to success in America. Blacks, they presume, want to succeed without doing anything except use the tax money paid by the hard-working ethnic populations.[38] This feeling probably accounts for the fact that the problem of Black Americans was ranked twenty-fourth out of a list of 27 major national issues in a national survey.[39] Schuman (1969) calls this White racism because Whites refuse to accept past or present responsibility for the prejudice and discrimination and general inequality in the spread of opportunities.[40] By applying the ideology of free will they avoid the reality of racial oppression and thus place the whole burden of Black subjugation on Afro-Americans themselves.

A similar ideology is that of universalism. This is the belief that race and ethnicity should not be taken into account in judgments about people and in the arrangement of institutions.[41] The theory that no important differences exist between Blacks and Whites in America—either biologically or culturally—is of recent origin. It gained prominance at precisely the time when Blacks began to insist that they did have distinctive attitudes, values, and lifestyles and began to question the validity and relevance of White culture. At the same time that Whites wanted to become color-blind, Blacks were demanding separate admission standards to schools and jobs. Thus the ideology of universalism must be viewed in the proper context. It is mostly an attempt by Whites to maintain institutional arrangements which embody the residual results of past overt racism. It denies that Blacks are an interest group or that Whites have had any responsibility for the racial oppression of Blacks for the last four hundred years.

Social Networks and Kinship Ties

This mechanism is one of the most important for majority group dominance and contradicts the myth of equal opportunity for success in America. In certain higher levels of the work world, social compatibility or comfort in social relations are decisive criteria in being considered for certain high-status positions.[42] Discrimination on the basis of sociability works against many groups but particularly to the disadvantage of women and Blacks—although for different reasons and to varying degrees.

In high-level business circles it is expected that management executives will go to the right clubs together, play golf, and socialize in one another's homes. Many of the biggest contracts in business are finalized at country clubs. (To this day many of these clubs still exclude Blacks and women.) It is in these settings that close primary relationships are formed between top management men who have control over corporate activities that influence the lives of people all over the world. In general these men are all from the right schools, belong to the same fraternity, and consequently are White, Anglo-Saxon Protestants.[43] This situation led C. Wright Mills to his conclusions concerning the existence and functions of "the power elite."

Even on lower occupational levels, kinship and friendship ties can be decisive. All other things being equal, knowing the right people is an important factor in obtaining certain jobs. In some cases this is the most important determinant of job placement. A number of people report that having the right contacts assured them their initial job placement.[44] This is where the isolation of Blacks from Whites works to the disadvantage of Blacks. Since Whites control the source of most employment, Blacks are able to compete only on objective criteria. Despite Weber's (1941) belief that the rise of modern bureaucracies prevented nepotism, ingenious individuals have managed to manipulate rational bureaucracies to serve their ends.[45] Even in civil service positions, allegedly based on merit, kinsmen and friends often manage to achieve a competitive edge over others.

The social taboos on interracial marriages had the latent function of depriving most Blacks of kinship ties that would allow them easier access to many occupations. Until recently they rarely had the opportunity to date a person of the dominant race since White parents controlled whom their children would meet, and fall in love with, by selecting certain neighborhoods, schools, and social clubs for them.[46] An excellent example of how kinship ties operate was revealed in the controversy over admitting Blacks to some of the craft unions. Many White parents complained because the traditional procedure had been to admit the sons of present union members on a preferential basis.[47]

Using social networks and kinship ties to gain admission to desirable jobs tends to invalidate the ideologies of equal opportunity and universalism. It illustrates the many different forms of racism and its embodiment in the social customs and practices that maintain majority group dominance along with political and economic methods. Each of these racist forms are interwoven into a complex web that keeps minorities under White domination.

Stereotyping

This is the adoption of generalized attitudes about the cultural traits that mold the personality, moral character, and value orientations of a particular group. In the case of Blacks it is the constant repetition of slogans and cliches about their alleged lack of industry, initiative, intelligence, honesty, and morality. While stereotypes may be applied to any distinct group, in a racist society dark skin is usually associated with negative values and white skin with positive values and goodness. In a number of studies where Whites were asked to impute characteristics to individuals on the basis of physical appearance alone, dark skin was usually associated with hostility, dishonesty, unfriendliness, lack of a sense of humor, slyness, etc.[48]

The stereotyped traits of racial groups often have no basis in reality. In many cases, no individual member of that racial group will have all the characteristics attributed to it. Stereotypes do contain some elements of truth although the reasons for their existence are rarely investigated. For example, there are some Blacks (and Whites) who are lazy because they are not motivated to work hard under a system where there are no rewards for industry. Even in the postslavery era, Blacks were relegated to the dirtiest, lowest paying jobs for which it is difficult to muster enthusiasm. When Whites encounter Blacks who are obvious examples of the inaccuracy of their stereotyped notions (e.g., intelligent, hard working, honest, etc.) they are usually dismissed as exceptions or a genetic mutation.

It is interesting to note that the stereotypes in America usually apply only to racial and ethnic minorities. Rarely do we hear stereotypes (except favorable ones) about White, Anglo-Saxon Protestants—with the possible exception of females. This reflects their power to control the dissemination of stereotypes about racial minorities and to effectively punish those who would say unkind things about them or their culture. Although stereotypes of Blacks are changing, the diversity within this group is still being ignored. White Americans now hold positive stereotypes of Blacks as entertainers and atheletes while ignoring their roles as scholars, artists, and scientists.

The practice of racial stereotyping functions to maintain contemporary status relations. Colonial inequalities are difficult to enforce unless members of the majority group continue to see their racial minorities in stereotyped ways. As Shibutani and Kian (1965) note, the unequal distribution of values becomes more difficult to defend once people identify one another as being basically alike.[49] However, it is precisely this function of racial stereotypes that is necessary for preserving the advantages of the majority group in competing for the social values of colonial society.

One of the most accurate analysts of this function of racial stereotyping was Gunnar Myrdal (1944). In his massive study of American race relations, he concluded that racial stereotypes are opportunistic and have the function to defend interests of the majority group. He noted that racial beliefs were not consistent and that that fact was illuminating and of highest importance. Specifically, he states: "It is no accident that popular beliefs are biased heavily in a direction unfavorable to the Negro people because they are steered by white people's needs for justification of the caste order." As examples he cites how White beliefs about Black laziness, lack of morals, criminal tendencies, etc., function to ease the conscience of the good, upright, White American when confronted with the slum conditions under which Afro-Americans must live. These beliefs also tend to portray Blacks as a threat to civilized society unless kept in their place.[50]

Tests and Qualifications

Tests are considered objective instruments that do not discriminate against groups on the basis of race, creed, color, sex, or class. They are increasingly decisive in admission to colleges, jobs, professions, etc. Through use of this basic requirement that individuals be ranked by their scores on these instruments, majority groups hope to maintain their privileges forever while avoiding the stigma of racism. However, tests inherently discriminate against racial minorities because (1) they usually contain a strong cultural bias, (2) minorities are often exposed to inferior schools that do not prepare them to compete equally with Whites on such exams, and (3) psychological factors such as the race of the examiner affect the test performance of minorities more than majorities.[51]

Most IQ tests and other standardized exams were originally constructed for White, middle-class populations. They thus work to the disadvantage of racial minorities who come from lower-class backgrounds and have different cultural values from the ones expressed in these tests. Because of the inadequate quality of so many Black schools, their graduates often do not have the basic reading and writing skills to pass such tests. Also, racial minorities are often intimidated by the presence of a White test examiner, which will subsequently affect their performance on these exams. In most cases the White student will face a White examiner with whom he can feel at ease. Even a Black examiner would not pose much of a problem since he has the security of his membership in the superior race.[52]

The important thing is to emphasize that these tests are not predictive of academic achievement or job performance, particularly for racial minorities. This could not have been more strongly demonstrated than when these test scores were recently waived for minorities entering college. Although some of these students have failed to complete degree programs, the majority of them have been successful in colleges where they could not have been enrolled under normal admissions standards.[53] As for job entrance exams, they are notable for their lack of relevance to the actual requirements of those jobs. Giving a test on English and math items to applicants for social work positions is one example. Most people learn the essential skills of a position in on-the-job training. Very technical occupations are of course an exception.

In recent years the controversy over the relationship between race and intelligence has been revived. The sole proof for the theory of the inherent inferiority of Black intelligence comes from the culturally biased IQ tests discussed above. In general the 15-point difference on IQ tests between Blacks and Whites is used as evidence of inherited racial differences in mental ability. Any discussion of this issue is fruitless because (1) the tests are culturally biased, (2) the variations within racial groups are greater than the differences between them, (3) Blacks and Whites are incomparable because of differences in learning opportunities, and (4) these tests are not accurate predictors of academic achievement or job performance.[54]

What is important is the use to which these tests, and theories about genetic differences in Black and White intelligence, are put. Lately a number of White-controlled universities and journals have given a great deal of exposure to the ideas of Arthur Jensen (1969)[55] and William Schockley (1972).[56] Both men claim that Blacks are deficient in certain mental skills and that this should be translated into some kind of public policy. Schockley, for example, has advocated sterilization of women in those groups (mostly Black) producing children of low intelligence capacity. He has even suggested that the number of Blacks who do score high on IQ tests can be attributed to the proportion of White genes they possess.

These ideas, which were once labeled racist, are now receiving exposure in such prestigious universities as Harvard and Yale, through the printed word in *Harvard Educational Review* and *Psychology Today,* and on television network shows. This is justified on the grounds of freedom of speech although it can hardly be overlooked that such civil liberties have seldom been given to others with unpopular ideas. Moreover, while White researchers with racist viewpoints can get exceptionally wide exposure for their ideas, Black researchers are unable to get the same exposure or research funding for a nonracist perspective of Black intelligence.[57] Another consequence of the focus on this controversy is that it is a diversionary tactic which shifts the issue to the question of Black responsibility for their own condition rather than internal colonialism.

Job qualifications represent another subterfuge in the strategy for majority group control. Racial minorities are obviously disadvantaged in competing for jobs with Whites when employers place heavy reliance on personal qualifications or skills that were not obtainable because of past racist practices. In some cases just requiring experience in a similar job category will exclude most racial minorities. Other structural barriers also operate against minorities. In universities where a publish-or-perish policy is in effect, racial minorities find it difficult to receive opportunities or promotions. While they may write scholarly articles, professional journals dominated by Whites will not publish them because of their radical or anti-White perspective.[58]

MAJORITY GROUP GAINS FROM MINORITY OPPRESSION

Traditional sociological views of minority oppression as a problem mask some of the gains majorities reap from the exclusion of racial minorities in the pursuit of American success goals such as money, power, and position. We are constantly told that majority group dominance is a natural tendency in human societies due to forces of xenophobia, stereotypes, cultural differences, and functional importance of roles performed. This explanation leads to the conclusion that the passage of time, greater communication, human relations education, and racial integration will decrease the problem or resolve it altogether. Such myopic thinking ignores a crucial element in the oppression of racial minorities: that the ethnic stratification system benefits all strata of the White majority and Whites do stand to lose something by the elimination of their racial privileges.

We are discussing separately here the gains of the White masses in contradistinction to the benefits reaped by the power elite from racial oppression. The advantages to the colonial ruling class have been described elsewhere. Basically these gains of majority groups fall into four categories: (1) economic, (2) psychological, (3) status-prestige, and (4) sexual and marital gains. Central to the understanding of these White gains under internal colonialism is the notion of racial privilege. Blauner (1972) defines privilege in terms of "unfair advantage, a preferential situation or systematic headstart in the pursuit of social values." He says that "white Americans enjoy special privilege in all areas of existence where racial minorities are systematically excluded or disadvantaged."[59]

Economic Gains

These are probably the most important White gains from Black subordination since they provide access to a larger share of the goods and services available. Ever since the era of slavery Whites have benefited from the exploited labor of Blacks. The slave trade, for instance, indirectly benefited the White middle-class in the form of an expanding economy that produced an increasing number of customers for the shopkeeper, markets for the small farmer, and clients for doctors and lawyers. It created jobs for White workers, and White indentured servants were permitted to escape plantation servitude solely due to the large supply of African slaves brought over to take their place.[60] This probably accounted for a large amount of White support for slavery.

After slavery ended Black workers came into direct competition with White workers. This fact accounts for much of the virulent White racism during the period immediately following emancipation and the failure of poor Whites and Blacks to remain united in a political coalition. The White worker believed that he benefited from restricting Black competitors for jobs. Ruling class Whites seized upon this fear of Black job competition to further their own interests. The result was the violent withdrawal of all Black rights and a rigid caste line based on race.[61] Boggs (1970) comments that "racism was real because there were real people with a stake in racism and these people were ready to resort to force to protect their stake."[62]

It appears that in the contemporary South the economic gains are greater than in other parts of the country. Glenn (1966) sought to investigate the manner in which Whites benefit from Black subordination. The process was relatively simple: to the extent that Blacks are relegated to low-paying jobs, Whites are allowed to avoid such work and increase their proportion of the higher-paying positions. In his examination of 1960 census reports he found that "the fact that whites in the Southern urbanized areas with large Black populations have unusually favorable occupational status and employment rates and higher incomes than other Southern whites is very likely the consequence of the presence and subordination of Blacks."[63]

Other researchers have made presumptions that the generally high living standards of some White Americans can be attributed, in part, to racial oppression and privilege. How much of it is neither clear nor proven. One economist came up with the figure of $15.5 billion as the White economic gain from racial privileges in employment, wages, education, occupations, and labor union monopoly.[64] One example of racial privilege at work is the proportion of Whites in suburban neighborhoods. Hermalin and Farley (1973) discovered that poor Whites far outnumbered rich Blacks in suburban communities because of the network of real estate practices, mortgage-lending arrangements, and governmental policies that prevent Blacks from obtaining the housing for which they are economically qualified.[65] Hence more decent housing was available to lower-income Whites.

White American gain from Black subordination is not as great as in classical colonial societies. In South Africa and Rhodesia, for example, the difference between Black and White income is 10 to 20 times higher.[66] The ratio of Blacks to Whites, is, of course, much lower. The number of Blacks in a given area usually affects the difference in racial income. In the United States the larger the number of Blacks in an area, the better the competitive position of low-status Whites. Where White employers have fewer White job seekers to select from the better the chances of White workers for receiving high-status positions. In analyzing data from the 1970 census, a trio of researchers found that Whites at the lowest socioeconomic levels appear to benefit economically from the presence of large numbers of Blacks.[67]

Whites also receive greater economic security from their racial privileges in the work world. When the economy is expanding Whites are given the lower rungs of better jobs and when economic conditions decline, as in a recession or depression, they are given preferential treatment for jobs formerly held by Blacks. For instance, during the Depression, there was a wholesale invasion of jobs held by Blacks by the White unemployed. They were usually assisted by employers, unions, and politicians. Blacks were ousted from occupations such as barbering, plumbing, and other new occupations they had just entered at that time.[68]

Psychological Gains

A number of psychological gains accrue to the White individual in a racist society. Internal colonialism permits him to act out these psychological needs against defenseless minorities. Racism provides some Whites with a feeling of psychological security in the face of feelings of personal inadequacy. They may feel weak and threatened by their environment but can take comfort in the fact that they can do things Blacks cannot do.[69] They may use Blacks as scapegoats by projecting onto them feelings of guilt from their own lack of accomplishment or success. Comer (1969) asserts that "racism is a low-level defense and adjustment mechanism utilized by groups to deal with psychological and social insecurities similar to the manner in which individuals utilize psychic defenses and adjustment mechanisms to deal with anxiety."[70]

Role analysis illustrates that playing the dominant role expands the ego. Individuals low on the status ladder may turn their attention to unfavored out-groups and derive from the comparison a modicum of self-esteem. Allport (1954) notes that out-groups are status builders because they have the special advantage of being in close proximity, visible, and holding a low position by group consensus, thus furnishing societal reinforcement for the White individual's sense of status enhancement. This is most easily observed in the racial pride of Southerners and their obsession with face-saving and self-justification, traits that derive from doubts about their position in the country-at-large.[71]

The low status of Blacks also permits frustrated Whites to displace their aggression safely. Blacks become scapegoats because they are available objects, not necessarily because they are the original source of the frustration. It is typical of a racist society that Whites can engage in neurotic, aggressive behavior toward Blacks without repudiation by other Whites while such acts toward other groups would be regarded as pathological. Frustrated, aggressive Whites may engage in certain aggressive behavior toward Blacks without provocation, for example, racial slurs, physical violence, etc.[72]

Status-Prestige Gains

Being White in colonial America automatically confers upon one a higher social status than any Black person regardless of the attributes or deficits possessed by either member of each race. According to

Glenn (1965), "The gains in prestige and self esteem by whites may be more important than the economic gains in perpetuating discrimination."[73] All Whites, regardless of how lowly they may be, gain a feeling of importance and superiority. One historian attributes the drive for status as a partial motivation for slavery. Stampp (1956) wrote: "Although the stress was on economic success, there were other gains associated with slavery to console those who did not achieve wealth. The desire for social prestige derivable from membership in a superior caste undoubtedly provided motivation and support for slavery among Northern and Southern whites, slaveholders and non-slaveholders."[74]

Besides being a source of status and prestige for Whites, the degradation of Blacks also permits them to increase their status in other areas, for example, in the type of occupation. The relegation of Blacks to dirty and servile work allows Whites to hold cleaner and more prestigious jobs. In areas where there are sufficient numbers of Blacks available, they monopolize such dirty jobs as janitors, porters, hospital orderlies, maids, etc. In some cases Whites go unemployed rather than accept jobs as domestic servants or janitors.[75] When White domestic servants are found in this country, they are usually foreigners.

The subordination of Blacks also permits Whites certain status luxuries that would otherwise be unavailable. White housewives, particularly in the South, are able to employ Black domestic help to cook their meals and clean their houses. Glenn (1966) notes that moderate income White families in the South frequently can afford a full-time servant whereas families with comparable incomes in other parts of the country can afford little or no domestic help. In fact his analysis of 1960 census data revealed that the employers who probably benefit most from Black subordination are Southern White housewives who employ domestic help.[76]

Sexual and Marital Gains

We have already discussed how the offer of intermarriage to members of the subordinated group is used to maintain their subordination, but that is a fairly recent trend and limited mostly to higher-status Blacks. Past practices have confined Black males to women of their own group while White males had access to females of both races. This was historically one of the sexual gains of White males. White females also benefited from this situation since Black women often bore the brunt of the double standard of sexual conduct. Women were expected to be chaste before marriage while men were permitted, and even encouraged, to engage in premarital sexual activity. To protect the sexual purity of White women most Southern White males began their sexual experiences with Black females. Black males, by threat of violence, were denied the same access to White women.[77]

Although this situation has changed considerably, Whites still enjoy certain advantages in the selection of sexual partners and marriage mates. It is Whites who define the standards of value for persons in the society. Since the criteria of beauty and sex appeal apply mostly to the White female, she is seen as the most desirable mate by males of minority races. That and her superior racial status lead many males to compete for her attention.

At the same time women select mates on the basis of their socioeconomic status. This means that White females are likely to favor higher-status minority males when choosing a mate for a serious relationship. This criterion, when applied by minority females, puts White males in an advantageous position since a greater proportion of them occupy positions of power and prestige. All non-White minorities appear to be affected by these factors since whenever they marry outside their group it is usually to a member of the White majority.[78] Hence Whites still maintain their racial advantage in the choice of sexual and marital partners even when free choice prevails. They are still more capable of marrying within their own group and also have easier access to the members of other racial groups as well.

UNDERSTANDING MAJORITY GROUP BEHAVIOR

To understand majority group behavior it is necessary to acknowledge that racism is learned behavior. For many Whites it begins at a very early age. Many White parents teach their children racist attitudes by their own behavior. Often they convey to White children their racist attitudes by referring to minorities as "those people," "niggers," "spics," "kikes," etc. White children who have Black playmates may be warned against associating with them.

The educational system also perpetuates the White child's racist socialization. In schools children are indoctrinated with myths of White supremacy. History books, for instance, often give the impression that many Blacks were happy with slavery. Stories such as little Sambo reinforce the conception of Blacks as childlike creatures. The language they learn usually upholds the idea that everything White is associated with goodness and the symbol Black is related to badness. Textbooks rarely include Blacks in anything but servile positions and this conveys the notion that the only people who matter are White.[79]

Until recently the communications media did their part to perpetuate racial stereotypes. The White-controlled newspapers rarely printed items about Blacks unless they had committed a crime. Moreover, it was a common practice to identify Black criminals by race whereas such was not the case with White criminals. In the communications media of television Blacks were conspicuous by their absence more than their stereotyped roles. The movie industry usually portrayed them in menial roles and as watermelon-loving and ghost-fearing creatures. American literature commonly placed them as servants to intelligent or wealthy Whites. Furthermore, most of the sociological and psychological works published accepted some part of the myths about their mental inferiority, character, or lack of culture.[80]

Given these aforementioned factors along with certain psychological forces of fear, insecurity, intolerance of ambiguity, authoritarianism etc., members of the White majority come to believe their superiority is absolute and unchangeable. They actually feel that their group dominance is the natural order of things and that no Black is or could even be the equal of the White. Along with the racial privileges they enjoy, and come to expect, they remain determined to retain their status as the superior racial group in a society which has structured those beliefs into an American creed.

DISADVANTAGES OF MAJORITY GROUP DOMINANCE

Although Whites enjoy certain gains from minority subordination in the short term, those advantages could be outweighed in the long run. Among some of the disadvantages are the following.

Working Class Disunity

Only employers benefit from divisions in the labor force. Conflicts between Black and White workers weaken both groups. Cheap Black labor acts as a depressant on White wages. The concentration of

Blacks in low-paying jobs may increase the number of such jobs. Instead of working together to gain a greater distribution of wealth to the working classes, Blacks and Whites expend their energy on competing for the available wages provided by employers.

Financial Costs

Since it is the working classes in American society who pay most of the cost of government services, Whites must bear the lion's share of the effects of racial oppression in the form of welfare, crime prevention, social services, and riot control. When racial segregation was still legal in the South, the duplication of facilities played no small part in that region's low standard of living for most of its citizens. The economic loss due to the failure to use Black talent effectively is immeasurable.

Political Costs

When the issue of race is stripped from the body politic, voters can pay attention to more relevant issues such as the inequality of wealth, political corruption, the quality of life, decline of the cities, etc. Voters will not find themselves in the position of voting for a man they believe represents big business interests but advocates a strong anti-busing program, dismantling social programs benefiting Blacks, and opposition to crime and welfare.

Loss of Cultural Diversity

Maintaining all-White institutions can lead to cultural stagnation. There are many things Whites can learn from Blacks such as expressiveness of emotion, compassion, fluidity of language, etc., which can be an asset. At the same time Blacks can learn from Whites certain techniques of organization, technical skills, discipline, and so on. In a multiracial society such as this one, there is no real benefit from the total dominance and pervasiveness of Anglo-Saxon values and cultural traits.

In sum, majority groups are dialectically linked to minority groups. Abolishing one means abolishing the other. That would mean a pluralistic equality where there is a fusion of cultures that form into a new society composed of only human beings. For the present time nationalism and racism will continue to divide us. As internal colonialism declines, race and culture differences without the implications of inferiority and superiority will form the basis of a new social order.

NOTES

1 Robert Bierstadt, "The Sociology of Majorities," *American Sociological Review,* vol 13, December 1948.

2 W. E. B. Dubois, *The Souls of Black Folk,* Fawcett, Greenwich, Conn., 1961, p. v.

3 Albert Memmi, *Dominated Man,* Beacon, Boston, 1968, pp. 185, 192–193.

4 Robert Chrisman, "The Formation of a Revolutionary Black Culture, *The Black Scholar,* vol. 1, p. 3, June 1970.

5 Milton M. Gordon, *Assimilation in American Life,* Oxford, New York, 1964, pp. 60–83.

6 Mae King, "The Politics of Sexual Stereotypes," *The Black Scholar,* vol. 4, p. 17, March–April 1973.

7 David Heer, "Negro-White Marriage in the United States," *Journal of Marriage and the Family,* vol. 28, pp. 262–273, August 1966.

8 Joseph Golden, "The Characteristics of the Negro-White Intermarried in Philadelphia," *American Sociological Review,* vol. 19, pp. 177–183, April 1953.

9 Kingsley Davis, "Intermarriage in Caste Societies,"*. American Anthropologists,* vol. 43, pp. 376–395, July 1941.

10 Louis T. Achille, quoted in Frantz Fanon, *Black Skin, White Masks,* Grove, New York, 1967, p. 71.

11 George Gallup, "Growing Tolerance Found Regarding Interracial, Interfaith Marriages," *The New York Times,* p. B.51, November 19, 1972.

12 David Heer, "The Prevalence of Black-White Marriage in the United States 1960 and 1970," *Journal of Marriage and the Family,* vol. 36, pp. 246–259, May 1974.

13 Nathan Hare, "Will the Real Black Man Please Stand Up?" *The Black Scholar,* vol. 2, p. 33, June 1971.

14 Robert Staples, *The Black Woman in America,* Nelson-Hall, Chicago, 1973, pp. 105–106.

15 U.S. Bureau of the Census, *The Social and Economic Status of the Black Population in the U.S., 1973,* Ser. P-23, no. 48, U.S. Department of Commerce, Washington, 1974, p. 113.

16 Bill Lane, "Are Black Swains Losing Out to Proximity Whites in Race for Hearts of Black Beauties?", *Los Angeles Sentinel,* p. B1A, January 28, 1971.

17 Erik Erikson, *Childhood and Society,* Norton, New York, 1950, pp. 72–80.
18 Douglas Davidson, "The Furious Passage of the Black Graduate Student," *Berkeley Journal of Sociology,* vol. XV, 1970, p. 205.
19 Frantz Fanon, *The Wretched of the Earth,* Grove, New York, 1963, pp. 167–189.
20 Raymond Kennedy, "The Colonial Crisis and the Future," in Ralph Linton (ed.), *The Science of Man in the World Crisis,* Columbia, New York, 1945, pp. 328–330.
21 Harold Cruse, *Crisis of the Negro Intellectual,* Morrow, New York, 1967, pp. 371–372.
22 Albert Memmi, *The Colonizer and the Colonized,* Beacon, Boston, 1967, p. 128.
23 Bertram Doyle, *The Etiquette of Race Relations in the South,* University of Chicago, Chicago, 1937, pp. 68–80.
24 Tamotsu Shibutani and Kian Kwan, *Ethnic Stratification,* Macmillan, New York, 1965, p. 318–321.
25 St. Clair Drake and Horace Cayton, *Black Metropolis,* Harcourt, Brace, New York, 1945, pp. 125–126.
26 Calvin Hernton, *Sex and Racism in America,* Doubleday, New York, 1965, pp. 127–129.
27 Fanon, op. cit., pp. 83–108.
28 Stanley Elkins, *Slavery,* University of Chicago, Chicago, 1968, pp. 81–89.
29 Mary Berry, *Black Resistance-White Law,* Appleton-Century-Crofts, New York, 1971.
30 Robert Blauner, *Racial Oppression in America,* Harper & Row, New York, 1972, pp. 31–33.
31 Edward Greer, "The Liberation of Gary, Indiana," in Peter Rossi (ed.) *Ghetto Revolts,* Transaction, New Brunswick, N.J., 1973, p. 280.
32 Gary T. Marx and Michael Useem, "Majority Involvement in Minority Movements: Civil Rights, Abolition, Untouchability," in Gary T. Marx (ed.), *Racial Conflict,* Little, Brown, Boston, 1971, pp. 424–439.
33 William Graham Sumner, *Folkways,* Ginn, Boston, 1906, p. 13.
34 Harry Kitano, *Japanese-Americans: The Evolution of A Sub-Culture,* Prentice-Hall, Englewood Cliffs, N.J., 1969.
35 Gordon, loc. cit.
36 Ibid.
37 Howard Schuman, "Sociological Racism," *Transaction,* vol. 7, pp. 44–48, December 1969.
38 Harvey Sarles, "On Racism in America," in John Szwed (ed.), *Black America,* Basic, New York, 1970, pp. 48–52.

39 Lloyd A. Free and William Watts (eds.), *State of the Nation,* Potomac Association, Washington, 1973, p. 35.

40 Schuman, loc. cit.

41 Robert Blauner, *Racial Oppression in America,* Harper & Row, New York, 1972, p. 267.

42 E. Digby Baltzell, *The Protestant Establishment,* Vintage, New York, 1964, pp. 318–325.

43 Baltzell, loc. cit.

44 Mark S. Granovetter, "Getting a Job: A Study of Contacts and Careers." Harvard University, Cambridge, Mass., 1974.

45 Max Weber, *The Theory of Social and Economic Organization,* Oxford, New York, 1941, pp. 329–336.

46 William J. Goode, "The Theoretical Importance of Love," *American Sociological Review,* vol. 24, pp. 38–47, February 1959.

47 Herbert Hill, "The Racial Practices of Organized Labor: The Contemporary Record," in Julius Jacobson (ed.), *The Negro and the American Labor Movement,* Doubleday, New York, 1968, pp. 297–298.

48 Bernard Berelson and Patricia J. Salter, "Majority and Minority Americans: An Analysis of Magazine Fiction," *Public Opinion Quarterly,* vol. 10, pp. 168–190, Summer 1946.

49 Shibutani and Kwan, op. cit., p. 314.

50 Gunnar Myrdal, *An American Dilemma,* Harper, New York, 1944, pp. 106–112.

51 Stanley Krippner, "Race, Intelligence and Segregation: The Misuse of Scientific Data," in Barry Schwartz and Robert Disch (eds.), *White Racism,* Dell, New York, 1970, pp. 452–464.

52 Edward J. Barnes, "Cultural Retardation or Shortcomings of Assessment Techniques," in Reginald Jones (ed.), *Black Psychology,* Harper & Row, New York, 1972, pp. 66–76.

53 For example, minority students admitted to the University of California campuses during the year 1972–1973 had median gradepoint averages of 2.52. Cf. *The San Francisco Chronicle,* p. 7, February 15, 1974.

54 Robert L. Williams, "Abuses and Misuses in Testing Black Children," *The Counseling Psychologists,* vol. 2, pp. 62–73, 1971.

55 Arthur R. Jensen, "How Much Can We Boost I.Q. and Scholastic Achievement?" *Harvard Educational Review,* vol. 39, pp. 1–123, Winter 1969.

56 William Schockley, "Models, Mathematics and the Moral Obligation to Diagnose the Origin of Negro I.Q. Deficits," *Review of Educational Research,* vol. 41, pp. 369–377, October 1971.

57 Frank L. Morris, "The Jensen Hypothesis: Was It the White Per-
    spective or White Racism?" *Journal of Black Studies,* vol. 2, pp.
    371–386, March 1972.
58 Robert Staples, "The Black Scholar in Academe," *Change,* vol. 4,
    pp. 42–49, November 1972.
59 Blauner, op. cit., p. 22.
60 Eric Williams, *Capitalism and Slavery,* University of North Carolina,
    Chapel Hill, 1944, pp. 19–29.
61 C. Van Woodward, *The Strange Career of Jim Crow,* Oxford, New
    York, 1966, pp. 67–109.
62 James Boggs, "Uprooting Racism and Racists in the United States,"
    The Black Scholar, vol. 2, p. 5, October 1970.
63 Norval D. Glenn, "White Gains from Negro Subordination," *Social
    Problems,* vol. 14, p. 175, Fall 1966.
64 Lester C. Thurow, *Poverty and Discrimination,* Brookings, Wash-
    ington, 1969, pp. 130–134.
65 Albert Hermalin and Reynolds Farley, "The Potential for Resi-
    dential Integration in Cities and Suburbs," *American Sociological
    Review,* vol. 38, pp. 595–610, October 1973.
66 Blauner, op. cit., pp. 25–26.
67 J. Sherwood Williams, B. Krishna, Singh, and Michael J. Miller,
    "Blacks and Southern Poverty," *Journal of Social & Behavioral
    Sciences,* vol. 20, pp. 62–71, Winter 1974.
68 Arthur M. Ross, "The Negro in the American Economy," in
    Arthur M. Ross and Herbert Hill (eds.), *Employment, Race and
    Poverty,* Harcourt, Brace, New York, 1967, p. 15.
69 Gordon W. Allport, *The Nature of Prejudice,* Addison-Wesley,
    Reading, Mass., 1954, pp. 348–349.
70 James P. Comer, "White Racism: Its Root, Form and Function,"
    American Journal of Psychiatry, vol. 129, pp. 802–806, December
    1969.
71 Allport, loc. cit.
72 John Dollard, *Caste and Class in a Southern Town,* Yale, New
    Haven, 1937, pp. 315–363.
73 Norvel D. Glenn, "The Role of White Resistance and Facilitation
    in the Negro Struggle for Equality," *Phylon,* vol. 26, p. 110,
    Summer 1965.
74 Kenneth Stampp, *The Peculiar Institution,* Knopf, New York,
    1956, pp. 29–33.
75 Blauner, op. cit., p. 24.
76 Glenn, "White Gains From Negro Subordination," p. 178.
77 Dollard, op. cit., pp. 134–172.

78 Milton Banron, *The Blending Americans: Patterns of Intermarriage,* Quadrangle, Chicago, 1972.
79 Bettye Latimer, "Children's Books and Racism," *The Black Scholar,* vol. 4, pp. 21–27, May–June 1973.
80 Shibutani and Kwan, op. cit., pp. 277–279.

SUGGESTED READING LIST

Allport, Gordon W.: *The Nature of Prejudice,* Addison-Wesley, Reading, Mass, 1954.
Baltzell, E. Digby: *The Protestant Establishment,* Vintage, New York, 1964.
Campbell, Angus: *White Attitudes Toward Black People,* Institute for Social Research, Ann Arbor, Mich., 1971.
Comer, James P.: "White Racism: Its Root, Form and Function," *American Journal of Psychiatry,* vol. 26, pp. 802–806, December 1969.
Dollard, John: *Caste and Class in a Southern Town,* Yale, New Haven, Conn., 1937.
Doyle, Bertram: *The Etiquette of Race Relations in the South,* University of Chicago, Chicago, 1937.
Ebony: *The White Problem in America,* Johnson, Chicago, 1966.
Glenn, Norval D.: "White Gains from Negro Subordination," *Social Problems,* vol. 14, p. 175, Fall 1966.
Gordon, Milton M.: *Assimilation in American Life,* Oxford, New York, 1964.
Howe, Louise Kapp (ed.): *The White Majority: Between Poverty and Affluence,* Vintage, New York, 1970.
Jones, James M.: *Prejudice and Racism,* Addison-Wesley, Reading, Mass., 1972.
Jordan, Winthrop D.: *White Over Black: American Attitudes Toward the Negro, 1550–1812,* University of North Carolina, Chapel Hill, 1968.
Lacy, Dan: *The White Use of Blacks in America,* McGraw-Hill, New York, 1972.
Memmi, Albert: *The Colonizer and the Colonized,* Beacon, Boston, 1967.
Schwartz, Barry N. and Robert Disch: *White Racism: Its History, Pathology and Practice,* Dell, New York, 1970.
Staples, Robert: "The Black Scholar in Academe," *Change,* vol. 4, pp. 42–49, November 1972.

Thurow, Lester C.: *Poverty and Discrimination,* Brookings, Washington, 1969.

Willie, Charles V., Bertrand M. Kramer, and Bertram S. Brown (eds.), *Racism and Mental Health,* University of Pittsburgh, Pittsburgh, 1973.

Yetman, Norman R. and C. Hay Steele (eds.): *Majority and Minority: The Dynamics of Racial and Ethnic Relations,* Allyn & Bacon, 1971.

Chapter 10

Social Movements and Social Change

When sociologists discuss social change in a society they commonly mean variations or modifications in any aspect of social process, pattern, or form.[1] It is a generic concept referring to the consequences of some type of social movement that alters the basic institutions and lifestyles of a society. Social change for Blacks is employed here in a more limited fashion. It is determined by basic and widespread changes in the conditions of life and status of the Black population. Perhaps it would elsewhere be labeled as a variation in the state of race relations since Black social change in America is rarely independent of the constraints of racial oppression or some degree of freedom from it. Thus social change for the White majority could have a minimal or different effect on its Black minority. Also, the same factors bringing about social change for the society as a whole may not always be operative for Blacks.

Our purpose in this chapter is to examine the area of social change as it uniquely affects Afro-Americans. There seems to be no constant element in change for this group except that they have constantly had to struggle for survival since their arrival on these shores. One cannot even see changes in their status as always bringing about progress since there have been regressions in certain historical epochs. Slavery was an erosion of their status as indentured servants and the system of Jim Crow put them in a worse position than during the reconstruction era. Moreover, although certain external events influenced their opportunity to effect positive change, they were usually brought about by some sort of independent struggle. Therefore, we also want to explore Black social movements and their ideologies as well as evaluate their dynamics and effectiveness. In discussing social movements we must keep in mind that one is automatically describing collective efforts of achieving social change. The two are really inseparable elements in a dynamic society.

THEORIES OF SOCIAL CHANGE

Change as a Function of Worsened Conditions

Commonly associated with Karl Marx, this theory asserts that as conditions get worse, the oppressed classes turn to revolutionary protest movements to bring about change in the social structure. It is the increasing misery of the working classes and the increasing alienation depriving them of satisfaction in their work roles that will motivate them to revolt against the prevailing system of capitalist rule.[2]

This theory has been challenged by many scholars because it does not conform to the historical records of social movements and social change. Davies (1969), for instance, has observed that a typical pattern that precedes revolts is a long period of improvement in conditions followed by a rather sharp decline. The greater the oppression of a group, the lesser the probability they will rebel. Groups subject to very brutal oppression tend to be concerned with day-to-day survival rather than protest.[3] This seems to be particularly true of Blacks. One notes that protest by Blacks, in general, was low-key during a long period after the end of the Civil War when they were preoccupied with satisfaction of their physical needs and avoiding lynchings and economic reprisals.[4] Even the alienation Marx spoke of does not necessarily result in protest movements to bring about social change. As seems true today, it can just as likely ensue in political apathy and indifference.

Rising Expectations

According to this theory, it is the rising hopes of a group that are unfulfilled that result in protests and revolts. Otherwise stated, as conditions begin to improve and expectations are raised for continued improvements, the failure of a society to adequately meet those expectations gives rise to group conflict and popular uprisings. It is the element of frustration resulting from the gap between expectations and achievement that is regarded as the key factor in bringing about social movements for change. As noted by Hoffer (1951), "People with a sense of fulfillment think it a good world and would like to conserve it as it is, while the frustrated favor radical change."[5] However, it is not solely the frustrations of a group that by itself bring about the eradication of frustrating conditions. Rather it is the coming together of a community of people to develop ideologies and strategies to alter oppressive structures and conditions.

As applied to Blacks, this theory is relevant when we consider that America's racial structure has been inflexible and accommodated few positive changes in Black life while certain circumstances in the society gave rise to a marked elevation in their aspiration levels. Certain dramatic advances such as antidiscrimination legislation, integration of the Armed Forces, and the Supreme Court ruling on school desegregation created the delusion that full participation in the American dream was possible. Subsequently, the widening disparity between aspirations and achievement intensified feelings of frustration and pent-up aggression. This pent-up aggression was then turned outward against the White power structure, which Blacks identified as the frustrating agent. Partial evidence supporting this hypothesis is available in the fact that civil rights militancy was stronger in the North than in the South, and among higher-status and urban Blacks than among those in the lower-class strata and rural areas.[6]

This hypothesis is not sufficient as a unitary explanation of social movements and change. Rising expectations do not have to result in protest and change. They can be transferred to some other form of behavior that is more respectable and safer. Some may attempt to accommodate themselves to the restraints placed upon their achievements by seeking to gain recognition and acceptance as outstanding members of a Black elite class. Others may turn their feelings of frustration and wrath toward members of their own group rather than the White ruling class. Moreover, if grievances are greatest among the higher-status members of a group, it is possible for an adaptive society to incorporate them into the society while continuing to exclude the more oppressed members of their group.

CAUSES OF BLACK SOCIAL CHANGE

Although there is no one factor that can be isolated as the primary cause of changes in the conditions of Black life, a number of contributing elements combine to form a typical pattern of change.

Attitudes and Values

In the case of effecting changes in Black life, the belief in democracy and equality of opportunity provided fertile soil for some demands for the right to vote, equality in employment opportunities, etc. These values, as applied to Afro-Americans, are held stronger in some segments of the society than others and during certain periods more than others.[7] It does not mean, necessarily, any strong White commitment to racial equality but it makes it difficult for Whites as a group to collectively organize and directly resist demands for basic rights due all American citizens. At the same time Black adherence to those beliefs gives impetus to their struggle to achieve liberation in a society which regards itself as a democracy. In other situations such as the ghetto rebellions, the values of materialism were subtly expressed in the looting of stores and the theft of merchandise. Because they are a minority, Blacks have achieved their greatest gains when the White majority's attitudes were most receptive to their demands and subsequently lost ground when there has been a conservative reaction to their protests.

Growth of a Black Middle Class

A strong Black middle class has been influential in that it has provided not only the leaders of most protest groups but in many cases the active members as well. Many of the original sit-ins and demonstrations were peopled by Black college students. Most certainly, the thrust of the nationalist movement has come from the Black middle class. As in other prerevolutionary societies, the middle class provides people with certain organizational and leadership skills. They are the individuals who have time to attend meetings and, most importantly, are somewhat independent of the White middle class economically, It is the middle-class Afro-American who writes and reads the revolutionary literature, organizes conferences, and sets trends in hair and dress styles.

Migration

Since 1876 migration has been a dominant feature of Black social change. During the late nineteenth century, there was a westward migration from the South to the Southwest. About the same time there were also some back-to-Africa movements that involved a small number of Afro-Americans. But the big migration took place around the turn of the twentieth century when large numbers of Blacks moved from the rural areas of the South to the cities of the South and North. Migration often brought about some changes because it involved contact with a new environment, exposed Blacks to a new racial environment, and created new problems. Some scholars have said that migration patterns caused the loss of a Black folk culture, transformed Black rural peasants into a landless urban prolitariat, created Black disunity, brought about Black political power, and changed the character of America's housing patterns. Many of these assertions probably have some validity unless one assumes America to have a unitary culture where the position of Blacks remains static regardless of locale. Another contribution of migration is that it decreased the isolation of Blacks who lived in rural areas and enabled them to form a more cohesive community of resistance because of greater communication with one another.[8]

Urbanization and Industrialization

The concentration of Afro-Americans in cities has had its positive effects. Cities have often been distinguished from rural areas by their greater emphasis on achieved rather than ascribed status. Because of their larger populations and impersonal character, individual merit is worth more than primary relationships. Hence, there was a faster growth of a Black middle class. The growth of industrialization also means that many Blacks were brought into the factories on an equal scale with White workers and unionism gave them additional benefits. Population increase and migration to the cities have made Blacks a dominant force in America's industrial centers. As a result, they are in a strategic position to gain certain types of minor political power and control over some of the society's essential resources.

Technology

Technology has had a profound impact, although much of it has been negative. For example, the technology that mechanized agriculture in the South around the turn of the twentieth century drove many Blacks off the land they had toiled for years. Presently, automation and cybernation threaten to make Blacks obsolete as workers in the industrial world. Yette (1971) claims that once an economic asset, Blacks are now considered an economic drag.[9] Both he and Willhelm charge that because they are now liabilities rather than assets to America's industry, the possibility of racial genocide is greater than ever. Willhelm (1971) asserts that "the arrival of automation eliminates the need for Black labor and racist values call for the Negro's removal from the American scene."[10] On the other hand technological developments gave us television, which was instrumental in enabling many White Americans to view racial brutality in the South in vivid color. It also made many poor Blacks aware of the affluent life of White America of which they were being deprived. Many observers of Black social change credit this medium with influencing Black demands and White acceptance of them.

War

While war may appear to be an inappropriate factor to cite as an influence in changing Black life, it has had its impact. It has been evidenced in three ways. First, it permitted Blacks to enter jobs from which they were previously barred because of a labor shortage during the period of international conflict. Second, to arouse patriotism in its citizenry and secure support for its wars, the government emphasizes that the United States is fighting to preserve democracy. Since its treatment of Blacks is in very blatant conflict with such a claim, it is more inclined to soften some of its racist oppression in order to gain national and world credibility. In the last two wars, which had significant Black participation, some concessions to Black demands were also necessary to maintain the morale of Black troops and insure their loyalty. Third, during a time of war the country has often been preoccupied or too weak to effectively resist Black demands for changes in their circumstances. Moreover, to preserve national unity during this time the government was more predisposed to make token concessions in order to avoid internal conflict that could endanger the war effort.

TYPES OF SOCIAL CHANGE

Up to this point we have been discussing social change in Black life without specifying exactly what the nature of that change is. While alerting the reader to the fact that we are not talking, necessarily, about major alterations in Black institutions or lifestyles, there are several areas in which change tends to occur.

Cultural Change

Changes in Black thinking, acting, and behaving can be observed most easily in the different hairstyles, clothing, names, food habits, etc., adapted. This type of change is often most prominent among members of the Black middle class, for example, using Black linguistic patterns, adopting an African name, serving soul food.

Economic Change

Making alterations in the activities of producing and consuming often means going from one mode of production to another, e.g., feudalism to capitalism, capitalism to socialism. For Blacks this type of change refers to growth of a large middle class, closing the gap between Black and White income, making the consumption of certain items easier for the poor through food stamps, Medicare, etc. Eliminating the system of Jim Crow opened up new consumer opportunities for Southern Blacks such as travel, going to formerly segregated theaters and restaurants, etc. Black capitalism, however, has hardly made an impact on the lives of most Afro-Americans since they still own less than 3 percent of the nation's business enterprises and take in less than 1 percent of its revenues.[11] The attempt at economic cooperation through the formation of cooperatives is significant for its future implications.

Social Change

Although changes in other areas are often brought into this umbrella-like category, it specifically means modification of the roles, values, and institutions that make up a social order. There are profound alterations in the values people hold, the occupations in which they work, how they socialize their children, and the way in which they interact, etc. Some would question whether there has really been any significant change for the Black population since they still, in general, hold an inferior status vis-a-vis Whites. While it should not be interpreted as any racial utopia, the United States has generally been forced to reorient its customs, institutions, and role behavior for its Afro-American inhabitants. Further, this change in the state of race relations pervades all regions and classes.

In the area of customs, Whites can no longer expect deference from every Black person they encounter. Indeed, they are more likely to receive belligerent responses from the Black youth population. Afro-Americans are no longer automatically placed in subordinate roles in their day-to-day interaction with Whites. Some may supervise Whites in their jobs, others date and marry members of the dominant racial group, and there are even some Blacks who have some degree of authority over Whites. The institutions of White America have been altered by the presence of Blacks as they have slowly, but surely, infiltrated most of them. Further the entrance of Blacks into certain White institutions such as schools and politics has helped to change much of their character.

Psychological Change

This area involves an alteration of ideas, attitudes, and orientations extant under the old system. Sometimes psychological change will precede other areas of change. Marx believed that it was the working class's sense of class consciousness that would precipitate the overthrow of the capitalist system.[12] However, his theory helps to explain awareness of oppression rather than the different modes of thinking that result from change in other areas. This type of attitudinal change has occurred among both Blacks and Whites. For Blacks it was reflected in the new sense of identity and self-respect they found in a Black nationalist orientation rather than the old assimilationist strivings. The slogan "Black is beautiful" conveyed the pride in their African heritage and a new sense of identity that was not White-oriented but reflective of their own racial identity. Other evidence of this psychological change can be observed in recent studies of Black self-esteem, the tendency of Blacks to relate to one another in a unique cultural fashion, and in many other ways. Among some Whites, particularly the youth, Blacks are no longer automatically regarded as inferior in status and behavior. In fact, their cultural lifestyles may be envied and even imitated. A recent poll among White Americans revealing that an increasing number of them approved of interracial marriages is indicative of a profound attitudinal change in the White population.[13]

Political Change

Here we are dealing with changes in the ways in which the society is governed and the people who govern it, i.e., the distribution of power in the society. Since political constituencies are made up of a multiplicity of interest groups, any change in the political structure is also an alteration of the priorities of a government. For the politically unsophisticated, the Republican party is regarded as probusiness while the Democratic party is considered the party of the working man. However, little change has occurred in this society as a result of changeovers in the political party running the government since they both represent the interests, to varying degrees, of the wealthier groups. Different priorities are emphasized by the two parties in order to garner votes and support for political campaigns.

Political control represents power. In that regard there has been little political change for Blacks in this country. What little political change has taken place has been in the form of gaining access to the voting franchise, being elected to prestigious but powerless political posts in large cities, and the ability to exact political patronage in the form of jobs and city services. However, Blacks have exercised political power by their independent struggles to gain control over their communities, by their protests against a society that penalizes them for the biological accident of their racial membership, and through their resistance to the forces of oppression they have faced since their arrival in this country.

BLACK IDEOLOGIES

Most social movements have ideologies to orient and defend their actions. Sociologists define an ideology as a relatively authoritative, closed, and explicit belief system that commands obedience from adherents, covers a wide range of situations, and is organized around one or a few preeminent values.[14] Black social movements have been conspicuous for the lack of an ideology or the prostitution of ideologies to serve a multiplicity of different and conflicting goals. Under the banner of nationalist ideology there are groups advocating socialism and capitalism, violent revolution, and cooperation with the system. These same movements have been heavily reliant on the charisma of a leader. Whatever he said was the ideology, not a guiding set of principles that were binding on all members of a particular group.

We also have to distinguish between ideologies and a social movement. The ideology is an articulation of ideals that set goals and guidelines for aspirations and policies. A social movement is the dynamic implementation of actions designed to reach those objectives. In some cases we have ideologies but not social movements. The ideology of Black separatism is a good example. While there are a number of Black separatist organizations, few are engaged in the active process of securing separation from Whites for its members or the masses of Black Americans. Similarly, many of the advocates of a Black capitalist philosophy are themselves not private entrepreneurs but salaried employees. While there may be extenuating reasons for this seeming contradiction, it does illustrate that ideologies are statements of ideals and not necessarily related to ongoing social movements.

Within the Black community there have been a number of ideologies proposed and followed. For the most part only a small minority of Afro-Americans have been adherents of a particular ideology. It seems reasonable to assume that most Blacks have simply desired liberation from the restraints of racial oppression rather than an ideological struggle over the nature of the society in which they live. This has probably been true of most groups throughout the history of the world. Revolutions have usually been carried out by a small minority with the tacit support of the majority. It is an ideology, however, that inspires that minority to take the risks that participation in an act of resistance usually entails. It is an ideology that motivates them to pursue a course they would not ordinarily undertake.

Among the most distinct ideologies followed by Afro-Americans are the following:

Assimilation

Various rationalizations motivate adherence to this philosophy. They range from those who believe that it is less difficult for Whites to discriminate against Blacks who are not concentrated in segregated areas and institutions to those who assume that racial integration will lead to widescale intermarriage and cause Blacks as a group to disappear. Since this ideology requires the cooperation of the dominant racial group, the means used were those that were normatively sanctioned or appealed to the conscience of Whites. As an ideology, it attacked the evils of Jim Crow and exhorted the virtues of universal brotherhood.

Black Power

The ideology of Black power appears to have initially been popularized by the novelist Richard Wright in his book of the same name. He was applying this concept to the emerging Black nations of Africa that were just gaining independence from their colonial rulers. Because he saw the potentialities of Black political organization, he urged Africans to throw off the shackles of White colonialism with the utmost expediency. The form of organization Black people require, he said, will be determined by the emotional and material needs of Blacks and this could be decided by Black people alone. The content determines the form, asserted Wright, and never again must the White world decide what is good for Black people.[15]

Almost two decades later the Black power ideology emerged out of the civil rights movement. The person most associated with the American version of the ideology, Stokely Carmichael, explained that Blacks could not secure justice by relying on their oppressor for it. New themes emerged from the Black power ideology that included (1) a rejection of the idea of integration as it was presently defined, (2) a rejection of having concerned Whites work in Black areas, (3) a questioning of gains to be made from coalitions with whites, (4) a rejection of the traditional Negro leadership organizations and their strategies, (5) a more direct orientation toward the Black masses, and (6) a more explicit rejection of nonviolence. The immediate goal was to enable Blacks to build up their own community and control it.[16] While Black power means were variable, they were outlined by a number of its spokespersons. Community control was the means, in most cases, through which Blacks were elected to political office.

The ideology of this movement was rather ambiguous in the beginning. It appeared to be more geared toward racial pluralism (i.e., coexistence of different groups) rather than separatism. Advocates of Black power planned to build enclaves of Black power like Lowndes County, Alabama, which could work together with Black power bases in Northern urban ghettoes to disrupt the system and achieve fundamental change. Since none of these Black power communities possessed enough power themselves to effect radical change, they planned to unite ultimately with White radicals to reconstruct the society along multiracial lines where racial integration would be a meaningful process for both Blacks and Whites.

Black power ideology did not last very long in that form and eventually evolved into different nationalist expressions, but it gave rise to the modern-day Black nationalist movement by its insistence that Afro-Americans could make gains only by taking their destiny into their own hands. Millions of Black people were inspired by the concept that they should develop the political power to take control over their political, economic, and social fortunes. This new Black consciousness was seen in the ghetto rebellions of the sixties. It was also expressed in the increased support among Afro-Americans for the liberation struggles in the colonial world, in the protests by Black high school and college students, and in the development of militancy and organization by Black workers and professionals. It probably had

more influence on Black cultural change than any other social movement. In the short period of five years it has revolutionized Black
cultural lifestyles. It most eloquently symbolizes the idea whose time
has arrived.

Black Separatism

This ideology calls for total withdrawal from White America. Where
to relocate differs according to the philosophy of the particular
separatist organization. Some advocate withdrawal to Africa while
others designate parts of the United States as a separate Black territory. In some cases the United States has been asked to grant a
certain amount of land anywhere to be used to establish a Black nation.
The demand for land, which would enable Blacks to physically separate
themselves from Whites, is a consistent goal of this ideology. Otherwise, Black separatist organizations may have entirely different orientations and programs. The Nation of Islam, for instance, seems to give
only token lip service to the idea of Black withdrawal from White
society while pursuing mostly a prostelytizing and economic program.
Meanwhile, the Republic of New Africa is trying to take over certain
Southern States where it wants to establish a Black Republic.[17]

Black separatism is an ideology that specifies means instead of
ends. The means is physical separation of Black from Whites because
a racist society is incapable of reforming itself. Separatists are a little
vague or sometimes unrealistic about the nature of the new Black
nation. The Nation of Islam does not really describe what kind of
separate territory it will create unless one is to assume that it will be
modeled after the Nation of Islam. Haraty (1969) responds to that
by asserting that "unless the separatists can offer a radically different
and infinitely more meaningful form of economic life, they cannot
hope to attract the Black masses away from Black capitalism.[18] However, one of the characteristics of an ideology is that it contains myths
that are attractive to its followers. Promising Blacks their own home-
land where they will be free and enjoy prosperity is but one myth
of the separatist philosophy.

Two Black scholars advance the thesis that the ideology of Black
separatism serves a useful purpose. According to Browne (1970), it
increases the options open to Black people. By so doing it could speed
up the realization of a harmonious pluralistic America. Moreover,

due to the ever-looming possibility of racial genocide, he says, separatism may be the only viable way to insure Black survival.[19] Forsythe (1973) argues that movements with a separatist orientation are tremendously important in terms of their mobilizing and therapeutic effects. They unleash a creative mental energy that is not found among those striving for assimilation. Furthermore, he asserts, Black separatism ideology decreases psychological feelings of marginality and inferiority while an integration orientation increases psychological deprivation because it has historically meant broken dreams, frustrations, and exploitation. On the other hand, a separatist ideology means pride, unity, independence, and power.[20]

While that may be the function of the ideology, it is quite clear that it has the support of few Blacks. Securing land from the ruling powers of America to establish a Black nation is quite unlikely. Genocide is a much greater possibility. The return of Afro-Americans en mass to Africa is also improbable. No African nation is prepared or willing to accept 30 million Afro-American refugees into its midst. Bennett (1970) makes the point that the choice of either integration or separation is a false one and leaves Blacks in an ideological void. Neither ideology confronts the real problem, viz., that racism cannot be dealt with in a climate of economic inequality because it is a function of labor, productive relations, money, and power. Neither separation nor integration deals with that reality but only with the question of whether Blacks are better off in the presence or absence of White people.[21]

Pan-Africanism

This ideology is one of the oldest and most comprehensive. Chrisman (1973) cites its basic premise as the belief that people of African descent throughout the world form a common cultural and political community because of their origin in Africa and a similar racial, social, and economic oppression.[22] It contends that political, economic, and cultural unity is critical to people of African descent in order to bring about an effective effort for the freedom and progress of the African peoples and nation. Pan-Africanism has evolved into this ideology, which is not universally accepted, as a result of several movements and conferences that have taken place over a number of years. Until 1945 it was largely dominated by Afro-Americans.

The origin of the term Pan-Africanism is traced to the first Pan-American conference held in London in 1900 and attended by 32 delegates—primarily Afro-Americans. A larger and more significant conference was held in 1919. Both conferences stressed the African heritage of New World Blacks and protested European colonial policies in African and Caribbean nations. As the representative vehicle of Pan-Africanist ideology, the five Pan-African conferences have not gone beyond stressing the need for an international community of Africans, the diaspora, and the protest against White colonialism in Africa.[23]

A revolutionary Pan-African ideology views the problems of African people on three levels: political, cultural, and economic. It sees the need for developing independent, Black-controlled political tools and institutions to bring about self-determination for the African continent and the diaspora. These tools and institutions will be employed to educate African peoples to a level of political consciousness which will mobilize them for a struggle against racism and imperialism and achieve their liberation. Culturally, it seeks to free them from the cultural domination of Euro-American values and institutions. An African culture and personality must be re-created and maintained to stabilize African-American institutions and form the guidelines for a value system that is revolutionary and humanistic. The economic aspects of Pan-Africanism reflect the traditional African values of cooperation and communalism. In an industrialized African nation and among the diaspora, this means following the principles of scientific socialism. Economic organization is geared toward meeting the needs of the people and not the profit motives of a small elite class of owners of the means of production.[24]

Other varieties of Pan-African ideology do exist. Among them are the two prominent African views. Nkrumah's Pan-Africanist ideology was based on the fusion of African-nation states into a centralized national federation in order to bring about rapid social and economic development in Africa. The other school of thought led by the leaders of the Ivory Coast, Liberia, and Senegal defined Pan-Africanism in economic terms and maintained that functional cooperation and policy coordination were a sufficient precondition for any form of African unity.[25] Among Afro-American Pan-Africanists, the ideology also differed. Marcus Garvey, for example, defined Pan-Africanism as the resettlement of Afro-Americans on African soil. Dubois was not in the separatist school of Pan-African thought and saw it as meaning Blacks should learn about their African past and coordinate their struggle with their brothers against the White oppressor.[26]

A common, and often studied theme, of Pan-Africanism is its African cultural orientation. By psychological identification with Africa, Afro-Americans gain a language, a history and identification, and a total humanity. By emphasizing the cultural unity of peoples of African descent, it ignores the crucial question of what kind of political and economic strategies Black people need. This has led to the charge by some Black scholars that Pan-Africanism is an all-inclusive ideology that accommodates all Black people of various and conflicting tendencies into its fold. It has been asserted that its apolitical character permits it to be used by enemies of the African revolution. The culturization of Pan-African ideology by reactionary elements in the Black community is perceived as a cheap substitute for a revolutionary struggle based on a scientific political belief system. As a result, claims Reed (1971), Pan-Africanism has become an elitist movement that attracts cynical, hustling elements who manipulate the symbols of the ideology to exploit the Black masses.[27]

Although the cultural element in Pan-Africanist ideology has been most discussed and served as the impetus for most of the Pan-African congresses, contemporary Pan-Africanists are focusing on ways and means of improving the socioeconomic conditions of Africans and Blacks in the diaspora. While Pan-Africanism has been much more than a search for cultural survivals in the diaspora, it has lacked a systematic theoretical body of knowledge on which to base a unified Black struggle. There is also the question of how relevant the ideology of Pan-Africanism is to achieving Black liberation in the United States. Whereas one can hardly question the necessity of Afro-American pride in and identification with Africa, the problems confronting this group must be solved in the context of the American form of oppression. Hence, Pan-Africanism must be viewed as only an interim movement in this stage of the Black struggle against colonialism and racism.

THE DYNAMICS OF BLACK SOCIAL MOVEMENTS

Although a number of Black protest actions might be characterized as social movements, the following are among the more significant and dynamic. In terms of their organizational character, the numbers of people involved, and the ultimate change brought about, they are the most prominent Black social movements of this century.

The Civil Rights Movement

There is no consensus on when this movement began but little disagreement exists that it had its greatest impact during the period 1960–1965. Nor is there much dispute that Martin Luther King, Jr. was its public spokesman. A number of events preceded the movement of the sixties and set into motion one of the greatest mass struggles against oppression. Prior to 1955 there were some cracks in America's racial caste system. The Armed Forces had been integrated by the executive order of President Truman in 1948; school desegregation in the South had been ordered by the Supreme Court in 1954; the Montgomery bus boycott became an international issue in 1955 as a solidified Black community struggled to desegregate public transportation in that city. In the early sixties student sit-ins and freedom rides began to spread throughout the country,[28] and the civil rights movement became a mass-based struggle. Throughout the country large numbers of the Black community organized to gain equal rights in all areas of American life. It differed from the previous Black protests because it operated independent of the traditional system and its leaders. The main strategy was nonviolent, direct action which was enunciated as an ideology by some Black leaders. However, nonviolence as a philosophy was never accepted by the masses of Black people. It was a pragmatic strategy geared to their situation as a racial minority. Since Blacks could not hope to win in a violent confrontation with the White majority, nonviolence at least gave them a moral edge over their oppressors. The important part of the strategy, however, was direct action, since it achieved change through a process different from those found in institutional political channels.[29]

Nonviolence as a strategy soon declined in its support among the Black masses. King had insisted that Black people must be nonviolent under any and all circumstances. He had adopted this strategy from Mahatma Gandhi, the leader of the Indian movement for independence from Great Britain. The major principles of King's nonviolent strategy were as follows: (1) it was not a method for cowards or weak people; (2) it seeks to win the friendship and understanding of its opponent; (3) the attack is aimed at the forces of evil rather than the evildoer; (4) the nonviolent resister is willing to suffer punishment but never to inflict it; (5) it is better to love rather than hate one's oppressor; (6) the universe is on the side of justice and the nonviolent ideologue has faith in the future.[30]

This strategy ultimately failed for a number of reasons. Among them was the decline of Black belief that their situation would improve, the self-restraint and sacrifice which proved too much of a burden, the emergence of competing movements with a new ideology that accepted Black self-defense, and the failure of nonviolent organizations to control and discipline their members.[31] Another primary reason was that the advocates of this principle sought to impose it on the oppressed but found rationalizations to allow exceptions by the oppressor. In the South the response of White mobs to Black protests was invariably violence, and their actions were upheld by the Southern authorities. Moreover, American society is basically a culture that sanctions violence and encourages it in its huge military expenditures, in its mass media, the toys it buys for children, and its history of violence against the Vietnamese, Japanese, American Indians, and Afro-Americans.[32]

History may show that the nonviolent civil rights movement was a necessary phase in the Black liberation struggle. At least it broke Black reliance on the traditional political channels to secure their rights. It involved the Black masses in a movement that formed a sense of peoplehood and eventually evolved into the powerful and ascending force of Black nationalism. Struggle is often of a long-range character and must go through different phases and forms before it culminates in total liberation. Angela Davis (1974) most accurately notes that "unfortunately, too many people fail to understand that it was because of what Martin Luther King had done that the Black liberation struggle was able to ascend to a different level, become more militant and to draw more people into the struggle."[33] However, it is still true that after all the efforts to seek reforms in American society on behalf of Black people, the masses of them remain subject to poor living and working conditions and still experience daily abuses based on their racial membership.

Black Student Movements

Although student political activity has had a long tradition in many countries, it has been notably absent in the United States. This was particularly true of Black students until the last twenty years. In the late fifties they actively joined the civil rights movement and sparked the era of sit-ins and nonviolent direct action protests. The reason for their belated entry into the Black liberation struggle can be traced to their parents' inculcating in them the belief that they were inferior to no one and had the same rights as any American. Within the civil rights movement they represented the most militant faction and were the first members to break away from the ideology of nonviolence.[34] They were the first members of the integrationist group to raise the cry of Black power and began to organize the Black community around the demand for self-determination. As a result of their previous activist involvement it was inevitable that their activities would be directed toward the colleges and universities of which they were a part.

Black student movements were at their peak during the years 1967–1971 and focused on a number of student concerns along with the welfare of the communities from which they had come. On predominantly White college campuses they formed Black student unions and associations and put forth certain demands before college administrators. These demands included separate admission standards for Black students, more Black faculty members, Black studies programs, separate facilities for Black students, and financial aid for economically deprived students. At Black college campuses they fought for liberalization of rules governing student conduct and a curriculum content that reflected the racial needs and character of the institution.[35]

The Black student movement spread to virtually all major college campuses in the United States. At each school the scenario was replayed over and over. Black students would make their demands and college administrators would be unresponsive. Collective student action would follow in the form of building takeovers, class boycotts, or demonstrations. After a period of conflict some compromise would be reached on the original student demands. Some of the actions were more dramatic than others, particularly at San Francisco State College, Howard University, Texas Southern University, and Jackson State College. Some of the student movements resulted in closing down the campus, faculty firings, and student deaths.[36]

Some observers have noted that Black student protest was inevitable because of the nature of the university. Stanford (1971) claims that the fact that the class interests of Black college students could not be fulfilled under a colonial regime caused them to become a revolutionary nationalist intelligentsia for the movement.[37] In a similar vein, Henderson (1970) asserts that education as a vehicle of upward mobility was virtually ineffectual for most Afro-Americans. In fact, he says, the educational system has been an important contributor to the perpetuation of the inequality experienced by most Black people. By its insistence that Black students be fitted into a White, middle-class model, it gave them a curriculum that failed to acknowledge the existence of Black people except as deviants and did not eliminate insensitive and racist teachers who know nothing about, care little about, and are untrained to teach Black pupils.[38]

Before declining its momentum around 1971, the Black student movement achieved a fair amount of success. Between 1967 and 1972 the number of Blacks enrolled in college doubled to 727,000; 18 percent of all Blacks aged eighteen to twenty-four were attending college in 1972 compared with 26 percent of Whites.[39] As Nathan Hare (1969) puts it, "Our cries for more Black professors and Black students have padded white colleges with more Blacks in two years than decades of whimpering for 'integration' ever did."[40] With those limited objectives achieved the Black student movement hit a low ebb for several reasons. The linkup with the community never really materialized and no revolution was ever won on a college campus. As a financial squeeze hit the nation's colleges along with a conservative backlash to student protests there were diminishing returns from student actions. Unlike the industrial world, the strike in a university is a political, not an economic, weapon. Politicians had little to lose by shutting down campuses or sending in the state militia to repress student rights. Because students did not know or could not attack the real sources of power behind the university, the movement was seized by persons who had no overall sense of purpose and consequently were incapable of offering a viable philosophy to keep the movement alive.[41]

However, the Black student movement did play an important role during its heyday. It took many of the ideas of Malcolm X, such as self-determination, the need to study Black history and culture, and the necessity to have education related to the needs of the Black community, and raised them as issues. The political and racial consciousness of many Black students was heightened by their participation in the struggle. By raising the issue of Black control of Black studies departments, they set good examples for the Black community's quest for control of its schools, the police, and other institutions. When they sought to establish links with the Black community they helped to destroy false class barriers between Black college students and the Black community. Perhaps the most important result of all was their attempt to use education not simply for self-betterment but to promote revolutionary change.

BLACK NATIONALISM

While there has always been some form of protest by Black people against the conditions of their life in this country, the most successful ones have been the militant struggles which forced concessions from the rulers. Movements that have depended on the moral conscience of this nation or relied on the good faith of Whites have met with little success. Freedom is taken from a people—it is never given to them.

Most Black social movements have been reformist in nature and aimed for some kind of integration into the mainstream of society. However, as long as it was profitable to exclude them from equal participation in American life, their efforts were frustrated. Therefore, Black people who had been here for four hundred years watched helplessly as White immigrants arrived in America and received the jobs, housing, and education that they were denied. To add insult to injury, these same White immigrants were pointed to as examples of what Blacks could achieve if only they would attempt to pull themselves up by their own bootstrap.

In the summer of 1964, the reformist character of Black protest came to an abrupt and violent end. The tranquility of the nation's race relations was shaken by the ghetto rebellions in the heart of America's cities. Black people began to redefine the causes and dynamics of their oppressed condition and started to move from their new understanding of White racism and how to eliminate its spectre from their lives. They rejected the American dream as defined by White people and galvanized into a powerful social movement known as Black nationalism.

Nationalism is commonly based on a nation-state concept. It emerges as a unifying force in the struggle to liberate the resources of a nation from imperialist control. Although Marx predicted that the class struggle was first and foremost a national struggle, the past twenty years of revolutionary wars have· been wars of national liberation. The conflict of interests has not been fought against the national bourgeoisie in countries like Algeria, Korea, and Vietnam but against French and American imperialism.

Moreover, nationalism is rarely found in the struggle of a numerical minority for liberation. Assimilationist ideology is more frequently the galvanizing force for minority social movements and such was the case for American Blacks. However, in the course of the struggle for assimilation many of the Black activists raised their level of political consciousness. From striving to become middle-class caricatures of White people, they rejected the concept of assimilation and began to forge a new identity for themselves. The central thrust of the Black liberation struggle became the demand for Black control of the Black community.

Nativist movements among Afro-Americans did not begin in the past twenty years although the most significant upsurge of Black nationalism has transpired in the post-World War II area. As early as 1828, a nationalist pamphlet, *Walker's Appeal,* by David Walker appeared on the American scene. Walker castigated the slaveholding Christians of "this Republican land of liberty" and exhorted slaves to slay their oppressors.[42]

One of the biggest mass movements of Afro-Americans was the nationalist crusade by Marcus Garvey. He built up a mass-based organization with the platform that what Blacks needed was an organization and a country. Since Blacks could not receive justice in a White man's land, they must return to the mother country—Africa. But this was an escapist philosophy which did not work too well for a people who had lived in America for over four hundred years. The government disposed of Garvey through imprisonment and deportation to his native land—Jamaica. He died in 1940 in London.[43]

Garvey was the precursor of another Black nationalist organization—the Nation of Islam. Under the leadership of Elijah Muhummad, this group found its greatest appeal to lower-class Blacks, many of whom had been imprisoned for a variety of crimes. Known popularly as the Black Muslims, this organization was characterized by religiosity, moral discipline, racialism, and the middle-class virtues of thrift, hardwork, and economic development of the Black community. Although possessing an anti-imperialist, antiexploitation character, the Muslims did not engage in political action and insulated themselves from both the culture and the everyday life of the Black community.[44] Perhaps their greatest contribution to the Black nationalist movement was the person who moved up through their organization, left it, and laid the foundation for the Black nationalist movement that is in motion today—Malcolm X.

It was Malcolm X who provided the groundwork for the Black liberation struggle now extant. Although his impact on the Black masses was greatest after his death, the revolutionary Black nationalists who waged their relentless fight in the Black communities and on the college campuses were his ideological heirs. Of all the Black leaders of the early sixties, it was Malcolm X in the forefront of an uncompromising stand against racism and capitalism who stressed that Blacks should have a positive concept of blackness; identify with the African continent psychologically; and run and control their own organizations.[45] The ideas of Malcolm X are approved by a large cross section of the Black population. Despite the ideological divisions in the Black leadership class, Malcolm X the man receives acceptance across the board. In part, this is due to his emphasis on pride in being Black, which has become a popular sentiment in the Black community. Conservative Negro leaders, however, find it possible to accept him only by making it appear that in his last months he was taking the road of compromise and reconciliation with the American establishment.

Yet there can be no doubt about Malcolm X's (1965) position in regard to the Black liberation struggle. Anyone who has read the speeches of his last days knows in what direction he was headed.[46]

From a narrow view of Black nationalism as a local matter, he developed an internationalist perspective of the Black liberation movement. He began to emphasize the link between the oppressed conditions of Afro-Americans and the colonial subjects of the Third World. It was his belief that the Black struggle in America was closely tied to the struggle between imperialism and the colonial world; that Afro-Americans would play a crucial role in helping to shape and inspire the worldwide movement for revolutionary change.

In the course of their struggle, there were twelve rules that Malcolm X believed Black people should follow:

1 Black people can gain freedom only through resolute struggle. This counteracts the idea that freedom will eventually come naturally.

2 The U.S. Government is a racist government and is not going to grant freedom. Black people will have to gain their freedom by themselves.

3 Gradualism is a hoax, and cannot lead to equality. Blacks should demand their freedom yesterday—not tomorrow.

4 Blacks must expose and oppose Uncle Toms. Negroes who support the system are also the enemy of the Black community. This rule reflects the beginning of a class approach—opposition against oppression, not a single racial group.

5 The Black liberation struggle must rely principally on Blacks and be under their control.

6 Strategy and tactics must be determined by Blacks. White liberals in particular, must not dominate in the decisions as to the thrust of the Black revolutionary struggle.

7 Blacks must develop their own leadership class and one that will be responsive to the desires and needs of the Black masses.

8 Internationalism, i.e., there must be unity among all colored peoples, who constitute a majority of the world's population, to fight United States imperialism and racism. The plight of American Blacks, then, is a human rights, not civil rights, issue.

9 Blacks must oppose both the Democratic and Republican parties. They both help sustain the racist system responsible for the oppressive condition of Afro-Americans.

10 Alliances are possible only when there is first unity among Blacks. Until Blacks have gotten themselves together, they cannot form alliances with other groups opposed to racial and class oppression. When joining other groups, Blacks must have equal status in the alliance.

11   Blacks must reject nonviolence as a response when under attack. They must employ active self-defense when confronted with violence, which will be initiated by the White ruling class.

12   The freedom of Blacks must be obtained by any means necessary. Blacks should not use unnecessary means but the means employed should be dictated by their efficacy and expediency.

While most nationalists claim Malcolm X as their own, there exist different nationalist tendencies in the Black community, with varying means and goals. These tendencies are classified into three basic types: bourgeois nationalism, cultural nationalism, and revolutionary nationalism.

Bourgeois Nationalism

The adherents of this philosophy believe that Black economic power can solve the plight of Black people. Setting up Black businesses and creating a new class of Black capitalists are their main goals. A positive attitude toward capitalism characterizes the bourgeois nationalists since they conceive of Black capitalism as a job-producing phenomenon for Black people, which in turn will alleviate other aspects of their oppression.

While the problem of jobs is a key one, two questions remain to be answered about Black capitalism as a solution: To what extent can Blacks develop a large-scale economic organization that will operate on a competitive level with the White owners of industry; and assuming they could accomplish their goals, what would be its effect on the lives of the Black masses?[47]

The answer to the first question is that the large-scale industrial development of the Black community does not appear to be a practical solution. To be competitive with White industry means Black ownership of banks, factories, real estate, and oil companies. This means the acquisition of capital—large amounts for the development of those economic institutions that will compete with already existing White industries. Advocates of Black capitalism do not presently have this capital, which they have tried to obtain from the government or large corporations.

Assuming that large corporations, for instance, will substantially aid in financing the development of competing industries is pure folly. The fact is that a few powerful capitalists are carving up the resources of this nation. In the era of monopoly capitalism, the captains of industry have formed combines and trusts that monopolize one particular industry or a set of different industries. Thus they are eliminating competition, not encouraging it—especially through financial assistance.

This situation forces Black capitalists into beginning on a small business level. Such a development is quite discouraging since almost 90 percent of small businesses started fail in the first five years.[48] The small businessman is simply unable to compete with large corporations in an era of monopoly capitalism. Thus, the prospects for small businesses in the Black community are not good.

If Black capitalism should succeed, one must still deal with the exploitative nature of the capitalist economic system. The primary goal of a capitalist is to make a profit; producing jobs is only a side effect of capitalist operations. Factories could not be run without workers and this is why people have jobs. When profits can be made without workers, as in the case of automation, then the capitalist dispenses with the worker. The problem of surplus value would still exist under Black capitalism because Black workers would produce the goods and a few Black industrialists would reap the benefits. This factor largely explains the anticapitalism nature of other nationalist groups in the Black community.

Cultural Nationalism

The cultural nationalists have as their main concern the development of a Black identity. Thus they concentrate on such matters as natural hairstyles, African dress and languages, and Black drama and literature. A degree of racialism is found among this group since they view the Black liberation struggle as a Black versus White confrontation.

Cultural nationalism has become a dirty word in certain circles because nationalist groups with a cultural orientation frequently eschew political analysis and activity. However, it is incorrect to assert that cultural nationalists are apolitical beings. In their writings and speeches one frequently finds attacks on capitalism and political oppression, but their organizational activity is directed toward the forging of a Black identity and they neglect the important task of politically educating the Black masses.

Moreover, Malcolm X saw the psychological identification with Africa as a means to an end, not an end in itself. There are some

cultural nationalists who believe that the reacquisition of their Black
heritage will ipso facto resolve the plight of Black people. It would
seem quite unrealistic to believe that what is essentially a political
problem can be solved by nonpolitical means.

Revolutionary Nationalism

The adherents of this philosophy believe that there must be Black
control of the Black community. While this is also true of the other
nationalist groups, there are some significant differences, mainly in
terms of means and ends. While the bourgeois and, sometimes, cultural
nationalists accept funds from the government to achieve their goals,
the revolutionaries state that the government must be reshaped to
meet the needs of the people. Thus they form their own political
party outside the Democratic and Republican parties. Their activities
are oriented toward achieving meaningful Black political power, not
being coopted into the present political system by becoming dependent on them for achieving economic and cultural goals.

Although all Black nationalist groups have only Black members,
the revolutionary nationalists more often accept short-term alliances
with White groups to achieve their goals. Usually, they unite around
a single issue such as demonstrations against a student strike at a university or the defense of victims in a political frameup. They have
also linked up their cause with that of Africans, Asians, and Latin
Americans fighting for the same demands. The common predicament
of White oppression also unites Blacks with Puerto Ricans, Chicanos,
and American Indians in the United States.

Because of its revolutionary analysis of the situation, this group
sees its goal as control of the political and economic forces in its
community. But those forces should be used by and for the people
in the community—not an elitist group of entrepreneurs. Unlike the
cultural nationalists, they conceptualize the problem in terms of class
oppression, with serious racial implications. Black revolutionaries, they
feel, will act as the vanguard to overthrow their capitalist oppressors.

The present state of the Black nationalist movement leaves something to be desired. Revolutionary nationalists sometimes get caught
up in the glamour of the forthcoming revolutionary struggle. There
is a great deal of emphasis on one of the means for liberation—the
gun. However, the image and activities of a revolutionary organization

cannot be identified with just the gun. To take control of the Black community, a revolutionary organization must understand the dynamics of the political-economic system and how it exercises its control over the masses of people. Once it reaches this level of political consciousness, it must educate and organize the Black community around the issues of housing, education, welfare, and the accountability of its political leaders.

AFRICAN LIBERATION MOVEMENTS AND SOCIAL CHANGE

The most salient characteristic of African liberation movements is that there are very few of them. In the last twenty years some 40 African nations have received formal political independence from their colonial rulers. With two exceptions, Algeria and Guinea, this independence was granted through peaceful negotiations with their European masters. As a result native Africans took over the political machinery that had been formerly manned by Europeans but the basic value orientation, social and political institutions, and philosophy of government and education remained the same.[49] Hence, what we find on the African continent today are three primary political segments: those areas where the imperialists and racists still endure, the regions characterized by neocolonial control, and the Africa where revolutionary transformations are taking place. Colonial Africa consists of countries to the south such as South Africa, Angola, Mozambique, and Southern Rhodesia. The neocolonial sector is composed of Zaire, Nigeria, Ethiopia, Kenya, and others. Revolutionary Africa is very small and primarily limited to Tanzania and Guinea.

In colonial Africa a White minority remains in obvious control of most of South Africa. There are 3.5 million White settlers who are economically exploiting 16 million native Africans and 250,000 Whites subjugating 5 million Blacks in Rhodesia. With a massive infusion of foreign capital and arms the White rulers of these countries have managed to maintain strong control over their African subjects. The United States, for example, sends 34 percent of its African exports to South Africa and 60 percent of its capital investments. Although the upholders of apartheid maintain that the natives are not prepared to accept equality with Whites, it is a simple fact of economics. Over 87 percent of the South African land area is occupied by the 19 percent of the population, which is White.[50] The low salaries paid native African workers allow almost all White settlers to lead lives of comparative affluence.

The neocolonial political structure of most of African society results from a combination of geopolitical and social factors. Instead of directly controlling African politics and economics, the European capitalists have installed educated elites to staff and operate the government. The consequence of Africans committed to European values and interested in having leadership roles has been a hopeless cycle of economic dependence on foreign capital in industry, finance, and agriculture. As a result there is no country in Africa with an independent economy. Those that are not in heavy debt to the Western capitalists must rely on either the Soviet Union or China. With this much control over the African economy, foreign interests continue to manipulate and dominate the African continent. African nations find themselves in the peculiar position of having formal political independence but unable to depart too radically from the policies and interests of the former colonial powers.[51]

Revolutionary Africa, Guinea, and Tanzania have adopted progressive, anti-imperialist and even anticapitalist measures. The noncapitalist sector of the economy has experienced a dynamic growth and the political leaders, Nyerere and Toure, have worked for the progressive erosion of the positions of international capital. In the country of Tanzania, for instance, the leaders have tried to re-create and adapt traditional African society based on rural socialism and self-reliance rather than imitate capitalist Western society, which is based on industry, urbanization, and outside aid.[52] However, both these countries are still weak in terms of economic growth and military strength and the survival of their respective nations has been threatened in the recent past.

The direction of change in Black Africa has been toward a neocolonial structure that has become even more unresponsive to the needs of the masses. Members of the African elite class have chosen paths to travel that are to their advantage rather than addressing themselves to the mass of grievances against the control of their natural resources by the rulers of international capitalism. The limitations of the native African bourgeoisie class have resulted in declining agricultural production, a decrease in their share of world trade, and an increasing dependency of foreign capital. Between 1960 and 1967 80 percent of that area's population had a per capita growth rate of from zero to only 2 percent.[53] Changing the situation through normal political channels has become even more difficult in the last decade. There have been over 30 coups in 17 of the 42 independent nations, which put military rulers in charge of the affairs of most of the major African states. Most of these military coups installed men who were more committed to the interest of foreign capitalists than their predecessors. Subsequent increases in the military budgets, the political power of the military, and widespread corruption all attest to the fact that those changes in governments did not represent any progress for the African peoples. Because the struggle of the African people had been for national liberation, the strategy of the former colonialists to substitute native Black faces for White ones has left the masses without an ideology or movement to fight against the neocolonial regime. Africans will have to be educated to the reality that they will also have to fight Africans before they win their freedom.[54]

It is in the colonial sector that we find the most dynamic social movement. Although African protest is in an incipient stage in South Africa it is beginning to emerge in mild forms such as strikes and demonstrations. Guerilla activity in Rhodesia has spurred the exodus of many Whites from that country and the White youth are becoming draft resisters. However, it is in the Portuguese-controlled colonies of Angola and Mozambique that the biggest and most successful African liberation movement is taking place. Since 1961 revolutionary groups have been fighting against the last vestige of classical colonialism still on the continent. Even with the aid of the United States government, Portugal has been unable to maintain its colonial position in Africa. Over one-fourth of the countryside of Mozambique is controlled by the Mozambique Liberation Front.[55] The drain of such a protracted war on Portugal's resources has led to a military takeover of its government. Even the new governing forces are resisting full independence to their colonized nations. It has the support of the United States power structure, which fears that the leaders of the revolutionary movement cannot be relied upon to set up a neocolonial structure capable of maintaining and protecting American investments in that area.

African liberation is still an ideal for most of that continent. The dream of a United States of Africa is far from a reality because the artificial boundaries created by the colonialists in the form of nation-states have diverted the African struggle into intense ethnic and national rivalries. The incapacity of the African rulers to deal with the plaguing problems of drought, famine, and poverty are related to the socioeconomic structure of neocolonial Africa and to the manner in which the wealth of that area is used and distributed. It seems quite clear that what is required for African liberation is a disengagement from international monopoly capital and this goal can be accomplished only through struggle against the native African elites who remain committed to colonial values and interests.

LEADERSHIP ROLES

As discussed in an earlier chapter, Black leadership has been a source of considerable controversy in the Black community. Yet every social movement needs and must select a leader who can become a personal symbol of the movement and a figure around whom others may rally, resolving or submerging their ideological and personal conflicts.[56] In the selection or rejection of Black leaders, Forsythe (1972) suggests that two methods are common: evaluation in terms of militance or nonmilitance and assessment in terms of national, class, and ethnic color origins. The militant leader is preferred because he is most aggressive in the pursuit of the movement's goals. In terms of national origins, some Black leaders (e.g., Garvey, Carmichael, and others) have had their leadership questioned because they were not native-born Afro-Americans. Ethnic-color criteria have been used because Blacks have never accepted non-Blacks as leaders in their social movements. At one point there was an attempt to deny leadership positions to mulattoes. In most Black movements, the leadership has come from the middle class although some of the nationalist leaders come from working class backgrounds.[57]

In most social movements, different types of leaders are involved. Since movements are often divided into phases, certain types of leaders may emerge at different times. Different leaders also have diverse functions as well as varying impacts on their followers. Although a number of leader types exist, there are three broad categories of leaders in Black social movements:

Charismatic Leaders

These are leaders whose authority stems from personal qualities rather than the power of any office or position they hold. This type of leader is seen as the creator of the movement and its ideas. He is oriented toward inspiring his followers by enunciating principles and slogans that call for sacrifice in a cause.[58] Martin Luther King, Jr.'s philosophy that if any blood is shed let it be Blacks is one example.[59] This kind of leader symbolizes courage and suffering through his actions, e.g., going to jail or fasting. Those falling into this category would include Elijah Muhummad, Marcus Garvey, and Martin Luther King, Jr. Another type of charismatic leader is the man regarded as a messiah, a man sent by God to carry a people to their liberation. Because many Black social movements have a religious basis, some of their leaders have been thought to be messiahs. However, the qualities that make a charismatic leader effective as a symbol of the ideology of the movement—idealism and spontaneity—often render him ineffective in the organizing and strategy-planning aspects of a movement.[60]

Administrative Leaders

A leader in this category puts stress on the practical aspects of a movement rather than its abstract goals. He is more inclined to make compromises with the opponent that the charismatic leader even if it means partial violation of the norms of the movement. It is his belief that it is more important to achieve some concrete aims than to claim honor and glory from the masses for his dedication to the values of the movement.[61] Often, the administrative type has a leadership position conferred on him automatically by the authority invested in his office. Hence the directors of the NAACP or Urban League are given leadership status regardless of the individual holding the office. Among other administrative leaders in the history of the Black liberation struggle have been Booker T. Washington and Whitney Young. The problem with some of these Black leaders has been that they betrayed the ideals of the movement because they were selected by and responsible to White institutions and interests.

Intellectual Leaders

This type of leader provides an elaboration and justification of the ideology and values of the movement. He is usually not an activist but through the printed word explains the myth and ideology of the movement, the methods to be used, and its potential for positive social change. His ideas often have their greatest effect on other leaders in the movement rather than its followers. It is in the category of intellectual leaders that Black movements have a rather unique character.[62] More often than not, the books and articles elaborating the ideals of Black social movements have been written by charismatic and administrative leaders. Because of the oral tradition of Blacks, and their low level of education, the masses were not much exposed to written ideas until the nationalist literature began to influence Black college students. Among the Black intellectual leaders there have been men such as Edward Blyden, Frederick Douglass, Frantz Fanon, Eldridge Cleaver, and James Baldwin.

PROSPECTS FOR FUTURE CHANGE

As a numerical minority struggling for full rights of citizenship in a society that had subjugated them for centuries, Afro-Americans accomplished a great deal more than can be observed on the surface. Not only did they force White Americans to restructure their attitudes toward, and relations with, them they sparked a whole series of protests by Whites against inequalities in this country and abroad. Still, there are limitations in any powerless minority moving for revolutionary change in a society where the potential agents of change, the working class, constitute a conservative bulwark of the nation's most exploitative values. Moreover, while what little gains Blacks have made were garnered through independent mass struggles, the White majority always had other options in responding to their demands. As long as the Black movements were directed toward equal participation in the social system as it existed, the power structure was able to accommodate them. However, once Blacks begin struggling for power to effect revolutionary change, other responses become potentially more possible. Hence we should consider that future changes in Black life could take several courses.

Genocide

This is the systematic destruction or extermination of an entire people. While many people consider Blacks, who warn against the possibility of this response by White America, as engaging in excessive rhetoric, several respectable scholars have written articles and books on the subject.[63] The basis for their argument is that Blacks have become a surplus part of the American labor force because of automation and cybernation. In a racist society which has no need for Black labor and which is faced with a dissident Black population, their removal from the American scene is possible. While such a possibility seems unlikely in a nation that has just made significant concessions to its Black minority, the potential of Black genocide should not be dismissed lightly. The United States is a violent culture that already includes in its history the extermination of almost all Indians East of the Mississippi River, the forced placement of Japanese-Americans in concentration camps, and a large-scale destruction of Korean, Vietnamese and Cambodian nationals.[64] However, Browne (1970) makes the observation that the present response to the Black labor surplus is to attempt to train them to perform some needed function in the economy.[65]

Black genocide can be achieved in more indirect ways and over a longer period of time, for example, through the eminently respectable method of family planning. Although this problem takes on a complex configuration, there are still attempts being made to legislate the compulsory sterilization of Black women. Even without legal authorization, reports are emerging about Black women being sterilized without their knowledge or consent.[66] A recent study found that births in the United States are declining most rapidly among poor Black and Chicano families. Between 1960 and 1970 the fertility rate of urban Whites decreased by 27 percent while that of Blacks fell by 37 percent.[67] There is some question about what, if any, action should be taken to stop this trend. Black women have the right to control their own bodies and refuse to bear more children than they want or can support. Yet one cannot help but notice that many family planning advocates are much more concerned with the large family sizes of the poor than of the rich. Also, their concern about limiting the number of children who must grow up in impoverished settings often does not extend to eliminating the basic causes of poverty.

As to the question of how possible genocide is in America, the Zebra case in San Francisco can be instructive. This involved a Black male, or group of males, who had killed 12 Whites and wounded 6 at random in a five-month period during 1973–74. Since the motives were apparently racial, the White community became alarmed and demanded that some action be taken to protect them. Mayor Joseph Alioto established what he called an Operation Zebra search throughout the Black community, looking for a Black man who fitted a vague description of the killer. What this turned out to be was a license for the police to stop and interrogate any Black male on the street. Those males who were stopped were given identification cards, a procedure reminiscent of South Africa's apartheid system. A group of Blacks in a movie theatre were jerked out of their seats and lined up in the lobby and searched. While the counsel of the Civil Liberties Union called it "a racist outrage," a hysterical White citizenry seemed ready to support any measures against the Black population if it promised any relief from the threat of a racial murder. Eventually the operation was declared unconstitutional.[68]

There are several lessons to be learned from the Zebra case. The first is that racism is still very much alive in America. No such measures would, or could, have been taken against the White population. It was only a powerless, and feared, racial minority that was subject to such indignities. Second, the implications of Operation Zebra were far-reaching. If the murders had continued, the operation could have been extended to a massive search of Black homes, establishment of a curfew for all Blacks, evacuation from the city, or White mob violence against the Black community. It cannot be overemphasized that these actions would be taken against all Afro-Americans because of the deeds of one Black male. Finally, the resistance of the Black community and its unity when under attack showed that the oppressive measures used in the past would not be accepted passively by Blacks who had undergone many struggles to gain some degree of human dignity.

Neocolonialism

This is a practice that we have discussed throughout the book. It is the positioning of a small elite class of Blacks in very visible posts, with little power, to obstensibly control the Black community or set an example of upward mobility and equal opportunity for the Black population. It is most evident in the Blacks elected to public office, Black capitalism programs, and the token number of Blacks occupying top positions in industry and government. Most of the gains won by Black social movements have gone to members of this group, who represent at most 10 percent of the Black community.[69] There is some indication that the number will not get much higher with increasing White resistance to affirmative action programs, job quotas, and poverty programs. The number of Blacks rising into the middle class will be declining in both number and proportion.

At the same time the proportion of Blacks below or just above the poverty line is increasing. In 1973 there were 31 percent of Blacks earning less than the poverty income of $4,500 compared with only 8 percent of Whites. The spiraling rate of inflation has particularly hurt lower-income Blacks who must spend a higher percentage of their earnings on two highly inflated items—housing and food. Despite public images of progress, Blacks have actually fallen behind Whites in two important areas in the last five years. Their family income is now only 58 percent of White family income—down from a high of 61 percent in 1970.[70] The gap between Black and White unemployment rates has widened and a large number of unskilled Blacks are locked in the ranks of the sporadically or permanently unemployed. As Blacks become more aware of their tenuous hold on the hard-fought gains of the sixties, neocolonialism as a strategy for muting Black protest will soon follow the fate of the institutionalized racial caste system.

Black-White Unity

While this would appear to be the most hopeful and logical response to the class-based oppression in American society, it does not seem an early possibility. The White working class is not disposed to any type of coalition or alliance with oppressed Blacks. Indeed, as Boggs (1970) has noted, the White working class, with the collaboration of upwardly mobile Whites, constitute the bulk of the counterrevolutionary force against the Black liberation movement.[71] Several factors account for this paradoxical situation. Swan (1974) has observed that Blacks are fighting for their humanity as well as more money, jobs, or political power. This has brought them into conflict with poor Whites who are solely struggling for better jobs, more money, and property within a capitalist framework. Although they struggle against the same system it is for different reasons.[72] Moreover, in a colonized society it is that layer of poor Whites who gain most from the racial privileges accorded Whites. In a racially equalitarian society it is the poor White who loses his advantages in jobs, employment, housing, and income by the elimination of racial differentials in those areas.

The groups of Whites most favorably disposed toward Black-White unity are ill-fitted to lead any challenge to the system. They are White middle-class youth, women, gays, and consumer advocates. However, none of these groups have a mass base—they have only a class base, and they are primarily members of the White middle class, not the working class.[73] Yet their potential for effecting change should not be understated. Within the White population a majority may soon be in what are traditionally regarded as middle-class occupations. Moreover, class is more a subjective than objective position. The discontent of these groups with the present politico-economic system is now being exhibited in apathy, alienation, and cynicism. As stated earlier, what will happen when the system of monopoly capitalism confronts its internal contradictions remains to be seen. One thing seems certain: as long as oppression and injustice exist, challenges to them will continue to emerge in different forms and on many fronts.

NOTES

1 Henry P. Fairchild, *Dictionary of Sociology*, Littlefield, Adams, Totowa, N.J., 1965, p. 277.

2 C. Wright Mills, *The Marxists*, Dell, New York, 1962, pp. 86–87.

3 James C. Davies, *Processes of Rebellion: The History of Violence in America*, Bantam, New York, 1969.

4 Doris Y. Wilkinson (ed.), *Black Revolt: Strategies of Protest*, McCutchan, Berkeley, Calif., 1969, pp. 8–12.

5 Eric Hoffer, *The True Believer*, Harper & Row, New York, 1951, p. 16.

6 Joseph S. Himes, "A Theory of Racial Conflict," *Social Forces*, vol. 50, pp. 53–60, September 1971.

7 Gunnar Myrdal, *An American Dilemma*, Harper, New York, 1944, pp. 3–25.

8 Herbert Aptheker (ed.), *A Documentary History of the Negro People in the United States*, vol. II, Citadel, New York, 1968, pp. 827–846.

9 Samuel Yette, *The Choice: The Issue of Black Survival in America*, Putnam, New York, 1971, p. 14.

10 Sidney M. Willhelm, *Who Needs the Negro?* Doubleday, Garden City, N.Y., 1971, p. 232.

11 Bureau of the Census, *The Social and Economic Status of the Black Population in the U.S., 1971*, Ser. P-23, no. 42, Washington, 1972.
12 Mills, op. cit, pp. 87–88.
13 George Gallup, "Growing Tolerance Found Regarding Interracial, Interfaith Marriages," *The New York Times*, November 19, 1972, p. B51.
14 Gary T. Marx (ed.), *Racial Conflict*, Little, Brown, Boston, 1971, p. 173.
15 Richard Wright, *Black Power: A Record of Reactions in a Land of Pathos*, Harper & Row, New York, 1954, pp. 342–351.
16 Stokely Carmichael and Charles V. Hamilton, *Black Power*, Vintage, New York, 1967, chap. 1.
17 Robert G. Weisbord, *Ebony Kinship*, Greenwood, Westport, Conn., 1973, p. 143.
18 Peter Haraty, "The Separatists' Fig Tree," *The Liberator*, vol. 9, p. 8, August 1969.
19 Robert S. Browne, "Separation," *Ebony*, vol. 25, pp. 46–52, August 1970.
20 Dennis Forsythe, "The Sociology of Black Separatism," a paper presented at the Annual Meeting of the American Sociological Association, New York, 1973.
21 Lerone Bennett, Jr., "Liberation," *Ebony*, vol. 25, pp. 42–43, August 1970.
22 Robert Chrisman, "Aspects of Pan-Africanism," *The Black Scholar*, vol. 4, p. 2, July–August 1973.
23 Clarence G. Contee, "Afro-Americans and Early Pan-Africanism," *Negro Digest*, vol. 19, pp. 24–30, February 1970.
24 Earl Anthony, "Pan-African Socialism," *The Black Scholar*, vol. 3, pp. 40–45, October 1971.
25 Ladun Anise, "Pan-Africanism and the Ideology of African Unity," *Black Lines*, vol. 1, pp. 17–18, Spring 1971.
26 Weisbord, op. cit., pp. 51–88.
27 Adolph L. Reed, Jr., "Pan-Africanism—Ideology for Liberation?" *The Black Scholar*, vol. 3, pp. 2–13, September 1971.
28 Wilkinson, op. cit, pp. 63–74.
29 Joseph S. Himes, *Racial Conflict in American Society*, Merrill, Columbus, Ohio, 1973, pp. 51–75.
30 Martin Luther King, Jr., *Stride Toward Freedom: The Montgomery Story*, Harper & Row, New York, 1958, pp. 102–104.
31 Himes, loc. cit.
32 Alphonso Pinkney, *The American Way of Violence*, Random House, New York, 1972, pp. 154–185.

33 Angela Davis, quoted in *Jet,* p. 15, May 16, 1974.
34 Howard Zinn, *SNCC: The New Abolitionists,* Beacon, Boston, 1964, p. 00.
35 Harry Edwards, *Black Students,* The Free Press, New York, 1970, chap. 5.
36 Cf. James McEvoy and Abraham Miller (eds.), *Black Power and Student Rebellion,* Wadsworth, Belmont, Calif., 1969.
37 Max Stanford, "Black Nationalism and the Afro-American Student," *The Black Scholar,* vol. 2, p. 27, June 1971.
38 Donald M. Henderson, "Black Student Protest in White Universities," in John F. Szwed (ed.), *Black America,* Basic, New York, 1970, pp. 256–270.
39 "America's Rising Black Middle-Class," *Time,* p. 19, June 17, 1974.
40 Nathan Hare, "The Case for Separatism," *Newsweek,* pp. 56–57, February 10, 1969.
41 George Napper, *Blacker Than Thou: The Struggle for Campus Unity,* Eerdmann, Grand Rapids, Mich., 1973, pp. 102–108.
42 David Walker, *Walker's Appeal in Four Articles Together with a Preamble to the Colored Citizens of the World but in particular and very expressly to those of the United States of America.* September 1829, p. 1.
43 Edmund Cronon, *Black Moses: The Story of Marcus Garvey,* University of Wisconsin, Madison, 1955, pp. 138–169.
44 Cf. John H. Bracey, Jr. et al., *Black Nationalism in America,* Bobbs-Merrill, New York, 1970, pt. 5.
45 George Breitman (ed.), *By Any Means Necessary,* Pathfinder, New York, 1970, pp. 33–67.
46 George Breitman, *The Last Year of Malcom X,* Merit, New York, 1967.
47 Ofari, op. cit., pp. 87–100.
48 Andrew Brimmer, "Economic Integration," *Ebony,* vol. 25, pp. 118–122, August 1970.
49 Ladun Anise, "Africa: Challenge of the Unfinished Revolution," *The Black Scholar,* vol. 5, pp. 2–9, April 1974.
50 "Apartheid and Imperialism: A Study of U.S. Corporate Involvements in South Africa," *Africa Today,* vol. 17, p. 00. September–October 1970.
51 Harold S. Rogers, "Imperialism in Africa," *The Black Scholar,* vol. 3, pp. 36–48, January 1972.
52 Giovanni Arrighi and John S. Saul, "Essays on the Political Economy of Africa," *N.Y. Monthly Review,* pp. 237–335, 1973.
53 Franklin Alexander, "A Critique of New Pan-Africanism," *The Black Scholar,* vol. 4, p. 11, July–August 1973.

54 Anise, loc. cit.
55 Arrighi and Saul, op. cit., pp. 378–405.
56 Lewis Killian, "Social Movements," in R. Paris (ed.), *Handbook of Modern Sociology*, Rand McNally, Chicago, 1964, pp. 426–484.
57 Dennis Forsythe, "A Functional Definition of Black Leadership," *The Black Scholar*, vol. 3, pp. 18–26, March–April 1972.
58 Hans Gerth and C. Wright Mills, *From Max Weber*, Oxford, New York, 1958, pp. 245–252.
59 King, op. cit., p. 102.
60 Killian, loc. cit.
61 Cf. Whitney Young, "He Was a Doer," *Newsweek*, p. 29, March 22, 1971.
62 Harold Cruse, *The Crisis of the Negro Intellectual*, Morrow, New York, 1967.
63 Willhelm, op. cit; Yette, op. cit.
64 Pinkney, op. cit., pp. 72–115.
65 Browne, op. cit., pp. 50–51.
66 "Forced Sterilization for the Poor," *The San Francisco Chronicle*, p. 19, February 26, 1974.
67 "Birth Decline Held Largest for Minorities," *Los Angeles Times*, pp. 1–10, June 18, 1974.
68 "The Zebra Killers," *Newsweek*, p. 27, April 29, 1974.
69 "America's Rising Black Middle-Class," *Time*, pp. 19–28, June 17, 1974.
70 Report of the Census Bureau, cited in *The San Francisco Chronicle*, p. 3, July 4, 1974.
71 James Boggs, *Racism and the Class Struggle*, Monthly Review, New York, 1970, pp. 91–100.
72 L. Alex Swan, "Nacirema Society: Capitalist and Colonial," unpublished paper, 1974, pp. 5–6.
73 William Strickland, "Watergate: Its Meaning for Black America," *Black World*, vol. 22, pp. 4–14, December 1973.

SUGGESTED READING LIST

Allen, Robert L.: *Reluctant Reformers: The Impact of Racism on American Social Reform Movements*, Howard, Washington, 1974.
Anise, Ladun: "Pan-Africanism and the Ideology of African Unity," *Black Lines*, vol. 1, pp. 17–18, Spring 1971.
Boggs, James: *Racism and the Class Struggle*, Monthly Review, New York, 1970.

Cronon, Edmund: *Black Moses: The Story of Marcus Garvey,* University of Wisconsin, Madison, 1955.

Cruse, Harold: *The Crisis of the Negro Intellectual,* Morrow, New York, 1967.

Forsythe, Dennis: "A Functional Definition of Black Leadership," *The Black Scholar,* vol. 3, pp. 18–26, March–April 1972.

Gibson, Richard: *African Liberation Movements: Contemporary Struggles Against White Minority Rule,* Oxford, London, 1972.

Himes, Joseph S.: "A Theory of Racial Conflict," *Social Forces,* vol. 50, pp. 53–60, September 1971.

Howard, John R.: *The Cutting Edge: Social Movements and Social Change in America,* Lippincott, Philadelphia, 1974.

King, Martin Luther, Jr.: *Stride Toward Freedom: The Montgomery Story,* Harper & Row, New York, 1958.

Mezu, S. Okechukwu and Ram Desai: *Black Leaders of the Centuries,* Black Academy, Buffalo, N.Y., 1970.

Napper, George: *Blacker Than Thou: The Struggle for Campus Unity,* Eerdmann, Grand Rapids, Mich., 1973.

Rustin, Bayard: "From Protest to Politics: The Future of the Civil Rights Movement," *Commentary,* vol. 39, pp. 25–31, February 1965.

Smith, Steward: *United States Neocolonialism in Africa,* International, New York, 1974.

Weisbord, Robert G.: *Ebony Kinship,* Greenwood, Westport, Conn., 1973.

Yette, Samuel: *The Choice: The Issue of Black Survival in America,* Putnam, New York, 1971.

Index

Marx, Karl:
  religion and, 163
  social change and, 281, 288
  social class and, 183
Marxist model of sociology, 14–16
Masculinity, falsetto singing as
    expression of, 70
  (*See also* Men)
Mass media:
  magazines, 93–94
  newspapers, 92–93
  racism in, 47
  stereotyping in, 272
  television, 38–39
Mate selection, 130–131
Matriarchy, as myth, 125–126
Matthews, Basil, 60, 119, 124
Mayo, Clara, 74
Mayors:
  coalition, 102–104
  small-town and ceremonial, 101–102
Mays, Benjamin E., 151, 164
Mbiti, John S., 152
Media (*see* Mass media)
Median income (1964–1971), 189
Medical research performed on
    prisoners, 238
Men:
  falsetto singing as expression of
    masculinity, 70
  fashion and, 71
  fathers, slave fathers, 118–119
    substitute fathers, 133
  income of, in lower-class families,
    126
  life expentancy of, 254
  labor force participation rate of
    (1960–1972), 203
  marriage as viewed by, 130
    shortage of educated men, 132
    socioeconomic status of males who
      intermarry, 252–254
  middle-class, skin color and, 199
  in nuclear family, 125
  in post-Emancipation families, 121
  widowhood among, 136
Memmi, Albert, 81, 250, 255
Mental illness, as sign of acculturation,
    139
Merton, Robert K., 221
Methodism, 155–156, 197
Michels, Robert, 108
Middle class, 189, 191
  Africanization of family and, 139
  Anglo-Saxon traits acquired by, 259
  bourgeoisie differentiated from,
    202, 204
  characteristics of, 192–193

Middle class:
  consumption patterns of, 128–129,
    195
  cultural patterns of, 59–60
  future of, 203, 204
  growth of: as economic change, 286
    social change and, 283–284
  housing of, 197
  interracial associations of, 198
  leaders provided by, 310
  leadership institutions representing,
    95, 96
  marriage in, 131–132
  men, skin color and, 199
  ordinary crimes committed by, 214
  origins of, 120
  police as viewed by, 225
  political behavior of, 196
  postslavery, 187
  recreation of, 196–197
  religion in, 197
  self-conception of, 198–199
  sexual revolution and, 137
  skin color and, 199
  women: fertility rate of, 123,
    195–196
    mate selection by, 131
    sexual behavior of, 127, 195
Middle-class families:
  as externally adapted, 127
  nuclear families as, 125
  number of, 126
  role performance in, 72
Migrations:
  1910–1920, 33
  social change and, 284
Militancy:
  religion and, 164–165
  of youth, 62
Militant preachers, characterized, 172
Military coups in Africa, 309
Military elite, 46, 48
Military officers, number of Black, 41
Mills, C. Wright, 10, 46, 261
Mindel, Charles, 125
Ministers, 169–175
  famous, 173–174
  historical development of, 170
  leadership positions of, 168, 175
  as leaders of slave rebellions, 154,
    158
  as link to African past, 158
  slaves pacified by, 155, 156
  stereotypes of, 171–172
  typology of, 172–173
  verbal facility of, 74
  who becomes, 170–171
Minor crimes, defined, 224

Roman slave system, 28
Roosevelt, F. D., 42, 99
"Root man", 75
Ruling class:
  cooptation by, 254
  racism perpetuated by, 250
  religion sharing common interest
    with, 163
  (See also Bourgeoisie; Upper class)
Rural women, fertility rate of (1967),
  122–123
Russuarm, John, 92

Sacred, the, defined, 165
San Francisco State College, 299
Scammon, Richard, 191
Scanzoni, John, 135, 167, 173
School desegregation, 33, 36–37, 41,
  47
Schools:
  Black English in, 74
  cooptation in, 254
  ethnocentrism in, 259
  performance of children in, 35–36
  racism in, 271–272
    schools fostering class inequalities
      based on race, 36
  (See also Education)
Schulz, David, 133
Schuman, Howard, 260
SCLC (Southern Christian Leadership
  Conference), 174
Seale, Bobby, 98, 237
Segregation during Reconstruction, 32
  (See also Desegregation)
Self-concepts:
  modified by liberation struggles, 81
  social class and, 198–199
Self-esteem:
  changes in, 288
  high level of, reference groups and,
    82
  personality development and, 79, 80
  socialization process and, 134–135
Self-hatred, personality development
  and, 79, 80
Self-identification, race as primary, 250
Self-respect, Black nationalism and,
  288
Sentencing, 230–231
Separatism:
  basic tenets of, 292–293
  dependency and, 257–258
Service stratum, 192
Sex roles, cultural variations and, 61
Sex taboos, strictness of, 72
Sexual behavior:
  of adolescent women, 129–130

Sexual behavior:
  development of heterosexual
    relations and, 128–129
  incest and homosexuality as, 137
  of middle class, 127
Sexual exploitation, 39
Sexual gains from minority group
  oppression, 270–271
Sexual image of ministers, 171–172
Sexual revolution, 136–137
Sexuality associated with female-
  headed households, 128
Seymour, Dorothy Z., 73
Shadow culture, 66
Sharecropping, 32
Shibutani, Tamotsu, 263
Simmel, Georg, immigration-
  assimilation cycle theory developed
  by, 6
Simple extended family, 124
Sit-ins, 91
Skin color, social class and, 199
Slaughter, Sara, 20
Slave revolts, 30–31, 154
Slavery, 27–31, 115–120
  as crime, 219
  dependency and, 257
  economic gains derived from, 267
  education under, 35
  end of, 30–31
  family during period of, 115–120
    free families, 119–120
    importance of family, 117–119
    marriage and, 116–117, 119
  food habits originating in, 71
  justification for, 29–30
  as most profitable source of labor,
    27
  peculiarities of U.S. system of, 28–29
  personality molded by, 79–80
  racism to justify and perpetuate, 46
  religion and, 153–156, 163–164, 166
  role of, in Black culture, 64–65
  slaveholders' values internalized by
    slaves, 224
  social class under, 185–186
  storytelling in, 75
Small-town mayors, characterized,
  101–102
SNCC (Student Non-Violent
  Coordinating Committee), 174
Social change, 280–321
  African liberation movements and,
    307–310
  Black ideologies and, 289–295
  Black nationalism and, 300–307
    bourgeois Black nationalism,
      304–305